AIN'T NO JAZZ IN KANSAS CITY

BRUCE RODGERS

ISBN (paperback): 978-8-8693-6664-1

Printed in the United States of America

DISCLAIMER

This book is a work of fiction. All names, characters, businesses, places, events. Situations and incidents in this book are either the product of the author's imagination or used in a fictitious manner. Any resemblance to actual persons, living or dead, or actual events is purely coincidental.

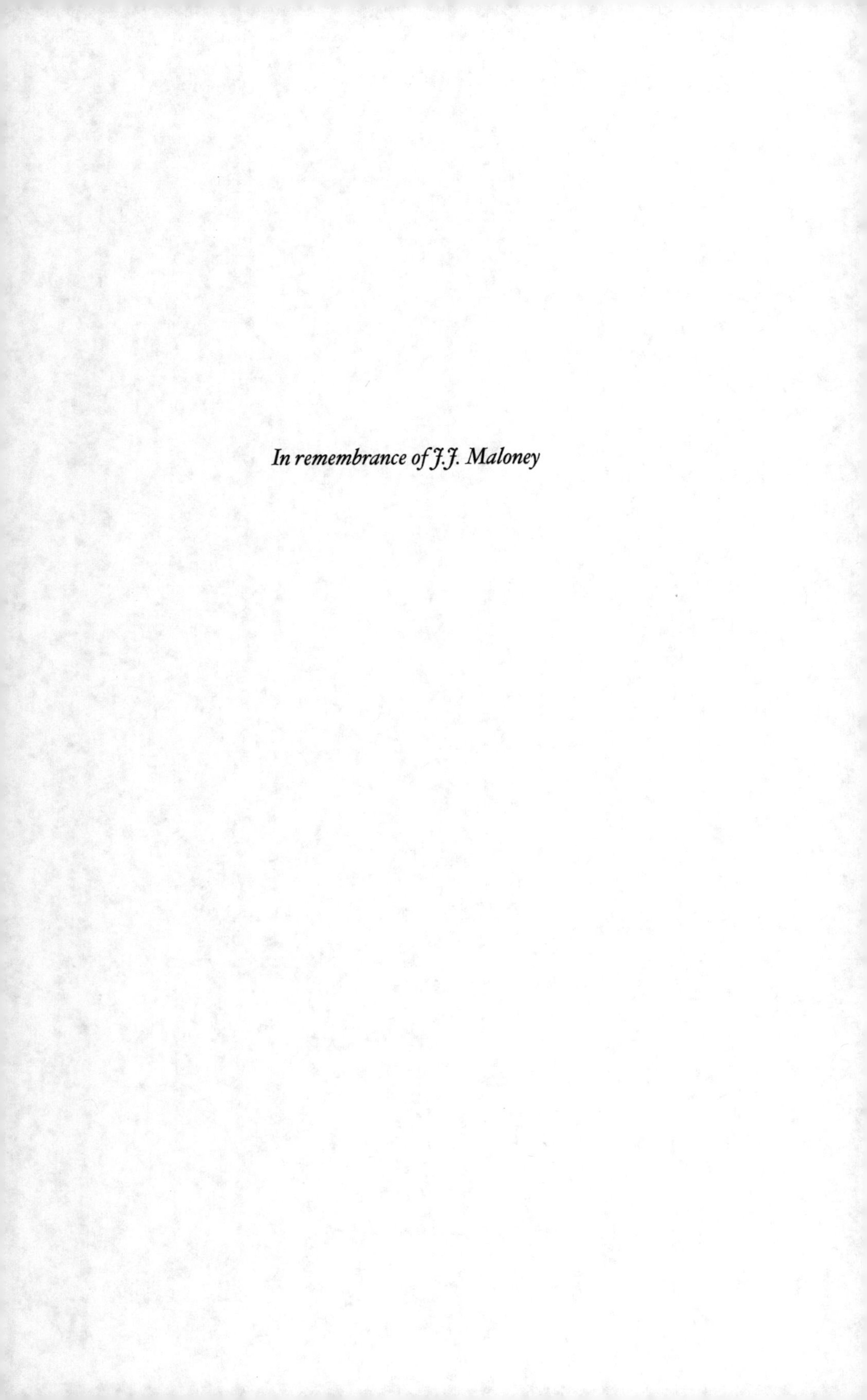

In remembrance of J.J. Maloney

CHAPTER 1

On a good night, the Repartee gave the city what it once was known for before disco suffocated live music. A place of singers and song, young lust and braggadocio, where inhibitions were adrift, and some sort of high could be found that would inject into the next day's conversation a jealous type of yearning from those not in attendance. But to some people in and out of the neighborhood, the block on which the club operated had been a cluster of sin no matter what type of gathering took place.

Such a message began with a line of small shirtwaist houses stretching up the block just west of the Repartee. A red neon sign that spelled out "MASSAGE" hung in the window of the house closest to the club. The sign was always lit, no matter the time of day. When at the stop across the street waiting for the Roanoke Boulevard bus, one could note that a customer never entered through the front door, be it lunchtime or early evening or around eleven when the last bus made its final circuit before heading downtown.

Young women who thought learning to be a masseuse was a step up from waiting tables quickly found out the reason why. The entry was through the back, just a few steps from the alley that ran the length of the block behind the houses. The alley connected to the parking lot for Nichelson's Diner, a twenty-four-hour eatery that occupied the south end of a cluster of buildings that wrapped around that corner of 39th Street and a four-lane, north/south trafficway. Patrons of the massage parlor could park in Nichelson's back lot, walk up the alley, and step quickly into the house, all the while running lines of conversation in their head to convince a woman's hands to do more than rub shoulders and back. Once such an appetite was satisfied, Nichelson's caught the other urge after a look through their menu.

The Repartee brought outliers to the area, part of other businesses on the same block that sold staples typical of a working-class neighborhood — a liquor store, a bar called The Pink Slip, and a carryout pizza shop. The liquor store added to the busyness on the Repartee's block. Narrow brown bags, the paper twisted tight around the neck of the bottle, left the liquor store early morning and late afternoon most days of the week, carried onto buses by riders shuffling home from menial jobs at a nearby hospital.

The Pink Slip was in transition. Retired and out-of-work old men from the neighborhood still came in the afternoons to suck down beer and shots and complain about their lives. But as the evening wore on, young men took to the stools to flirt and brag. They paid no mind to the few old men who stayed on to drink as if making a last stand for territory they always thought was theirs.

West of the Slip, the Repartee occupied the second floor above an office used to help people with their income taxes. It was closed for a good part of the year. The entrance to the club was through a narrow door at sidewalk level next to the tax office. A sign spelling out "Repartee" in cursive marked the door, the only indication a first-time patron had to find the club. Upstairs, when he wasn't using his van to make day time deliveries, Corey Edwards worked the door several nights a week.

On his nights, to get ready for the night, Corey would move a tall stool and high-top table away from the door. Once satisfied, he'd pull out a pack of cigarettes from his back pocket and begin looking for an ashtray. As doormen go, he was on the small size, under six feet, though a couple of years wrestling on his high school team had broadened his shoulders and thickened his arms.

A mean look wasn't in his nature. Instead, Corey used a smile and steady glare from his piercing blue eyes to deflate trouble. Males had a hard time finding fear in his eyes, while females wanted to know more about him. Corey straightened up when he saw Mike walking toward him.

One-time comic Mike Smith leased the upstairs space, once a church, after cashing a life insurance policy paid out on his stepfather. His plan was to open a comedy club. Hope for success rode high, causing indecision as to what to call the place — Mike's Upstairs Comedy? Smith's Laugh-A-Long? Stand Up Palace? All sounded lame.

He settled on Repartee after remembering a fellow comic congratulating him on his "repartee" when dealing with a heckler at a club in Des Moines. Mike liked the sound of the word, a little exotic and outside the midwestern norm. People would remember it, he thought, and then wonder what it meant. Mike liked that. The name stayed after the comedy club faltered and when Mike brought in live music. Most of the club's décor from its earlier church days remained.

The wooden, pew-like benches, left behind by the World Salvation Church, sat in rows in the rectangle-shaped room. Small, four-foot-high pedestal tables marked the rows of benches at one end. Three aisles took people to their seats. One aisle, against the far wall, had a small shelf running its length for drinks and ashtrays. Men liked to stand along that wall, watching the band, looking for women who might want to dance.

In front of the seating, a small laminate dancing space contrasted with the wooden floor that covered most of the club. Overhead lighting illuminated a one-step elevated stage that could hold a good-size choir or six-piece band comfortably or give a comic, especially one dying in front of an audience, plenty of room to pace. The front door, where Corey checked IDs and took the cover charge, was to the right of the stage. Stepping in through the doorway, a patron could take in most of Repartee at first glance.

At the far end of the room was the bar, minus bar stools, with the waitress area to one side near the register. Mike didn't like people sitting at the bar. It meant that their backs were usually to the stage. By standing at the bar, people likely turned around and surveyed the crowd before them — guys checking out women as they walked down the hallway leading to the restrooms. At the bar, it was also easier for a woman to find a guy she might have spent time with from a previous night.

Steps on the far corner of the bar led up to Mike's office. An intercom box near the cash register connected the bar to the upstairs. With another bartender, the office was a refuge for Mike, especially when he got tired of the noise and the flood of questions and compliments from regulars and people who felt they had to know him.

He put some good money into lighting and the speaker system. The Repartee's low ceiling helped push the music out from the stage. Musicians readily took to the place, making Russell Manger's job as a promoter easier both to build personal prestige and to attract girls wanting an introduction to a particular musician. Some nights with music, drink, smoke, and the dance-hot bodies, the effect was near religious, maybe not unlike the energy the World Salvation Church had brought with it before the Repartee.

At max, the Repartee held four hundred, but it rarely got there. Still, Mike could turn a little profit and pay the band at half-full, especially with him bartending, Becky working the floor mainly for tips, and Corey at the door for the few bucks and free drinks.

Usually, Mike waited for Corey to go to the bar to get the change box and say his hellos. But as Corey watched Mike cross the club's hardwood floor, he could tell there was something going on that night. Mike always had a fluid motion in how he moved despite his top-heavy weight and large frame. That steady bodily flow made Mike seem more compact than he was, less of a big presence from a big man. Only when Mike raised his head and shoulders as in anger or laughter did his bearing enlarge. Now Mike moved quickly and more deliberately.

Corey thought Mike was basically a good guy, him proving it at times, at least for Corey when Mike rattled off a joke or impression from behind the bar after that night's crowd had opened their wallets.

Now, from Corey's perch on the stool, as Mike walked toward him, it wasn't going to be a trip down memory lane to his old standup routine. Mike had something on his mind.

"Hey, Mike, what's up? Some comps coming in for early drinks?" Corey said with a smirk.

Mike shook his head. "Always a smartass, aren't you. No, a guy is going to drop off a sack tonight to you.".

"What kind of a sack?" Corey was not particularly intrigued but a little confused.

"I don't know. A SACK!" said Mike, irritated. "Probably a brown paper sack, like a ... a lunch sack, you know." Mike glanced at the upstairs entrance, then over his shoulder back toward the bar.

Not sure Mike wasn't playing some sort of guessing game, Corey asked, "What guy? What does he look like? And what's in it?"

Mike raised his head and leaned in, his round, jowled face above Corey. He placed one hand on Corey's thigh, squeezing until Corey squirmed. "Look...a guy, just a guy with a sack. And don't ask what's in it." Then, bringing his face even closer to Corey's, Mike added, "Just get it from him, okay?"

Corey nodded. "No problem, Mike."

Mike stayed close to Corey. Corey smelled the whiskey and leaned back. Mike gave him a tight smile, stood straight and turned, then hesitated and turned back toward Corey. He looked long at Corey, something he really didn't do when he hired him. Then, it was just a favor to Russell because he was Russell's friend, and Russell said he was good with people.

"Listen, you're a pretty good doorman for a guy without any real bulk. You're a smooth talker, people like you, the girls like you — and for that, you get free drinks all night, fifteen bucks, listen to some pretty good music and have a shot at getting laid. Now, just listen and stop asking questions. Just take the sack and wait for someone to ask you about it."

Corey liked being a doorman. "Sure, Mike, whatever you want. Sorry. Okay, a guy with a sack. What do you want me to do with it?"

Mike lowered his shoulders. "Nothing. Don't look inside. Don't open it. Don't leave it lying around. Just stash it somewhere close where you can find it. And if a girl shows up and asks about something from Mike — me — give it to her. Now you got this?"

Mike glared at Corey. "And don't hit on her."

"Okay, I got it," said Corey.

"Good, man." He slapped Corey's shoulder and walked to the bar.

Corey lit a cigarette. *For this, he wanted me to come in early to talk. Fuck, probably some shit going out the door...or in the door. Who cares? Like I don't know or want to. Stupid way to do it...in a sack to some chick, but like I could care. Ain"t my deal.*

With another drag on his cigarette, Corey heard a noise coming from the stairs. He walked over to the top step and looked down. "Is this the only way in, man?" said a guy pulling up a two-wheeler stacked with two Roland amps. "Yep. Sorry, man," said Corey. The roadies were here. Time to get the change box and start on this night's free drinks.

Any thoughts about getting a sack at the door left Corey when he saw Becky standing on her toes, leaning over the bar. Viewing her backside, her jeans tight over every curve, was a good way to begin the night, he told himself.

CHAPTER 2

"Hi, Becky," Corey said as he came up behind her at the server's station. The wiggle of her butt as she wiped the bar tempted Corey to touch her. He didn't.

Becky Williams had tight, curly red hair, done up big, permed out. Her skin was a milky cream color. Her bright green eyes lay on her young face like two pieces of jade buried in soapstone. Her look lacked sharp contours, just a slight tightness at her cheekbones that broke open when she smiled. Becky wore little makeup, only lipstick, usually an off-red color that made her small mouth appear a little larger. She had a model's body with thin, long legs and a runway walk to go with it. Her breasts were small; it was her face that caught a man's eye. The sexiness was immediate, and there was confidence in her that signaled classiness.

Corey planned to ignore her when he first saw her waiting tables. Too pretty, he thought. It was Mike's modus operandi in the way he wanted to push drinks. But Corey still asked about her in a casual, uninterested way.

She was Greg Zurkee"s girlfriend, a horn player jazz musician trying to make it in a dance-club-DJ-disco-holdover town, wanting steady work and making a name. Becky and Greg lived together. His band, Good Riddance, played the club regularly. Mike, of course, had an interest in Becky, so he booked Greg's band on weekday nights a couple of times a month as maybe a way in. The band's following was loyal but small. The music was tight, with standards some fusion but nothing experimental or left field. Most times when Good Riddance played, Corey wasn't even needed at the door, and sometimes Becky had the night off to listen to Greg. Mike bartended, making sure he always complimented Becky on how good the band sounded. Watching Mike soften in front of Becky had Corey sometimes laughing to himself and thinking, *Stand in line, man.*

It was Becky who first approached Corey. It was during the band's first gig at Repartee. Mike wanted Corey at the door, not sure how many of the city's jazz lovers would come. He overestimated.

Becky wanted to meet Corey for nothing else than to tell him she would soon be waiting tables. She wanted him to know her so that maybe she could get a few of her girlfriends in the door without paying the cover. Musician friends had said he wasn't a big guy or loud in how he dealt with people, and she noticed he was good-looking. Becky hadn't had a lot of guys, but she knew enough about certain types, ones she tried and wouldn't go back to, the ones where insecurity sucked away their sweetness, leaving a mark on her face. To her, Corey was a little different. He had a softness that didn't quite mesh with the door-man's job.

She first found Corey sitting on a stool by the front door, looking around the room and wondering why he was there for such a small crowd. When he saw her making her way across the floor, he gave her a quick legs-to-head look and a faint smile. He figured she was going to ask about where the women's john was. Sometimes, the question was for real; other times, he guessed it might be an opening for something else.

"Hi, I'm Becky," she said in a bouncy schoolgirl manner.

Corey lifted an eyebrow and then, with a squint, took in all of her face. "Howdy," he answered. "What's up?"

"I'm going to be waiting tables starting tomorrow night. Thought

I would introduce myself since you're the doorman. I'm Becky Williams."

"Yeah, I got that. Mike said something about hiring you. Nice addition, I must say."

Becky laughed, throwing her head back, her big red hair bouncing about. "Thanks!"

Corey couldn't help but smile back. "You part of the band?" Corey asked, knowing the answer was likely yes.

"Boy, you get right to the point," said Becky. "No warm-up."

"There's plenty of foreplay under the right circumstances," said Corey. He couldn't help but smile, hoping she wouldn't walk away in a huff.

"Wouldn't know, but I'm sure others would," Becky shot back, lifting her head up a little and looking directly at Corey. Then she moved away but stopped after a few steps. "The women's restroom down that hall?" she asked, pointing back toward the bar.

"Yeah, that way," Corey said. "I'll see you around," he said as she moved away.

"I'm sure," Becky said, looking back while bringing her hand up to her face and running her fingers under her hair and behind one ear. "Nice meeting you."

Corey watched her walk away. He waited for an exaggerated wiggle from her. There was none.

CHAPTER 3

pstairs, above the bar, Mike sat in his office behind a metal desk. Marcus sat across from him in an overstuffed leather armchair, his muscular size making the chair look small. He was an easy 250 pounds with a wide frame that made his six-foot-two height almost unnoticeable. "Charcoal" was his nickname in high school, and he took it as a compliment. Marcus was proud of his dark skin. He grew a beard, which he kept neatly trimmed because he thought it enhanced his color. He accepted the anger sometimes shown in his sculpted face and ebony eyes, and he knew the fear White people had of his appearance. Only men his size or bigger would challenge him, and only Black women were unafraid.

The two men sat in a messy place. Stacks of band press kits, cassettes, and LPs were piled on one end of a couch. An ancient paper-folding machine sat at the end of a table near boxes of envelopes, reams of colored paper, and an electric typewriter. Each month, the bar did a mailing announcing the bands for the month. The walls were covered with posters and photos of Mike with various musicians, along with a few comedy club posters from second-tier Chicago and St. Louis clubs. Comic "Mike Smith" was always listed below the headliner or even lower. The clutter hinted that business wasn't bad, but Mike knew he needed it to be better.

"You got it lined up?" asked Marcus.

"Yeah, I do," said Mike. "But what's this sack shit going to prove?"

"Lewis wants to know if this peckerwood is okay. That's all."

Mike ran both his hands through his thick, curly hair. He grabbed his chin with his right hand, pulling down on the skin as if he had a goatee. Then he opened his hand and rubbed his chin across the palm, and his eyes widened as he thought about the plan. "How's giving him a sack with a rolled-up white rag in a baggie with talcum powder going to prove he's not a narc or whatever?"

Marcus clutched the armrests. "Look, Wonder Bread," he said, lowering his voice and leaning forward. Mike didn't flinch. "This is what Lewis wants and what he thought up. The sack will be folded a certain way — marked or something — in a way Lewis will know if someone opened it or squeezed it or whatever. When Michelle picks up the sack and brings it back to Lewis, he can check to see if this yahoo touched it or opened it and looked in."

"And what if he does and sees the rag in the baggie of powder? What's that prove?" Mike asked in a way that didn't show fear.

Marcus didn't answer right away. He looked hard at Mike. He had sized him up before. Mike's hands were big like his, and even though he was only a little over six feet in height, Marcus figured he could throw and take a punch. But Marcus wouldn't let it get that far unless Lewis wanted it done.

Marcus began slowly, on purpose, dragging out the words. "If he opens the sack, looks in, and sees the rag, tastes the powder, he's going to know it's a test ... one he failed, and he won't be back here. He'll know we're on to him. He fucked up. We'll know he's working for the cops..."

"Or just stupid," Mike interjected.

"And we can assume they'll try something different later, and we'll be real up about it. Watching people close. Lewis says business is going to pick up, and he wants this to be a solid enterprise. He's got his own people to answer to. Now, do I have to keep goin' on with this? You got it, cuz?"

Mike thought the plan was bush league, and he had wondered from the first meeting with Lewis if he someday he'd have to take on Marcus. If nothing else, Mike knew he could out-think the guy. Mike fell to the temptation to push the tension along.

"What if he looked in because he's just curious, that's all, and it has nothing to do with anything other than the guy didn't listen to me about not opening the sack," said Mike, gesturing the words out with his hand close to his face. "The guy drives a delivery van for a living, wants to be a writer, or a musician or some artsy shit. He's an okay guy, smart but maybe a perpetual loser, but okay. Russell Manger, the guy who books bands, vouched for him."

Marcus was getting bored. Mike reminded him of mouthy White guys he used to slap around when he loan-sharked for Lewis. And this doorman, he meant nothing. Marcus would just as soon have some fun breaking a couple of his fingers with a ball-peen to find out if he is what he is, but Lewis wants to keep it calm. "I'm gone," Marcus said while standing up. "Like if this honkey says anything about the sack thing, call me. You dig? If I don't hear from you, I'll be by tomorrow night."

At the office door, Marcus stopped and turned back to Mike. "Let's do this right, White man, or I might be running this joint." Marcus then smiled.

Mike propped his elbows up on the desk and folded his hands under his chin. Marcus was scary, yeah, but Mike liked to play a little with him. Still, there was no getting away from the guy. He had made a deal with Lewis. He hoped Corey didn't open the sack.

With Marcus gone, Mike looked at the time on the wall clock. No rush. He began rubbing his forehead, thinking back. Three months ago he was broke with the club circling the drain, but at least he didn't know Marcus or Lewis or played sack games in some drug drama. Now, he had some money and a promise of more to run his club, but the attention and applause that he used to crave seemed even more elusive than ever, especially if he had to play patty-cake with ball-busters like Marcus.

It was ten till seven. He moved some papers to reveal the month's music calendar under the desk's glass top. He paused without looking. *Oh yeah,* he thought to himself. *Thursday, Good Riddance on the bill. I was the one who set it up this way.* A small crowd was expected. He'll bartend and have time to watch Corey at the door. Mike swiveled in his chair and pressed the intercom button on the wall behind him.

"Becky?"

"Yes, Mike?"

"I'll be down in a few minutes with the money for the register. Do an inventory of the bar to see what liquor we need and make sure the beer coolers are stocked. You know the drill. Have Corey help you carry some bottles from the back room if need be."

"Okay, Mike," Becky said in a hurried tone.

Mike hesitated at turning the intercom off. Corey likely was at the bar. The guy had a thing for Becky for a reason Mike easily understood. He often thought of having her himself, knowing he could move Corey aside in a heartbeat. As for Greg — he wouldn't have to know. Still, Mike didn't like tappin' the help — too much potential for drama. He had plenty of drama already. Still, Mike kept the intercom on.

"That guy who came down from Mike's office, who was he?" Corey asked.

"Now you pay attention," Becky said. "I don't know, but he kind of gave me the creeps. And he gave you a weird look."

Corey also noticed a quick but hard stare from Marcus. "Yeah, not in my circle of friends."

He didn't want to think about it too much. He was working on Becky.

"Maybe he's the rep for the musician's union. I know...maybe he's demanding more money for Greg's band!"

"Oh, shut up," Becky said. "You're not funny. Let me check the bar."

Becky stopped folding napkins. She began counting beer bottles in the cooler, then she hesitated for a moment, thinking of what Corey had said. Sometimes, she made more money than Greg on a night waitressing than him playing his trumpet. Corey looked at the blank expression on her face, wondering what she was thinking about.

"Union rep," Mike repeated to himself as he switched off the intercom. "I wish." *Funny, that's what I thought when Russell wanted to talk about — union scale for bands — when he called after booking a few bands into the club. Good luck with paying that ... maybe at a downtown hotel lounge.*

CHAPTER 4

Mike had met him at the Repartee early one afternoon. Russell Manger always wore slacks, a dress shirt, and expensive shoes when most of the rest of his world kept jeans and tees. It signaled a touch of oily arrogance in him. He slicked his thinning hair back and had a neatly trimmed goatee. Russell looked the part — a smart guy who made money from others. Mike led him to the bar after waiting for him at the front door. He didn't want Russell in his office. Mike wanted to make a point to keep the hierarchy in place.

"You want coffee or maybe a drink?" Mike asked.

"Neither. You got some tea? Green tea?"

Who asks for tea in a bar? Mike wondered. *Geez.* "No tea, sorry."

"A glass of water will be fine," Russell said.

Mike scooped some ice cubes into a glass and added water. For himself, he reached over for the coffeepot.

"How are things, Mike?" Russell asked.

"Things are going. A couple of those bands you booked brought a good crowd, especially that reggae band...err, Island Sound. Good band. Got people up dancing and drinking."

Russell smiled. "Yeah, they're good, real good. I don't handle them all the time. They got their own way about 'em. Maybe someday. They got a new album coming out in a few months. Could try to book them right after its release, an album release night."

"Yeah, that could be good."

Mike stirred his coffee with a straw. Russell took a sip from his glass. "Don't want to be too inquisitive, Mike, but how are things going revenue-wise?"

"Yeah, well, you know," Mike said with a shoulder shrug. He sized Russell up again. Mike was aware that every time he talked with Russell, he sized him up. He always had to figure out what the guy's angle was because he never appeared to be into what he was doing just for his love of music. Mike decided to open up a little, maybe get to the point of concluding what Russell's game was.

"Look, Russell, you're no dummy. I agreed to let you bring in some bands here because I needed another way to get people in to spend money. As a comedy club, I can't compete with that club in Westport, and the circuit itself is still too small for this part of the Midwest. Unless you got the bucks, this town isn't going to attract big names. And for local talent, that doesn't rise much above guys pimping on each other on street corners about getting or not getting laid."

"Gee, a little bitterness there, Mike," said Russell, his eyes fixed on Mike.

"Yeah, I know. Maybe that gives you an indication of where I'm at."

"What about you getting back up on stage? Heard you were pretty good."

"Now, where did you hear that, Russell?" Mike said as he took a sip from his coffee.

Russell felt defensive. "I don't know, just heard, that's all." He took another drink to relax. "I get around, Mike. Know people. Your name came up on occasion. I thought about promoting comics. One has to diversify, and I'm ambitious, Mike. But I still want to help people showcase their talents."

"Yeah, yeah, Russell. Screw the flattery. My coffee is getting cold. What did you really want to talk about?"

"You have a nice club here, lots of potential..."

"Get to the point, Russell."

"Okay," Russell answered softly. Mike's anxious, maybe near the brink, Russell told himself. "Mike, I know an investor. He likes music and wants to help make the Repartee the premier music club in town. I can arrange a meeting."

Mike stared at Russell. *An investor could mean conflict. An investor could mean money and an eventual way out of this.* "I don't know about having an investor, Russell," Mike said. "I like running things myself."

"Oh, he's not that much of a hands-on person," said Russell. "Just an entrepreneur type, a guy with a fondness for music. Not all that terribly wealthy but has money to invest and, honestly, wants a return."

"So he figures he can get a return by investing here?"

"Yeah, he does," said Russell.

Mike thought about it. *Could be legit. Could be a legitimate music lover with money. And it could be some hood looking for a place to launder money, put one of his guys inside, and run a few girls out on the side.*

Russell pushed a little, knowing Mike was running through the possibilities. "Mike, an investor, would help you update the place, expand the stage lighting, and add a soundboard. Some of the better-known bands want a place they play at to have a soundboard."

"Yeah, I know," said Mike. "The sound system works but could be better."

Mike kept his eyes on Russell. He told himself that just talking with this investor wouldn't hurt. Maybe. "What's this investor's name?"

Russell didn't let Mike's stare bother him. He knew Mike was genuinely interested. "Can't say right now. I got a little stake in this, too, Mike. You agree to consider the investment; I get to keep booking bands. I'll set up a meeting; you'll know then who he is."

"You can keep booking bands here now," said Mike. "I don't need an investor for you to do that."

"No offense, Mike, but that's only if you stay in business."

Mike reached for some brandy to add to his coffee. "We all set for this month for bands?" he asked.

"All set, Mike."

Mike took a sip from his coffee. "Meet here or somewhere else?"

"Probably here, Mike."

"Set it up for a couple of weeks from now."

"Mike, it will be a good thing, you'll see," said Russell. He tried not to show any excitement.

"Yeah, yeah," Mike answered, waving his hand toward the door. "But don't take me for an idiot." Russell knew it was time to leave.

Mike watched Russell strut to the door. "Piss-ant," Mike murmured to himself. He didn't like it, not all of it. Sure, he could lie to himself and believe this investor was some bored rich guy with a love of music and a shit-pot of money. But no. It was likely some guy wanting a foot in the door, seeing something here he couldn't see. Mike felt anger. Then he told himself that he didn't really care. *Fuck this town. Try something different, bring some life, and all I get is aggravation and a string of phone calls from vendors wondering when this or that will be paid. What the fuck ... let this investor take it over as long I get a few bucks out of it and an eventual way out of here.*

CHAPTER 5

Corey was carrying a case of beer to the bar when he saw Pinky standing by the stage. He wore his usual green Army field jacket, collar up. The jacket hung on his thin frame, its bulkiness making Pinky appear to lean forward either when in motion or standing still. But it wasn't that. The scar tissue on his back, a reminder of when docs removed the shrapnel, made him standing straight up with his shoulders back difficult. The pain, or fear, gave his face a hallow look, the skin drawn tight around his eyes that appeared like gashes above high cheekbones and below long dirty blond hair, which always fell over his forehead. Pinky waved to Corey and started walking toward the bar. Corey held up his hand and mouthed for Pinky to stay there.

"Got to talk with this guy," Corey told Becky.

"Another union rep?" she answered with a forced smile.

Corey grimaced and walked to meet Pinky. "Hey, Pinky. What's up?"

"Corey, my man. Thought I stopped by to see my roommate ... my man." Pinky was his jittery self.

"Okay, man. What do you want?" Then Corey remembered. "You got it? You owe your share of the rent, remember? It's late."

"That's why I stopped by," said Pinky as he pointed at Corey. "A job. To cover that. Did you ask Mike about me being a bar back?"

"No, I didn't," said Corey, waving one hand in Pinky's face. "We went over this. Mike can't afford a bar back. The guy knows how to bartend, and if he needs help on a big night, he brings in a girl. With that, he's the bar back. I didn't ask because I knew the answer."

Pinky swung his body back and to his left as if dodging a punch. "Ah, man. I was hopin'."

"Look, I told you this. But I think you were half-lit when we talked about it. Man, you got to slow down with the drinking. Get in a VA program or something. You're going through the disability checks and not paying the rent, and I can't keep fronting you your share. Maybe someone down there can help you out."

"Okay, preacher man," Pinky shot back, raising his voice. "I hear you. Can you spot me ten?"

"Ah, Jesus, man. Like I'm a bank," Corey said in a whine while touching his back pocket.

"Come on, bro. This ain't for a bottle. I need a burger or something." Pinky waited, then reached into his jacket pocket and pulled out a pack of cigarettes.

"Give me one," Corey demanded. Pinky held the pack out, snapped it against his hand, and Corey pulled one out. Pinky lit Corey's cigarette, then his own. Both men took a drag. "Ten for a burger...yeah, right."

"A burger tonight and one tomorrow," Pinky said with a smile. Then, in a more serious tone added, "The disability check will be here on the 15th. You'll get my rent share then."

"Meanwhile, I've got to dodge the landlord."

"We both do."

Corey reached for his wallet. "Here's five. Go collect aluminum cans or something for the rest."

"Thanks, man," Pinky said with disappointment while folding the bill into his hand. He pointed to the bar. "Hot chick. You doin' that?"

"I wish," Corey answered while looking back at Becky. She was busy behind the bar.

Pinky turned and went down the stairs to the street. Corey went back to the bar.

There, Becky asked, "Who was that?"

"Roommate."

"You always give your roommate money?"

Narrowing his eyes, Corey said, "I see you were checking it out. No. We're friends."

"Oh, I see," Becky said, lifting her chin and looking up.

Corey let it go. He knew what she was implying. She was getting back at him a little. He studied her mouth and lips. He wanted to kiss her.

"Hi," Becky said loudly as she looked pass Corey to the entrance door. It was Greg. He was carrying a small amp and his trumpet. He put them down by the stage and walked to the bar. Without looking at Corey, he walked behind the bar and embraced Becky. "Hey, baby."

Corey turned away as they kissed. The band was setting up. Might as well step outside for a minute. He figured it would be a slow night, betting on an older, mellower crowd. Then Corey remembered. *The sack is coming.* "Huh."

CHAPTER 6

Pinky walked west on 39th. He moved quickly, shoulders slumped, head down. Barely five-nine, he took long, quick strides nevertheless, covering ground easily. He walked like a man who walked a lot, with no hesitation in where he was going.

Bain's Liquor & Groceries was four blocks up, not far from the house he shared with Corey. Ordinarily, he'd stop in the liquor store by the Repartee and then grab a shot at the Slip, but Corey might come down from the club and see which way he went. *Don't need more crap from him about rent. With the five-spot and his loose change, I could still get a cheap half-pint at Bain's. Then maybe walk by Lou's to see if anyone was smoking a doobie at the back door. Catch a buzz, and with what's left over from buying the bottle and with some sweet-talk to Lou, maybe he would even let him get a small beer to cap off the night before heading back home.* Pinky liked the plan.

A block up from the Repartee, Detective Steven Jensen watched Pinky walk by from an unmarked car. "So, what do we know about this clown?" Jensen asked without turning to look at his partner, Malcolm Frederick.

Jensen expected to do another eight years and retire. He pushed the weight limit set by the department and was prematurely gray. He fit the stereotype of a fat, sloppy, cynical White cop derided by the generation that came after him.

His partner, Frederick, was tall and thin and kept up on the latest fashion trends to go with his small Afro, a hairstyle his Black brothers were moving away from. He viewed being paired with Jensen as either an inside joke by the personnel department or window dressing in the name of diversity.

Frederick sighed and squinted as he followed Pinky. "Not that much. His name is Peter James Grayson, but he goes by the nickname Pinky. He's a Vietnam vet, Army, has a drinking problem, doper but nothing hard, at least not yet ... usual mix of issues dealing with having been in. But nothing major. A few fights, disorderly, kicked out of a couple of bars, a couple of arrests for public drunkenness, on disability. Took some shrapnel in the back."

"In other words, another loser vet," said Jensen. "Jesus. Why can't these guys get it together? I was over there. Came out okay."

"You were in the Air Force, there in 1965 before the real shit started," said Frederick. He was irritated, having heard the comment before.

"At least I went."

Frederick shot a hard look at his partner. "My lottery number was high. I dodged motherfucker!"

"Okay, okay," Jensen said quickly. "Let's drop it." He looked at his side-view mirror, down the street toward the Repartee. "If this club has attracted the attention of Marcus Rudd, and therefore Lewis, there's got to be a reason. We got any kind of plan on this?"

"Not really," said Frederick in a calmer voice. "Could it be Marcus wants a piece of the club, somewhere to hang? I bet the owner — we know who owns this place?"

"Some comic guy...moved here from out of town," said Jensen. "We'll get more information tomorrow. But something's got to be stirrin'. Marcus doesn't make social calls without a reason."

The two detectives sat in silence, and then Jensen asked, "What's Re-part-tee mean? What is it, Italian or something?"

Frederick looked over at Jensen. "No, man. I think it's French."

"Okay, wise ass, what does it mean."

"Like a witty answer to someone's remark ... kind of a return remark, you know, a sharp comeback to an insult."

"Oh," said Jensen, drawing out the word "re...part...tee. Like what I do with you when you pimp on me."

"Yeah, that's right, Jensen. Like you do me," Frederick said in mock resignation. He then turned his head and looked out his side window.

Jensen pulled a cigarette from a pack on the car's dash. "What kind of music they play in there, Mr. Know-It-All? Do they play any country? I bet it's rock and jazz, right?"

Frederick thought about getting out of the car and walking around a bit. Instead, he just opened his car door as Jensen lit his cigarette and said, "Country maybe, but Jensen, there ain't no jazz in Kansas City. Such hipness left when Count Basie and Charlie Parker left town."

Jensen laughed and said, "So country took its place!"

"Yeah, Jensen, so did cowboy hats." Frederick started to get out of the car.

"Come on, Frederick. Let's get back on point. So, we see this Pinky guy leaving the place ... before it really opens."

Sitting back down and closing the car door, Frederick added, "Maybe he knows something. We could introduce ourselves or just wait until this guy Pinky fucks up, which he's bound to do, I figure — and then have a talk. Or find someone else or ..."

"Does he drive?" Jensen interrupted.

"No. Lost his license, doesn't have a car."

"Does he have a girlfriend?"

"Not that we know of ... Does anyone have a girlfriend these days?" Frederick asked.

"Not really, at least for some. For studs like you, Frederick, it's pussy galore."

"You got that right, Jensen. You finally got something right about your partner."

Jensen ran the middle finger of his right hand down the side of his cheek at Frederick as he watched Pinky disappear over a hill. He then reached for his coffee cup, perched on the car's dashboard, and flipped the cigarette out the window.

Frederick gave Jensen a look of disgust.

"So, he likes a little dope, does Pinky, and likes to drink," said Jensen after taking a sip. "Takes money for those habits. He probably wouldn't pass up some sort of a deal if he thought he was getting a little something in return."

"Probably not," answered Frederick flatly.

"Let's put it on the to-do list." Jensen then looked back over his shoulder. "Want to stop in for a quick one at the Slip? I like making the homos nervous."

"Jensen, if we're going to investigate what could be going on at this club, don't you think we shouldn't be seen hanging around near it? At least not yet."

"All right," said Jensen. "You got a point. Let's call it a day."

CHAPTER 7

Mike closed the door to the desk safe and spun the dial. He had the cash for the night. When he got downstairs, the band was beginning its sound check. Becky was talking with Greg on the stage. She turned and saw Mike. He motioned for her to come to the bar.

"Pick out a jazz or light rock cassette and get some sounds going on the tape deck," he said when Becky came behind the bar.

Corey wasn't around. Mike checked the wall clock above the bar. It was twenty to eight. He'd open the doors at eight whether the band was ready or not. Get some drinks in some people. Greg might get the band going before nine, or maybe not. Didn't matter. The bands are paid to begin at nine with two breaks if they want, and most do. Usually, the musicians come to the bar for their free drink. If not, Mike makes sure they know to take the pot outside. He doesn't want the smell drifting through the place, giving people temptation. Most musicians remain discreet, going downstairs by the street or behind the building; anything else stays backstage.

With Greg's band, there was little worry that drugs would make their breaks stretch out, causing a stir within the crowd. Whatever Greg's band members did, it was not done during a gig. As for the help

... Becky never drank while working, and with Greg playing tonight, she'd hustle to close out to leave with him. Neither struck Mike as big druggies except maybe for a few lines on a mirror before a romp in bed. For that, with Becky, Mike told himself he would give coke a try again.

Corey, on the other hand, would give anything a try, particularly if it led to party time with a girl. But since the warning from Mike — after he noticed Corey disappearing backstage one night during a band's break and then pinching and rubbing his nose throughout the night — Corey had left it alone while working the door.

"You get fucked up, and door money ain't right, and you're out of here, pronto, for good," Mike told Corey.

That night, Corey decided that one doesn't push against Mike.

Mike settled himself into a bartender's role, wiping down glasses and filling the wash and rinse tubs with water. After walking the floor, Becky came back up to the bar as Mike made a pot of coffee.

"Where's Corey?" he asked.

"I think he went outside for a minute. His roommate showed up earlier."

"So what? He's talking with him outside?" asked Mike.

Becky smiled and shrugged. "I don't know, Mike."

Mike gave her an irritated look, then saw Corey come back into the club. "There he is. Tell him to come up and get the door money." Becky turned and walked in Corey's direction. Halfway, she whispered to Corey, "He's not in a good mood."

At the bar, Corey smiled. "Just outside getting some air, Mike."

Mike looked at him. No red eyes, no twitchy nose. Corey didn't look like he had done anything he had been warned about. "Here's the door money. Remember what I told you earlier."

"Yeah, the sack. Don't worry, Mike, I'll do want you want."

Mike figured he would. Mike stared at Corey as he settled in on his stool and put a metal box with the night's door money for change on a shelf behind him. *Though Corey had talent somewhere at something, he was just wasting time because he thought with his dick too much.* At one time,

Mike could relate to the guy. As for tonight, Corey will follow through because this place is his party outlet, Mike told himself.

Still, this whole sack thing was simple yet overblown. He wouldn't know if Corey looked in the sack or not. Corey could leave it alone, and Lewis could still claim he looked in. Next thing, Corey's out, and a goon like Marcus is sitting at the door and the whole vibe of the place changes. But maybe Lewis doesn't want the vibe to change; that's the reason for the sack test.

"We agree to this, and there won't be any disruptions, Mike," Lewis said early on at their one and only meeting. Marcus drove Lewis in one Sunday morning to meet Mike.

CHAPTER 8

Lewis didn't' leave his suburban home much except for an occasional night downtown with his wife. He grew up on the eastside, carving out some territory along Truman Road and then branching out from there. He started with muscle, getting a take from the local businesses for protection against "the nasty elements of the neighborhood," as Lewis always put it to a reluctant business owner. With Marcus at his side, it didn't take too much persuasion.

With some capital, Lewis upped operation to loansharking and then to drug dealing. Smart and thinking ahead, he bought into some legitimate businesses, building a respectable front, leaving the flashing cars and stable of girls to others. His drug business remained discreet as he moved away from the transit hassles of marijuana and concentrated more on the growing attraction of cocaine. Its appeal to many classes of people gave Lewis insulation from too much scrutiny as multiple layers of people did the legwork.

Mostly, his operation stayed in certain areas, not pushing against the Italians in the north or the Mexicans on the west side and leaving the ghetto hustlers to peddle their hard stuff and attract the cops. If Lewis found a little beachhead somewhere outside his usual sphere of business, he'd let the other players know and cut them in if necessary to avoid any disruptions. If someone complained or got greedy, he'd deploy Marcus, whose street cred nobody questioned.

He made contributions to local politicians and sometimes attended charity fundraisers. He liked the respectability that came with such events, but, in practice, he stayed on the back wall away from the media lights. Lewis had a patient, thoughtful approach. He liked things to be calm.

Mike first heard of Lewis when he had trouble getting his liquor license. After three trips to city hall to find out what the delay was a clerk whispered to him that he ought to contact Lewis Richardson for help. "The guy has some juice where needed," said the clerk.

Once the license came through, Mike forgot about the suggestion. But when Russell introduced Lewis to Mike, he again remembered what the clerk had said.

"Mike," Russell said, his arm outstretched and pointing toward Lewis. "This is the possible investor I talked to you about, Mr. Lewis Richardson."

Lewis reached toward Mike to shake hands. He wore a polo shirt, dark slacks, and a light-colored sports jacket. His short stature, broad smile, and cinnamon skin shade were disarming. He wore glasses. Mike didn't know whether it was because he had bad eyesight or just wanted to look smart. A slick Black guy in country club threads, Mike said to himself. Marcus stood next to him, expressionless.

"Mr. Smith, a pleasure to meet you," said Lewis.

"Yeah, same here," answered Mike, looking at Marcus. They shook hands.

"This is Marcus Rudd, my associate," said Lewis. "He assists me in my business dealings."

A hood with his muscle, Mike told himself immediately. *Should have known.*

The thing is, how much of a hood was this guy? Could Mike co-exist for a while until he had some money to leave this town? The only way, Mike told himself, was to know as little as possible about what Lewis wanted from his investment, then plan for an exit.

It was more than music and money as an attraction for Russell. It was power. The twerp, as he was sometimes called, was ambitious.

"Russell has said a lot of good things about the potential of your club," Lewis started in as Mike motioned for them to sit down. He then walked around his desk and eased into his chair. Marcus took a few steps away from the two toward the door, intently watching Mike.

"Oh, Russell," said Lewis, turning to him. "Would you mind if Marcus and I talked with Mike alone?"

A look of hurt flashed across Russell's face. "No problem. I'll wait downstairs at the bar," he said.

Lewis looked around Mike's office. "Your office has a homey but masculine feel, Mike. I like that. A reminder of your past career and what you're doing now. I take it there's no female influence in your life."

"I get a little here and there, and that's about it," Mike said.

Lewis nodded. "I, myself, am a family man. My children are in private school. We have a nice, custom-built house in the suburbs, a pool, and a well-stocked bar. I occasionally entertain with my wife. You should find a steady girl and come out sometime when we have such an occasion."

"I'll keep it in mind," said Mike.

Lewis smiled at Mike. *He wasn't intimidated,* Lewis told himself. *I like that. The nervous, intimidated types are usually stupid, prone to make mistakes, and easily rattled if the authorities put a little pressure on them. This could work out without too much interference on his part.*

"Russell is quite the go-getter," Lewis began. "He's got a good ear for a band that could go somewhere and a good feel for where that band should play. Don't you think, Mike?"

"He does pretty good by me. Seems to know what he's doing."

"Precisely," said Lewis. "So when he mentioned to me that your club was a good place for bands, a place that the public liked and gravitated to, I listened."

"I'm sure," said Mike.

"But Russell wasn't quite sure how long he could book at the Repartee — by the way, an interesting name for a club."

"Some people say that, but there's a little bit of a reason for the name," said Mike.

"I would guess it's a comeback of sorts ... maybe a resurgence, a counter to some kind of negative, I would guess. Am I correct in my assumption?"

"Maybe, but maybe you're putting too much into it. It's a word I like, that's all. Thought it would be a good name for a club."

"A comedy club, that is. That didn't work out, did it?" said Lewis as he leaned back into his chair.

"Yeah, that's right, it didn't work out," said Mike sharply. "The town isn't ready for it."

"I would agree," said Lewis in an even tone. "This town is barely ready to move beyond the disco era into live music again. But, Mike, you are pushing that along. You're a pioneer of sorts, an entrepreneur of the arts."

Mike looked around his office. He looked at Marcus standing near the door. They exchanged blank stares. "Look, Lewis ... Mr. Richardson, Russell said you were interested in investing in the promise of this club. I'm interested in talking about taking on investors. Can we get to that point?"

"Is the situation more urgent than I thought, Mike?"

"No," said Mike. "I can keep going, but I need improvements, a soundboard, better lighting, some funds to market the club and maybe attract some national performers. Step it up a bit."

Lewis nodded. "Good plans, Mike. But tougher if you don't have the needed money to up your game. Plus, what happens if there's problems?"

"What kind of problems?" Mike asked.

"Well, say, for example, that metro liquor distributors tighten the requirements for a line of credit, or beer deliveries get a little erratic — some of those trucks can be prone to break down. And those city fire inspectors ... sometimes they can really be by the book in their inspections, and you sure wouldn't want an underage person being caught in your club drinking. Being shut down a few days can hurt."

Mike said nothing. He tried not to show defeat in his face. *It was either to let this guy in or slowly drown. Lewis wanted into the club for some reason. But he likely had no one to run it, at least not right now, or otherwise, he wouldn't be here. Russell didn't seem the management type and Marcus would scare people away. So, Lewis needed Mike for right now. A little leverage, for the time being*, Mike figured.

"Yeah, problems can pop up," Mike said. "Having a professional around to deal with them is important, someone who doesn't lose focus on giving patrons an entertaining venue to spend their money. Good management is important for investors who recognize the value of what they're investing in, and customers want a place they feel comfortable in." Mike looked beyond Lewis to Marcus.

Lewis gave Mike a smile. "I like this beginning basis of mutual understanding, Mike," he said.

Mike turned his hands upward and nodded.

Lewis opened his jacket and reached inside the breast pocket. He pulled out an envelope and held it as he said, "Our discussion has been fruitful, Mike. As a businessman, I obviously do my research even before entering into discussions on a business deal. So, Mike, I assume you know I know a little about you."

Mike pulled his chair closer to his desk. He put his elbows up, hands under his chin. Lewis was like another club owner telling him he would go on late, telling him his material wasn't that good, but with the crowd well into their drinking, it didn't matter that much. "Maybe you should get a stage name," they would sometimes suggest, "something where the last name sounds Italian or Jewish — builds a little anticipation. Everyone knows a 'Smith.' With a last name like yours, you might be fighting harder for a laugh." *Club owners — they always need to give you shit before they pay you.*

"Here's some proof of my intentions to invest, Mike," said Lewis as he slid the envelope forward across the desk.

Mike looked down at the envelope. "How much of an investment are you making, Mr. Richardson?" asked Mike, grinding out the words slowly.

Lewis stood up, not liking the way Mike asked the question. He reached over and put a hand on top of the envelope. "It's five thousand, Mike. A start on what you want to do with the club." Then Lewis added, "Or it could go toward helping pay the cost of keeping your mother in that nice retirement home and paying for her medications."

Mike looked up at Lewis. *Maybe someday I could beat this guy to a pulp,* he told himself. *Or maybe I could survive long enough to get something out of this and split. Mom needs her comfort, but at some point, she will die.*

Mike stood up. Marcus took a step toward the two men. Lewis raised his hand to motion Marcus to wait.

"I always like my investors to do their research," said Mike. Lewis looked puzzled. He continued almost cheerily. "I always thought business deals worked when both parties do what they had to do to share in the benefits of the deal."

Lewis nodded.

"And for my part, I don't need to know much for that arrangement to work well. But I need a comfort zone too. Otherwise, you never know what could happen."

Lewis gave Mike a smile. He knew he could fuck with Mike and slowly push his business into the ground. But Lewis didn't want to wait, and maybe Mike didn't really want to know what Lewis' reason for using the Repartee would be. It wasn't hard for Lewis to guess when someone was in dire need of money; loan sharking made one a quick study. If things get complicated, Marcus could step in, but from what Lewis observed, Marcus might have to bring his A game.

"Like you, Mike, I like business deals to go smoothly, with each party knowing what they have to do to make money."

Mike smiled and reached down and picked up the envelope as Lewis lifted his hand from it.

"Marcus will handle the details of my investment, Mike," Lewis said. He turned and walked toward the door, then stopped. Without turning around, Lewis said, "Maybe we'll meet again, Mike, socially if this business deal goes well. You could get an invite to a party at my place. Bring a girl if you find someone special."

Mike shrugged. "That's a big maybe."

"I'm sure it is," Lewis said while walking through the door behind Marcus.

CHAPTER 9

ain's Liquor & Convenience was in what was left of an old 1930's gas station. The pumps had long been removed, the outdoor lift gone, and black asphalt poured, surrounding the small building on three sides. As Pinky opened the heavy front door, the owner, Gary Bain, called out from behind the counter, "Got to have money to buy something, Pinky."

Despite approaching middle age, Bain still had a youthful athletic built, like one would have with a love of cycling or soccer, where constant movement kept the stomach flat and the legs shapely. When he came out from behind the counter, Bain could attract the notice of either sex, though it was men he thought about. Only when he put on his readers to count change or do inventory did one begin thinking about his age.

Pinky gave him a look of disdain. Ever since Gary had let him slide after catching him pocketing a candy bar one night when Pinky was a little high, he thought he had the right to always give him shit. "Aaww, stick it, Gary. I got money. Give me a half-pint of Jim Beam."

Gary laughed, then turned around to get the bottle. Pinky dropped the wadded five-dollar bill on the counter. "Two-fifteen," said Gary, reaching for the bill.

He un-wadded the bill, gave Pinky his change, and bagged the bottle. Before Pinky could turn around to leave, Gary asked if Pinky wanted to make twenty dollars.

"Doin' what?"

"I'm putting in another cooler in the back to hold more beer. I need someone to move some junk out to the dumpster and clean up the area before they bring in the cooler. Probably less than a half day's work. You interested?"

"When? What time?"

"Sunday morning when it's slow...be here around eight."

"Okay, yeah, I could do it, even if it's grunt work," said Pinky. But Pinky was leery. Is this guy for real, or just planning an opportunity to put the moves on me? He put out sort of a gay vibe.

"I appreciate it, man, but you have to stop giving me shit every time I come in. Otherwise, fuck it."

"Okay, I'll think about it," said Gary with a smile. "And I'll even throw in a candy bar with the twenty if you do a good job."

Pinky flipped him off as he walked out, now not sure if he'd show up.

As he neared Lou's, Pinky looked to the bar's back door to see if there was anyone standing around talking and passing a joint. It was a warm fall night. No one was there. Either Pinky's timing was off, or it was a slow night at the bar. He walked into Lou's through the back door as most regulars did.

Carolyn Wishman was behind the bar, not Lou. Pinky smiled — no problem getting a free beer or two from Carolyn. As Corey's on-again, off-again girlfriend, Pinky had seen her come and go from their house, and sometimes he had seen a lot of her as she readied herself in the morning for her day job. She didn't seem to mind that the bathroom door was half-open when she got out of the shower.

"Hi, Pinky," Carolyn called from behind the bar.

"Ah, sweetness in the flesh," Pinky said. He forgot about Gary. His mood lifted.

Carolyn smiled, put her hands on her hips, and said, "What ya have?"

"You know damn well, lady, what I'd have, but my roommate would kick me out."

"I was talking about what to drink, mister," said Carolyn. The smile stayed on her face as she pulled a beer from the tap and placed it in front of Pinky. "Come from the Repartee?"

Pinky reached slowly into his pocket as if to pay for the beer. Carolyn motioned to stop. "Yeah, your old man is working hard, sippin' on a drink and watching the band set up."

"Did he say he was swingin' by here before I closed?"

"Didn't say," Pinky answered.

Carolyn was unaffected by his answer. "I'll stop by you guys' place after I get off," she said to herself as much as to Pinky.

He watched her move down the bar to wait on another customer. Though she was just over five feet, she moved her backside as if taller, bringing on a look from most guys. She had a tight, subtle swing to her hips, more pronounced when she threw her head back and ran her fingers through her long, thick black hair. Her breasts were ample, and she used her cleavage well to coax the tips, picking out blouses for that purpose. Pinky found her hot yet respected her and Corey's relationship as much as he could. He didn't move on women, even loosely tied to another guy, but he thought Corey didn't give her the respect she was due.

Still, Pinky didn't know much about her. Corey didn't talk about their relationship. When the two did fight, Corey — to his credit — didn't lay the blame on Carolyn. Differences didn't seem to linger, probably because Corey was always interested in more than one woman. Pinky knew this; Carolyn suspected it.

What Pinky knew about Carolyn was that she worked a part-time day job and took a class or two at the community college in addition to a couple of nights at the bar. Old Lou, the owner, liked her and trusted her. Corey once said she had grown up in the city's northeast side, a community with a long history of being a tough place to grow up in. When Carolyn talked about herself, she always quickly mentioned her brother, Michael, the guitar player and wannabe rock star. If Carolyn didn't have much hope for a future with Corey, she dreamed of her brother making it. She seemed more mother than a sister to Michael.

Pinky knew he didn't bring much to the table when it came to her or any girl. Memories of the war gave him an ongoing excuse to get drunk, and he took to it when he could. Money was a constant hustle, and he had no real plan about anything, much less keeping a woman in his life. But if Carolyn ever *really* broke up with Corey ...

Pinky turned on his stool when he heard the break of balls from the pool table in the back room. "Some guys have got a two-dollar nine-ball game goin'," said Carolyn, walking back toward him. "If you go back there, make sure the money stays off the table, please."

"No problem." Pinky grabbed his beer and headed to the back room.

Steve Lawton was lining up a shot on the nine. A fresh-faced college kid looked on anxiously. Steve stroked, and the ball fell cleanly into the corner pocket. He chalked his cue and walked back toward the college kid to await the money.

"I've lost twelve dollars to you. I can't keep playing," said the kid, slapping a couple of bills into Steve's outstretched hand.

"Okay," said Steve with a shrug. He turned and saw Pinky. "You want in, Pinky?"

Pinky took a sip from his beer. He didn't particularly like Lawton, a sometimes construction worker and street-level dealer. The guy was a Neanderthal of sorts: big, a braggart and intimidating. But Pinky wasn't afraid. The war had done that. If you survived, it meant the jungle had sucked any fear from you.

"Yeah. Let me get a stick."

They started at two bucks and a beer each game. Pinky couldn't afford to lose. He had only two dollars and change in his pocket, so he went all out, winning the first three games and letting the beers collect on a nearby table, pacing himself in how he drank.

After the fourth game, Lawton spoke up. "Let's play for five."

"Okay, Steve."

Lawton won the next game, leaving Pinky with around two dollars again after paying out. When he broke at the start of a new game,

Lawton scratched the cue ball and left the nine-ball hanging just outside the side pocket. Pinky had an easy combination shot for the win. After that, Pinky won five in a row — thirty dollars up. Pinky couldn't help but have a smile on his face.

"You never shot that good in your life," Steve fumed. "Most of it is fuckin' luck with me leaving you good. I'm fuckin' done." And Lawton slammed his cue stick on top of the pool table.

Pinky said nothing, but he kept his cue stick in his hand until Lawton walked out of the bar, kicking a chair on his way. Pinky gave two beers to a couple of guys who had been watching the game, then walked back to the bar.

"You got him mad," said Carolyn. "The guy's a hothead, Pinky. You have to watch out when you deal with him. Stay in the bar for a while."

Pinky was in a mellow mood — a few beers in him and some money in his pocket. He looked into Carolyn's eyes, searching for that hint of interest he hoped was there. "If you ever get tired of Corey..." Pinky let the words trail off.

Carolyn smiled and reached out to touch his hand. "We might be too much alike, Pinky," she said, walking away.

Lawton sat in his pickup a while, thinking about waiting for Pinky. "Skinny motherfucker," he said to himself. He could bust up the guy, but he wasn't sure he wouldn't come after him later. A lot of rumors floated around about Pinky and his combat experience in Vietnam, and the guy seemed unhinged in public on more than one occasion. Still, Lawton didn't like losing at anything. *Next time I play him, I'll get in his face more.*

Lawton started his truck and turned right toward the state line. He'd stop for a couple more at the Two States Lounge before heading to his apartment on the Kansas side.

Carolyn's remark stayed with Pinky. He could keep it lingering by having another beer or walking to another neighborhood bar. But that meant spending money, paying the full tab to drink. No. It had been a while since he had bought himself a meal. He decided to walk back east to Nichelson's. Meatloaf sounded good. Pinky felt hungry, and he felt the weight of the half-pint in his jacket. It was still early. He could always go back to drinking.

"I'm going to go get a bite down at Nichelson's," Pinky said to Carolyn as he downed his beer.

"Okay. Be careful," she called back as Pinky walked outside into the night air.

CHAPTER 10

Nichelson's drew people throughout midtown and beyond, being one of the few places that served decent food around the clock. They tolerated partygoers leaving either the Repartee or Westport, the entertainment/retail district a mile to the east.

On an early Saturday morning, after the bars closed at 2 a.m., Nichelson's could extend a night's enjoyment. A passerby would be easily drawn to peer into its long rectangular window, magnifying the crowd outward as they waited for tables, mouths moving silently, people bringing their barroom laughs, exaggerated stories, and repeated invitations to supposedly all-night parties with them.

Lighted to the extreme, as if to evaporate the liquor running in people's veins or cleanse a stoner's bloodshot eyes, single men would squint around the room, pick a pair of women, then wobble up to the booth to spin a line of introduction. He had mere seconds to make an impression and slide in next to one of the girls or be barked back to his booth by one of the waitresses moving through the narrow aisles.

Donni O'Connor held court at the lengthy front counter. She was a tall, dark-haired woman — six-three or more — tall enough that her red and white uniform always seemed a little small on her frame.

Glasses and heavy makeup dissolved any distinct features other than a long face framed by light brown hair done in the early '60s flip. Her large hands and a small, faint "USMC" tattoo on her right forearm could get a customer wondering, sometimes leading the eyes to search for Adam's apple above Donni's buttoned-up blouse.

Few things escaped her during her shift. Those in some sort of a search knew that. With a tilt of her head Donni could direct the cops to an obnoxious customer in need of an escort out. Taxi drivers looked to her to find a nearly passed-out pickup. For those who showed her respect over time and left a decent tip, be it a woman or man, Donni could then direct her gaze toward another like-minded soul wanting touch. Only those seeking to score drugs were ignored. Donni figured that most at that time of night brought their high — or low — with them, and she and Nichelson's were there to help them cope or come down if the effort was wanted, and they behaved.

She didn't seem to have a love interest or any special person in her life. The other waitresses took their direction from her, but Donni was never part of those periodic clusters when two or three waitresses gathered quickly at the coffee machine to whisper about this customer or that, or laugh quietly at some drunken idiot trying to find his mouth with a hot cup of coffee.

When Corey came in alone, he always sat at the counter. He liked the way Donni moved behind the counter, her slow glide and deliberate girly motions to get a glass of water, refill a coffee cup, or lay a plate of eggs and hash browns before someone seemed choreographed, a dance that got more precise and comfortable as the night wore on. He never asked if she was someone else before the glasses, the makeup, and the waitressing. He never heard anyone ask her about it.

Some never noticed the tattoo or big hands; many were taken back by her physical presence, something that would cause most men, even big men, to pause. Only Black men hit upon her occasionally, seemingly not intimidated by her size but rather attracted to her because of it. She could force a slight smile at a pickup line and sometimes place her index finger on her lower lip and bat her eyelids in an overly girlish way, but she always ended the chase with "Honey, you ain't big enough for me" and then turn her back and walk away.

The few times Donni looked at Corey directly, he pondered the meaning. Eventually, he decided her infrequent, direct look upon him meant he was okay, that he didn't need to go beyond a "hello" or "How ya doin' Donni?" and then order his coffee and breakfast. If he wanted something more from her, he could ask. But until then, Corey would just always leave a big tip.

CHAPTER 11

By the time Good Riddance took their first break, a good-size crowd had settled in. The band was building a solid following, a little older than the usual Repartee patrons: newly established college professors, single young executives with money, small business owners — music consumers with a real or perceived sense of sophistication.

Corey watched Mike work the bar. He was hustling as people crowded in. *I bet he's reaching into his bartender's skill book,* Corey thought, *and wishing he had a larger wine list. It's a crowd that likes martinis and can read a wine label.* Corey grinned. Already, Mike had Becky behind the bar making her drink orders herself.

A couple of band members walked past Corey to go outside for some air. Greg stood off the stage, watching Becky behind the bar.

"Good crowd tonight, man," Corey said, loud enough for Greg to hear.

Greg turned around. "Yeah, yeah, it is." He came over and stood by Corey, still watching people at the bar. They were about the same height, Corey a little bit stockier with hair cut shorter. "You're Corey, right?" Greg said.

"Yeah. The door guy."

"Becky has mentioned you. I'm Greg Zurkee," he said, sticking out his hand.

Corey shook it. "Very good band. Smooth and tight."

"Thanks. We try — excuse me." And with that, Greg started walking toward the bar.

Seemed like a good guy, Corey thought. *Definitely into Becky*, and he could see why Becky liked him — good-looking, polite, talented, and a musician. *Musicians always have girls. You could be a bass player uglier than Bigfoot and get a girl. It's just the way it is. Painters — artist types — got girls too. Down the list of attracting groupies were writers.* Maybe that's why Corey didn't write much like he should or told himself he should. He smiled at his own analysis. He then thought of Carolyn and wondered if he would see her tonight.

For Corey, there wasn't much to do after the first set. Those who wanted to be there were there. Late-night stragglers looking for a pickup usually don't show — with a jazz band, it's mostly couples. The crowd's older makeup made any arguments over a woman or a drunk getting in someone's face unlikely. Corey looked around the room. Not one, not one pair of single women, just a couple of stray guys who were either diehard jazz fans or wondering why they came when there weren't any available women. Cory grabbed his beer mug and walked to the bar. The drink rush had ended, and band members were making their way back to the stage.

"Hey, Mike, can I have another?" Corey said, putting his mug on the bar. Mike took it without a word and came back with a refill. "When is the bag supposed to show?" Corey asked in a whisper. Mike gave him a disgusted look.

"I don't know. Just do what you're supposed to. And don't the fuck talk about it?"

Corey frowned and took his beer. *Jeez, you'd think the guy would be in a better mood — he seems to be making money tonight.* Corey walked back to his stool. As he sat down, he turned and saw Becky coming toward him with her waitress tray. She looked like she wanted to talk.

"Ready to hit the floor already?" Corey said.

Band members were settling in for another set. "Aren't they just great tonight? Greg is so talented. Russell is looking into some places that might work for the band."

"Oh yeah, where?" Corey asked in a deflated tone.

Becky looked at him funny. "Aren't you happy for us? I mean, as a writer, you want success too, don't you?"

"I do," said Corey with meaning.

"Russell said Omaha and Des Moines have some clubs that book jazz bands, even Oklahoma City."

"Yeah, I've read where some early jazz musicians actually built on their reputations in Oklahoma. What a weird place for jazz."

"Oh, I wouldn't know but it's exciting, better than just playing a few places here in town and having Greg work his day job." Becky's eyes sparkled as she watched Greg blow lightly into his trumpet to clear it, then turn to his band members to see how close they were to starting the next set.

"Would you travel with the band if he hits the road?" Corey asked.

"Maybe, sometimes, but probably not often. I still have classes to take."

Corey nodded. He told himself he needed to know when Good Riddance was out of town.

The band started, and Becky moved away to work the floor, giving Corey a big smile as she did. Corey watched the band get into Nat Adderley's soul jazz number, "Stony Island." The crowd stirred, and a couple of women began pulling their dates onto the dance floor. The band sounded good.

Corey took a few steps away from the front entrance to get a better view of the band. Greg's playing was impressive, and people were connecting to it. He held his horn up high as if he wanted the notes to bounce off the ceiling and into the crowd. Corey didn't see Russell walk in and didn't know he was there until he felt a tap on his shoulder.

"Here," Russell said, holding a brown sack, the grocery store type with handles. He brushed the sack against Corey's leg.

"Hey, Russell," said Corey while looking down at the sack. "You're the guy?"

"Just take it," Russell said.

Corey took the sack and looked around. Most everyone was still watching the band as they closed the song. He turned back around and saw that Russell had moved into the crowd, cutting across the dance floor to the other side of the room. Corey stood there. He looked down into the sack and saw another smaller sack inside. He walked back to his stool and shoved it into the darkness by the steps leading to the stage.

Corey was a little unnerved. He really liked being a doorman. He met girls, felt a little important, and liked talking with the musicians. At times, he got invited to after-gig parties; the drugs were free, and sometimes, a girl settled on him when her other pursuits ended. He knew he was a minor part of the city's music scene — it was better than driving a delivery truck.

But he wasn't sure about the sack thing. Corey figured it was probably weed or coke. But for who and why this way? Was this going to be a regular thing? *If this is all I have to do, maybe it's okay,* he told himself. Corey wondered if he should talk more to Mike about it, to know about what's going on. And Russell ... the guy was close to being a snob, not the gofer type. It seemed strange he would be doing this — whatever "this" was.

For the rest of the band's set and into its second break, Corey just sat on his stool, occasionally looking over his shoulder to make sure the sack was still there. At one point, he caught Mike staring at him from the bar. Corey gave him a weak wave, which Mike did not acknowledge.

As Good Riddance got into their final set, Michelle Freely walked in through the entrance. She was wearing a tight black dress over a curvy figure and in high heels. Her straight, dyed-blonde hair fell back behind her shoulders, away from the low neckline of the dress. Corey looked at her and then took his eyes down.

"Here to pick up something from Mike," Michelle said dryly.

"Oh, yeah," said Corey. He then got down from the stool and reached around to get the sack. "Here you go."

Michelle took it with a forced smile and turned to walk out. She hesitated and then looked back. "You're kinda cute, sailor," she said.

Corey blinked and smiled, then took another quick glance at her breasts. She caught his look, then walked away.

Downstairs by the front door, Marcus waited for her. He held open the passenger door to the black Cadillac Seville for her. She put the sack at her feet, kicking it to one side. Marcus got in and asked, "Any problems?"

"None. Just a guy who checked out my boobs like all guys do." Michelle then pulled down the sun visor and looked at herself in the mirror, touching the corners of her mouth with her little finger. Marcus was expressionless. He checked the side mirror and then pulled away from the curb.

CHAPTER 12

Pinky was on his third cup of coffee in Nichelson's. The meatloaf dinner was worth the walk. He sat at the front counter, intrigued by the looks of Donni but trying not to stare. Corey had mentioned once or twice about this "big woman" who worked the counter. Pinky was interested in talking with her, though he wasn't quite sure why.

The place wasn't crowded. The bars were still open, and it was a Thursday night. Pinky was nearly sober by now; the beers had worn off, and with the coffee buzz, he was a little hyper. Things could start racing through his mind, stuff he didn't want to think about. "Fuckin' 'nam," he murmured aloud to himself.

"What's that?" asked Donni as she walked by.

Pinky looked up. Donni towered over the low counter. She had a deadpan look on her face. "More coffee?"

"Yeah, warm it up." Pinky cupped his hands around the cup as she poured. "You worked here long?"

"Couple of years?"

"This all you do?"

"My, my, what a nosey little man," Donni said in mock surprise. "Yes, dear, this is all I do."

"I don't mean anything by it. Just talkin'." Pinky took a sip of the hot coffee. Donni stood in front of him. She had put the pot of coffee down on the counter, still holding on to it. Her other arm stretched out along the counter. If Pinky looked up from his coffee, he'd be looking right into Donni's midsection. He sensed she was waiting for him to talk more.

"My roommate comes in here a lot."

Donni stepped back from the counter and turned around to put the coffeepot back on the warmer. She looked down at the counter in both directions. The two other customers seemed content, no one motioning for her to come to them.

"Oh yes, who is that?"

"Huh, Corey, Corey Edwards. You know him?"

"Sure. Cute Corey. He's in here a lot at night. Works the Repartee, doesn't he?"

Pinky nodded.

One of the counter customers waved to Donni. "Excuse me, dear," she said as she walked away, grabbing the coffeepot.

Why am I talking to this weird, transvestite, big woman-guy? Pinky wondered. How long has it been since he touched something soft other than himself? He felt the left breast pocket of his field jacket for the half-pint. He then glanced at the big clock above the entrance to the restaurant. It was almost 1 a.m. The Repartee would be closing. If he hung around a little while longer, he could maybe catch Corey leaving the club and get a ride back to their house. But if he had picked up a girl, Corey wouldn't like finding him leaning up against his van looking for a ride. And if he had a girl and Carolyn showed up at the house ... Pinky visualized a scene he didn't want to happen. He decided to walk but sensed his conversation with Donni hadn't ended.

Donni had made her way back to Pinky. "So that little dimpled-chinned Corey is your roomy, eh? I see him sometimes in here with — what's her name —Carrie?"

"Carolyn," Pinky said.

"Carolyn, then. When he's with her, he sits at the counter. She seems such a sweet girl. When he's with someone else, he sits in a booth. Tell me, does he ever think with his other head?"

Pinky let out a quick laugh. Donni oozed sarcasm. Pinky liked that. "The guy's got charm looks ... if he had money, he'd be a real prick."

Donni smiled and flicked one hand at Pinky. "Now, dearie, you're his roommate, and he must be some sort of friend."

"I guess."

Donni looked again down the counter. Pinky heard some people coming into Nichelson's. It would get busy soon.

"Maybe I better settle up," said Pinky, pulling a ten from his pocket. Donni took the bill and took the ticket to the register. She came back with Pinky's change. "More coffee?" she asked.

Pinky shook his head as he stood up. Taking the money from Donni, he left a dollar on the counter, pushing it forward. "See ya," he said. She nodded back.

Outside, Pinky paused before turning down the alley that ran south of Nichelson's and behind Repartee, the massage house, and up to the next block. He could use the alleyways to keep off the street. Pinky didn't get the half-pint put into a brown bag. In the alleys, he could take a drink without worrying about a cop cruising by.

Corey stood at the door as people slowly filed out. He looked at people's hands to see if they were leaving with a glass or bottle, politely taking it away if he saw one while saying, "Thanks for coming." Russell had stayed through the third set, which was unusual for him. His habit was to do the rounds at some of the other clubs in the city with live music, though there weren't that many. Russell liked being seen. As he left the Repartee, he shook Corey's hand without a word. Corey felt something in his hand as they touched. He quickly slipped it into his back pocket. He had a good guess what it was and was surprised by the gesture. Corey hadn't asked and hadn't done anything for Russell.

Band members were milling around on stage, lighting cigarettes, and talking among themselves as to how the night went. It had been good. People stayed to listen and dance when it was the right tune. They showed appreciation and the band responded back. Sharing space with talented artists can leave contentment or want. The audience left contented, the band fulfilled, and Corey ... he felt, as best he could determine for himself, guilty.

He was wasting time he had told himself during the band's final song. Here was talent on stage; here was him sitting on a stool. He wasn't much more than what he was. Where Greg spoke of himself through his horn, Corey sat sipping beer and eyeballing women. There wasn't much of a comparison, and Corey knew it. He had published two small features in a local arts magazine. As much as he talked about being a writer, actual writing, it seemed, only got in the way of getting laid. The thought seemed like a line from a bad poem.

With the crowd gone, Corey took his empty mug to the bar. Becky was out on the floor, going from table to table, picking up the empties. Greg was unplugging the mics. Mike was wiping down the bar.

"Can I get one more, Mike?" Corey asked. Mike had a beer poured and bought it over.

"Did you see who brought it?" Corey said, touching his pants pocket.

"We'll talk about it later," Mike said. "Now, check the johns, make sure nobody's in there hiding or too sick to leave and pull the trash bags to take outside with the rest to the dumpster. After that, lock the front door. When the band's ready to go, help them with their gear and then lock up again."

Corey wondered why Mike had to repeat the same instructions every night he worked.

In the women's restroom, Corey pulled out a small piece of aluminum foil folded in a square. He unwrapped it, pulling back the foil and then the inside wax paper. There was enough cocaine for three or four lines. He quickly refolded it and put it back in his pocket. To him, it confirmed what was going on with the sack.

Corey wasn't going to turn down free coke, but he was uneasy about it. He thought about talking with Russell but then decided against it. He had dealt a little grass here and there to get his supply for free, but he didn't really like the scene or being around dealers. Twice, he had been burglarized, and people he didn't know had shown up at his door asking to buy. The peace/love thing was long gone; guys had guns to go with their scales. It was about money and partying, and Corey would rather others take a big risk.

Corey took the trash bags to the back stairwell. When he came back to the bar, Mike was pouring shots for the band and Becky. It was his usual celebratory toast to a good night. "Come get yours — we're waiting on you," he said to Corey.

Mike raised his shot glass. "Here's to a good night of good music and good people — and I made a few bucks." Glasses went up, and everyone downed their shot. Mike handed Greg the band's money. Greg and the band thanked Mike and walked toward the door. Corey followed to help with whatever needed to be carried down to their van and to lock up.

"I'm leaving too," said Becky. "Mike said it was okay." She gave Corey a big smile and squeezed his forearm. Greg was down the stairwell, his back to them.

Corey was surprised by the touch. She was interested in him, but he would have to work hard to get her more interested. Some charm and the right opportunity might make it happen, at least temporarily. Corey watched her bounce down the stairs to catch up with Greg. *Fine lady*, he told himself.

Back at the bar, Mike was waiting for Corey to return. He anticipated that Corey would want to talk about the delivery of the sack. "Look," he said, "I'm not going to get into it. You did fine tonight. Keep doing that, don't talk about it, and everything will be copacetic."

Corey nodded. "Okay, Mike."

On the way home, Corey's mind stayed on things at the bar; Mike, Russell, and Becky — and himself. He wanted to turn on some music at his place and have something to eat and a beer. Maybe he could open his journal and write about what was on his mind or pound away on the typewriter at that short story he was two pages into. Or he could swing by Lou's to see if Carolyn was closing up. They never seemed to make plans to be together; it just happened. Corey liked it that way. He decided not to see if she was there. If he couldn't sleep, he'd call her apartment.

CHAPTER 14

Lou Levin came down from his upstairs apartment, like he always did when Carolyn worked, to help her close the bar. He was grateful to have her. She was honest. Maybe not so good in her choice of boyfriends, he would tell himself, but honest. He could hear his wife, Marge, now gone, badgering him to make sure he always was doing the young lady right.

"Now, are you paying her enough?" "Is she okay by herself down there running the bar?" "Does she have a nice friend she could bring to brunch? I could make latkes with fish." Lou smiled as he lumbered down the back stairs. He missed his wife.

Lou unlocked the back door, stepped in, and found Carolyn counting the money. "Good night?" he asked.

"Not bad, Lou."

"Any problems?"

Carolyn thought of Pinky and Steve but decided it wasn't worth telling Lou. "Mellow night, Lou."

Lou walked the place, pushing a chair or two up against tables and turning off the pinball machine and the lights above the two pool tables. When he got back to the bar, Carolyn had the night's receipts in the deposit bag.

"Want to count?" she asked.

"I'll do it in the morning, hon. I trust you." Lou looked around the bar once more, then turned back to her. "Want to have a good night's drink with an old man?"

Carolyn smiled. She was very fond of the man. "Thanks, Lou, but I've got to go."

"What's the hurry?" But Lou knew it was Corey. Carolyn had all the radiance of a woman in love. He had seen it in his wife their first time, and he knew he had it all his life — and still did when he thought of Marge.

"That boy treating you good?" he asked.

Carolyn didn't answer. She looked up and down the bar. Glasses were clean and put away, tubs empty, coolers filled, ashtrays stacked, bar wiped — everything looked good for the morning.

"Okay, none of my business. But a man's a man when he treats a woman right."

"I know, Lou. He treats me well. Maybe I just want more now."

"More is good in love, hon. It can smooth out the rough spots, makes the togetherness hold."

Carolyn didn't respond. While she had great affection for the old man, he could overdo his philosophizing. Lou knew that and had to remind himself that the young find their own way — the good ones always do, the rest, maybe just a crapshoot.

"Okay, enough of the wise old man stuff. Everything looks fine, Carolyn. Got your tips?"

"I do, Lou."

"Okay, then," Lou said as he escorted Carolyn to the front door. "Where's your car?"

"Right in front," said Carolyn.

He wanted to say more about what he thought of Corey. That he could hurt this pretty young woman or, worse, push her back to the place she had worked herself out of. The guy was a womanizer — a hungry wolf after anything with a skirt. Marge would ask and then warn Carolyn to stay away from guys like Corey. Carolyn would likely listen to Marge more than him. Marge was always in everybody's business, especially a young girl's business. Lou — he didn't know how to intrude gently into the life of a young woman. He would just hope it turned out okay or be able to help if asked.

Lou turned the lock. Carolyn smiled at Lou. The outdoor lights and their reflection of the window glass made her eyes sparkle more. She kissed him lightly on the cheek. "See ya," she said as she moved quickly to her car. Lou watched her get in, heard the car start, and watched as she pulled away. He then turned and walked behind the bar. He got a glass and poured some brandy. He then shuffled over to a table and sat down.

This time of the night was tough on Lou — the emptiness, the absence of voices, nothing to do but think. He remembered coming down the bar at night to get away from Marge's badgering about this or that. She was always in some person's life, telling Lou all about it. When she worked the bar with him, she'd know everyone's name, the names of their kids and where they worked. It wouldn't be long before she'd know their troubles, and if it were something Lou could help with, she would talk about it and talk about it until he did do something, as much as a bar owner could do. Lou chuckled to himself. If they had had kids together, it might have been worse. He took a sip from the brandy. Right then, Lou would give his right arm to hear a little badgering from Marge.

CHAPTER 15

Corey's blue Dodge van was in the driveway when Carolyn pulled up. She knocked at the door. Music could be heard behind it. "The Logical Song" by Supertramp was playing on the stereo.

There are times when all the world's asleep
The question runs too deep for such a simple man
Won't you please tell me what we've learned
I know it sounds absurd, but please tell me who I am

It was loud enough to drown out her knocking. She turned the knob. It was unlocked. Carolyn exhaled, and she stepped in. It was a small frame house two bedrooms downstairs and a converted antic bedroom upstairs. Corey took the downstairs but shared the kitchen with Pinky. One of the bedrooms was his office of sorts with a desk, electric typewriter, bookcase, and file cabinet. He kept the door closed most of the time. When Carolyn first started seeing Corey, she'd ask how the writing was going. She didn't ask much anymore.

Carolyn walked into the kitchen. Corey had his back to her, making a sandwich at the counter. She reached around his waist, pulled in close, laid her head against his back, and squeezed. Corey flinched for a second. "Hi," she said in a low voice. Corey stopped what he was doing, stood still, and closed his eyes. He reached around with one hand and squeezed her behind.

"Want one?" he asked. He felt her shake her head no. Corey then slowly turned around, breaking her embrace.

Carolyn stepped away then put her purse on the kitchen table. "There's a beer in the fridge," said Corey. "Or I could roll one."

Carolyn walked back into the living room and turned the music down. Back into the kitchen, she said, "Gee, Corey. Like, I haven't looked at enough beers tonight. And I'm not really in the mood to smoke."

Corey shrugged as he bit down on his sandwich while looking at her, trying to size up her mood. "Good night?" he asked through the chewing.

Carolyn sat down, looking straight at him. She didn't know if she loved him or not. She really liked him, thought about spending her life with him, having kids, a house — all the regular stuff. But at that moment, he was just a jerk stuffing his face. He never brought up the future — their future. Was there one? But she liked him. He was easygoing in most ways; nothing seemed to faze him, even when she told him about the rough spots in her past — if he remembered any of it.

"Pinky upstairs?" Carolyn asked.

"Yeah, I guess. I heard him come in. If he's awake, he'll probably come down for another beer soon."

Corey stared intently at Carolyn. He figured she was in one of those moods, building to a point when a woman pushes a man to see if it's worth staying around. Corey waited for the expected opening question. He didn't want her to walk out.

"What are we doing here, Corey?" Her voice was circumspect. "I kinda like to know where we're going. We've been seeing each other for months, and I still don't have a key. I've got to knock on the door, afraid of what I might be interrupting." Anger flared in her voice.

Corey put up his hand, palm out. "You stumbled into something one time, early on, before our relationship settled in. It hasn't happened since."

"What hasn't happened? Me catching you with someone else, or you screwing someone else?"

Corey threw his head back as if dodging a slap. "Whoa!" She was on a roll. He ran his fingers threw his hair. Carolyn waited for him to speak. Corey just looked at her, assessing what to say. He still wanted her. He remembered the cocaine Russell had given him, the folded square still in his pocket. Maybe a little toot would help change the subject. Maybe not.

"You know I have lots of chances with guys, especially at the bar," Carolyn continued. There was hurt in her voice. "But I don't do anything 'cause I'm always thinking of you, of us." Her voice quivered. "I guess, I guess, I love you."

She looked at him, afraid of what she said and waiting for him to come and hold her. To say he loved her. Corey had a look of concern. He shifted his weight from one foot to another, still leaning against the kitchen counter. Carolyn grabbed her purse and walked into the living room toward the door.

"Wait," Corey called out. "Please, sweetheart, wait."

Carolyn stopped. She kept her back to him. Corey came up behind her like she had done to him earlier. He pulled her close and pushed his face into her hair. He kissed the back of her neck. Carolyn stared at the front door. He could feel her breathing. *I'm not going to cry,* she told herself. Corey put his hands on her shoulders and gently turned her around. He brought her in toward him, looking at her.

"This is honest, Carolyn," he said, "as honest as I can get."

Carolyn waited, afraid of what he was going to say.

"I don't know if I love you. I don't know. But I don't want you to leave, and I want you in my life. That's all I know." Carolyn was silent. "Yes. Stay. Stay with me — don't go. We'll get up early. I'll make breakfast, call in to say I'll be late to work, and then we'll go get a key made. Okay? Then you can go get some of your stuff and bring it over."

Carolyn had hoped for more. But it was enough. He could hurt her, she thought, hurt her bad. But she loved him. There wasn't any doubt. Stay or go. If she told him what he said wasn't enough, she would hurt now. But if she stayed and she caught him with someone else, it would hurt more then. But he could be true; he could someday say he loved her. Taking a chance always comes from a want.

Corey had expected an immediate response to what he had said. For a moment, a feeling of panic came over him. She might leave.

Carolyn looked into his eyes. "I'll stay … and I want the key."

Corey let out a breath and pulled her in for a kiss. Just as he did, the stairwell creaked. Both turned and saw Pinky coming down from upstairs.

"Whoa, am I interrupting something?"

Corey and Carolyn broke apart. He kept her to his side, arm around her shoulders. "Yeah, you are," Corey said.

"Aw, man, sorry. Just wanted a beer." Pinky walked into the kitchen.

Corey and Carolyn looked at each other. "Come, let's go into the bedroom," said Corey. He took her hand.

"Night, Pinky," Carolyn called out.

"Yeah and turn off the stereo when you head back upstairs, will ya, please?" said Corey.

Pinky waved back at them. He wondered if the makeup routine was for real. How long before another crisis in the relationship? He shrugged as he stood in front of the opened refrigerator. He liked Carolyn, but she was a sucker for thinking a guy like Corey would be true. But then, what did he know? He would have to go buy it if he wanted to get laid again. But then he would have to get some kind of a steady job to afford the nut. Pinky let out a "Ha," shook his head, and took a drink from his beer. He let the refrigerator door close. Obviously, a woman wasn't a big priority these days. Pinky took another drink and wondered what it was.

Standing there, beer in hand, he heard giggling from Corey's bedroom then a big knock as something large banged against something else. It was Corey's headboard hitting the wall as he and Carolyn fell into bed. Pinky opened the refrigerator again and got another beer. The bottles clanged as he held them in one hand while turning out the kitchen light. Pinky walked by the stereo. The Supertramp album had finished.

Carolyn and Cory lay naked in his bed with a sheet over the top of them. One arm was under her head, her back to him. His free hand moved up and down her side, to her back, butt, and legs, following the curves of her body. He kissed the back of her neck, his hand reaching around to her front and then between her legs. She turned. They kissed again and again. He kissed her cheeks, her forehead, her eyes. He nibbled at her ears, moved down to her neck and then to her breasts, then reached lower and, with one hand, opened her legs again. He moved to her belly button, then down further. She had shaved that morning, leaving a little patch. His tongue parted the outer lips, lifting higher to flick at her aroused clitoris and then bite gently all around her vulva. His hard penis stabbed at the sheets, making him bring it up to his abdomen so he could lay flatter on the bed between her legs. Her eyes stayed closed. She arched her back. He lifted her higher. He always liked this from the very first time, and he tried to master it. To Corey, this was his control for a while, then hers when he went inside. His mind settled only on her, enjoying her, glad she was enjoying him. She was going to let him do what he wanted, and hopefully, then, he would take his time when he came up to enter her so she wouldn't think of other things except him.

CHAPTER 16

t was Sunday, around 8:30 in the morning. The parking lot at Bain's Liquors was empty. Jensen needed cigarettes. The two detectives had spent most of the night parked down the street from a lumberyard on Southwest Boulevard. They had gotten a tip that a van with marijuana was going to hide a few hundred pounds in the yard for eventual distribution. The van never showed. It was a phone-in tip that both men now knew they never should have taken seriously.

"Want some coffee?" Jensen asked Frederick as he got out of the car.

"Naw. Get me some gum."

Jensen walked in and saw that Gary was behind the counter. The always-friendly Bain chirped, "Howdy, sir. Can I help you?"

Gary knew the detective, and after being reprimanded for using the word "detective" in an earlier greeting of Jensen, the storekeeper avoided the word, at least publicly. Still, to Gary, with it being early Sunday morning, most neighborhood folks — if any were in the small store — could figure a guy in a crumpled brown suit buying cigarettes and looking like he'd been up all night wasn't on his way to pray at church.

"Give me a pack of Camel Lights and some of that gum," said

Jensen, pointing behind the counter. He reached into his pocket, pulled out a money clip, and began to unfold dollar bills.

"No problem," Gary said, holding his hand up and smiling. Jensen hesitated to drop the bills onto the counter when he heard a sound in the back room. Pinky came out of the doorway and asked Gary, "You want me to take those boxes in the corner to the dumpster?"

"Probably. I'll be back there in a minute," Gary answered. Pinky turned and went back into the room. He didn't bother to look at Jensen.

Jensen recognized Pinky from a few nights earlier. "Come here, Gary. Come outside — I want to show you something," Jensen said loudly, hoping Pinky would hear his request from the back room. He put his money back in his pocket. Outside, Jensen pulled Gary over to the passenger side of the detectives' car so Frederick could hear the conversation.

"That guy is cleaning up for you. He works for you?" asked Jensen.

Gary looked at both detectives, one then the other. "Why? He do something wrong?"

"No, Gary. We're just curious. Saw him walking down the street one night, real late."

Gary figured the two cops had something in mind for Pinky. He felt protective. "He's okay, regular neighbor guy. Like everyone, he tries to get by," said Gary. "I just like to help him out every once and a while when I can." Gary smiled. The two detectives looked at each other.

"So, he doesn't work a steady job," said Jensen.

"Not really. He's on disability, a Vietnam vet. You know that war messed up a lot of guys. I haven't heard anything real bad ... maybe kinda volatile when something sets him off." Gary smiled again while looking at Jensen. "But I don't think he's been in any real trouble."

"We know, we know," said Frederick. "See, my partner here is a vet himself." Frederick continued, pointing at Jensen. "He's been to 'nam and takes an interest in fellow vets, wants to make sure they're handling the pressure of being out, you know."

Gary relaxed and slowly nodded as if picturing Pinky in some therapy program.

"See, Gary, cops aren't all about bangin' heads," said Frederick.

"Yeah, just let us know if you think he might need some ... err, guidance or referrals," said Jensen, handling Gary a card with his phone number. "And don't let on that we're asking about him. Don't want him to get paranoid or anything for no reason. You know, vets need to stay calm, reintegrate back into society."

Gary tightened his smile. He wasn't quite sure if what Jensen was saying was the real reason for their interest. But he wanted to believe it was. After all, it was Jensen and Frederick — the rumor went — who pushed for more patrols in the neighborhood, especially near his store. "Okay, sounds right. I'll let you know. I like the guy. But finding out more means I would have to get to know him a little better."

"Yeah, we know, Gary," said Jensen.

The men shook hands, and Gary went back into the store. Jensen got behind the wheel. "That guy is a fucking trip," said Jensen to Frederick as they drove out of the parking lot. "I need to wear a raincoat when I talk with him."

"Why? Afraid you'd come all over yourself?" said Frederick, laughing.

"Fuck you, Malcolm. But it's funny that he thinks we had something to do with the increased patrols in the area."

"Some people will believe what they want to believe," said Frederick.

"And with that, the guy doesn't let me — us — pay for anything. I mean, I could get my cigarettes, milk, whatever there for free, at least for a while."

"Are you sure his generosity only has to do with him thinking we boosted the patrols?"

Jensen looked at Frederick with a smirk. "He's not interested in me. I'd bust him up."

Frederick grinned. "Yeah, you're right. You're such a hunk."

The detectives headed back downtown. They agreed to drop in at Bain's once a week.

Back behind the counter, Gary thought about what the two detectives had said. He guessed that helping a vet wasn't their only motive.

Something was up. Whatever their motive was, it wasn't the same as Gary's. To him, offer a little help then Pinky might come around a little more, things could lighten up, something might develop.

Gary turned and walked toward the back room. "Hey, Pinky, how you makin' out?"

Pinky spent all morning cleaning out the back room at Bain's. Thankfully, the store got busy later in the morning with the after-church crowd, and Gary pretty much left him alone. He finished up by noon and got his twenty dollars. With it, he bought a six-pack and another half-pint. Gary frowned while running it up on the register.

"This your lunch?" asked Gary sarcastically.

"Look, man, don't preach. I did the job and appreciated the work. What I do with the money is my business. I can function fine. If you need some more work done, let me know."

Gary thought for a minute, wondering if he should suggest future steady work. He decided to. "There are times when I need another clerk," he said. "I need time off too, you know. Is that something you could do? And to be honest ... sober?"

"Cleaned up the back room all right, didn't I?" Pinky said. Then, extending his arms and hands out in front of him, he added, "Didn't get the shakes, did I."

This is getting old, he told himself.

Gary didn't laugh. "Yes, you did good work. It's fine. Not trying to insult you. We'll talk more, okay?" Gary stuck out his hand. Pinky looked at him, then lifted his arm and made a fist. "Right on. Let me know," and he walked out of the store.

He took his time. Pinky figured Corey and Carolyn were up and left to get breakfast, or Corey was cooking. He cooked a mean breakfast, part of the lasso he used to snarl women. Of course, he already had them there anyway — *maybe there was guilt in cooking for a woman you just fucked for completely selfish reasons.* Pinky backed away from the thought. Such bitterness didn't mix with his mood. He hoped the kitchen was free, snickering to himself how working a straight job made him hungry for food.

Corey sat on his bed, watching Carolyn brush her hair. She swung her head back and then forward, her black, wavy hair falling one way and then another. She was beautiful. He would be an idiot to push her aside. But he had had other beautiful women, so what made Carolyn different? Maybe it was him that was different or getting there. Here he is, thirty, driving a truck during the day, working a few nights a week at a club, really doing nothing while wanting to write, get published, get something other than being an ordinary schmuck. *Maybe a steady girl, maybe being only with Carolyn, would help. Getting her that key to the place sure lightened things, and man, did she ride me. She's happy this morning. Me too ... maybe because she is.* Cory let out a "humph."

"What's that, babe?" Carolyn asked.

"Oh, nothing, just thinking."

"About us?" Carolyn asked teasingly.

Corey grabbed her from behind. "Still got time for a quickie," he whispered into her ear. Carolyn turned around, came close as if to kiss him, and then quickly bit him gently on his lower lip. Corey jumped back. "What's that for?"

"For later," Carolyn said. "You going to remember the key?"

Corey nodded and smiled. "Yes."

They decided to part ways for the day and then get together in the early evening. Carolyn was going to her apartment to check in with her brother. Corey wanted to drop by the club to see if Mike was there. He wanted to know what nights he worked the coming week and maybe find out more about what was going on. Things seemed to have changed at the Repartee.

The next day was the start of the workweek — him in his van making deliveries, Carolyn at her day office job.

CHAPTER 17

After the sack drop on Thursday night, Mike had expected to hear from Lewis or at least Marcus the next day. He didn't. A few days later — Saturday — Marcus called wanting to come by the club. Mike met him down at the club's front door in the early afternoon. They walked up to Mike's office without speaking.

Marcus eased his big body into the chair in front of Mike's desk. He gave Mike a long stare. Mike stared back, thinking maybe this was some sort of test, or maybe Marcus was gathering his thoughts, or *maybe the guy just needed to take a shit.* Mike smiled.

"What are you smilin' at, motherfucker?" Marcus asked.

"Hey, just tryin' to get in a good mood. What's the word?"

Marcus leaned back into the chair. "Lewis thought it went okay. Your guy didn't seem to touch anything and didn't say anything stupid. Lewis thinks he might work out but still isn't sure. We're looking around for someone else, maybe."

Mike wasn't surprised at what Marcus said. Wriggling off the hook with Lewis once he had his resources together or getting to a place where he could be left alone enough without thugs scaring the clientele is a process.

"Okay. But if there's a new doorman, please let it be an ordinary-looking guy."

"Why?" Marcus asked in a sincere way.

"'Cause I don't want people feeling like their walking into a place where someone's going to wrestle them to the floor and pull out their gold fillings. This place — believe it or not — has a good vibe because it's about music, and people can come in and wrap themselves around that."

Marcus' questioning look was gone. "Lewis doesn't give a shit, and neither do I."

"I wouldn't expect anything different. But tell Lewis — no, ask Lewis — to hold off for a little while. Corey only works three or four nights a week. The rest of the time, I watch the door and have an extra girl working the bar. No need for that to change right away."

Marcus seemed to ponder what Mike had said and began another long stare at him. Mike put his head down and rubbed his forehead, waiting for the big gofer to say something. Mike looked up. Marcus had gotten up from the chair and was standing by the door. "I'll see you in a few days," Marcus said as he left.

Mike walked down to the bar. He popped open a beer. He'd give this whole thing a year or two at most, time enough for him to pool some money together. He'd need it, maybe for a lawyer if things exploded apart and then to start again if he had to do some time. That thought chilled him. He wondered if an ex-con doing standup had some sort of appeal to booking agents, especially if he tailored his routine around it.

Or, if not, in time, duck out of town and let Lewis have it all. It would have to be a pretty good chunk of change and done without Lewis thinking he had scammed him somehow; otherwise, Marcus would track him down. With some improvements and pushing the scene along, the Repartee could be the happening place with money rolling in. Still, Mike could plead high overhead while putting some money away. The key was not to ask too many questions and act like he didn't really know what was going on. Let Lewis run his coke. Mike decided he'd run the club, just prepare for when it felt like it was time to leave it all behind. Overall, the need was to be cool until then as to not attract the heat.

CHAPTER 18

Russell stood on the balcony at Michelle's midtown apartment. Before him lay Volker Park and to the north, across a large expanse of green, the neoclassic Nelson-Atkins Museum. Ten years or so ago, Volker was a happening place, a place to chill, score some weed, maybe protest something or other — usually the war — and listen to some half-ass musicians. Then the cops and city figured it out.

Russell was waiting for Lewis to send Michelle off on a shopping trip. "Hustle Bird" by the Ohio Players pushed its disco-rock sound out of Michelle's stereo. Russell couldn't help but bob his head a little to the beat.

"Aw, baby, can I have some more?" pleaded Michelle.

"Damn, I just gave you three hundred ... how much more?"

Michelle came close and rubbed up against Lewis, reaching down to his crotch. She was an inch or two taller than Lewis, noticeable by her long legs. Her blonde hair was kept long and rarely pinned up or back. Short shorts were her favorite dress around the apartment, especially when alone with Lewis. They were easily dropped to the floor, and such an invite kept Lewis from again complaining — for a White girl — she was putting on weight. Going out, Michelle preferred short one-piece dresses or shorts with color leggings. "Another hundred?" she asked softly.

"Damn!" Lewis said, pulling off two more fifties from the wad of bills he had in his hand. Michelle squeezed him lightly, grabbed the money, and turned for the door. "Don't be too long," said Lewis. "After Russell, I'm going to watch some b-ball, then I expect you back before I leave to go back home. Got it?"

Michelle waved as she left.

Lewis put on sunglasses and walked out onto the balcony. "Damn bitch always hitting me up," he said.

Russell turned and looked at Lewis. Russell didn't really care about Lewis' relationship troubles. "Nice view," he said.

"Yeah, should be considering what I'm paying. Damn, girl cost me a lot of jack but man, can she fuck." Lewis looked at Russell. "Tell me, Russell, do you give a fuck if a girl can fuck?"

Russell seemed startled. "Sure I do, Mr. Richardson ... sure."

"I don't know, man. People tell me you're the wheeler-dealer type. More interested in money than wetting your dick. Am I right?"

Russell got uncomfortable and thought about what he had to say to change the conversation. "Yes, Mr. Richardson. I want to make money, and I want to promote music, and, as you know, I look for ways to do that."

Lewis pulled down his sunglasses and looked at Russell. "You're the cool cat, Russell. Now let's talk motherfucker."

As they sat down in the living room, the doorbell rang. Lewis opened it and let Marcus in. Russell sat expressionless on the leather couch. Lewis made him nervous, but he told himself he could handle it. It was a means; doing what Lewis wanted was a way to make money and become the music promoter extraordinaire he wanted to be, maybe with a record label. Yet, Marcus could flat terrify him. Russell swallowed, remained expressionless, and said, "Hello, Marcus."

Marcus gave him a blank look and sat down in a chair facing Russell. Lewis was in another chair next to Marcus. A teakwood coffee table was between the two men and Russell. On it was a flat porcelain tray and a small jar with white powder in it. Russell took that for cocaine. He occasionally glanced at the jar as Lewis and Marcus leaned in close and whispered to one another.

"Your man Corey seemed to do all right the other night, Russell. Didn't mess with the shit," said Lewis. "Now we continue."

Russell nodded; not sure what Lewis meant.

"How tight are you with him?"

"We went to the same high school. I knew him then ... ran into him at bars later. He helped me with some promoting when I was booking bands at that warehouse space on Linwood. We know each other, talk some, nothing special."

"Did he ask to work at Repartee, or did you just get the job for him?"

Russell thought a moment. He couldn't really recall one way or another. "He asked me about working there."

Lewis looked over at Marcus. He got up from his chair, walked back behind the couch, and put his hand on Russell's shoulder. Russell stiffened.

"I think you know what we've got going here, Russell, my man. You did well with the Repartee connection. Now you help me more. I help you more. Capeesh?"

Russell nodded. "I understand, Mr. Richardson."

Lewis liked that Russell addressed him with a "mister" even though he was a funky-ass White boy.

"You're going to help me move some product. We're going to transfer it out of the club with someone in a band to various other places out of town, places where that band is booked to play — booked by you, the promoter, and I can help you with that. You get a cut of what the band gets playing, a slice for setting up the movement of the stuff, and in the process building a rep as a Midwest music promoter. Dig?"

Russell's eyes widened.

"Now, it's going to go through you. You set it up, deciding on which band and which band member can handle it — carry it along. You give that guy a cut from your end. You keep me out of it, obviously. Nothing flows back to me." Then Lewis added calmly, "If it does,

Marcus here might cut your dick off, stuff it in your mouth, and sew it shut."

Marcus smiled.

Russell stiffened up in his seat. He didn't want to look at Marcus. "I understand," he said in a squeaky voice.

Lewis continued. "Certain clubs will get a hold of you with dates. You book the right band with them to bring the shit to them. You won't know beforehand who that person is or how to get the shit to him. Marcus will tell you the procedure before you leave town to go there. Any fuck-up on the way falls on you."

"Do I travel with the band?" Russell asked, gaining composure.

Lewis shrugged. "You just got to make sure the shit arrives and gets to the right person. Ride along or show up by yourself; it doesn't matter. They'll know to contact you or the guy in the band you made the arrangement with. Again, any fuck-up, and you deal with whatever, and then me. Things go good, and the payoff is juice and jack for you."

Russell stared at Lewis and then glanced at Marcus. Both men had a smug look. A part of Russell didn't want to be there. He didn't want to hear what he had just heard. All he wanted to do was promote music promote bands. He loved music. He loved the scene, bringing the sound to people, bringing new music to people, hanging out with musicians, learning the history of music and musicians, and having people come to him with news about this band or that. It wasn't about making a lot of money or dope. It was about the music, making this town about music again, doing something worthwhile, and getting a rep.

"Hey, White boy, you in on this or not?" Lewis asked.

Russell knew he had to be in. He could not be in. There were less than a dozen places in town to book live music, even counting the suburbs. Lewis could lock him out; he had the muscle. Then what? Dreams for himself were dreams for the city, he told himself, for music, for the musicians he knew that had talent. If he stayed out, then, for sure, it would all belong to Lewis. Russell felt like a sideman in a band put together by Lewis, and if he wanted to stay on stage, he had to learn the tune Lewis had written. "Yes, Mr. Richardson. It sounds good to me."

"Good, man, good," Lewis said. "Now Marcus will be getting a hold of you sometime soon with some details. Obviously, what's been said here doesn't go beyond this room. Got that motherfucker."

Russell nodded. He then looked down at the coke on the table.

Lewis smiled. "Lay out a line or two for yourself. Seal the deal."

Russell tapped out some coke on the tray, then took out his driver's license, using the edge of it to break up the small clumps and separating out the coke into two lines. Lewis watched with a bored look. The arm on the stereo's turntable lifted; the last song from the Ohio Players album *Rattlesnake* was over. Lewis looked over at Marcus as Russell divided out the cocaine. With two lines in front of him, Russell reached around to his wallet to pull out a bill. He stopped as Marcus leaned forward and handed him a straw cut in half. Russell snorted the cocaine up quickly. He then leaned back on the couch, pinching his nose and sniffing. "Man," he said, rolling out the word slowly.

"Yeah, Russell. We don't step on our blow but a little. It's real clean shit," said Lewis with a grin. He watched Russell rub and pinch his nose again, then again. Lewis then stood up. "Okay, treat's over. We'll see you later, Russell, my man."

Russell stood up slowly, smiled at Lewis, then nodded to both men, leaving quietly without a handshake, rubbing and pinching his nose as the apartment door closed.

For a moment, Lewis and Marcus were silent. Then Lewis said, "I think that fucker will do all right. He's smart enough and hungry enough not to fuck up. And the dude could do some good things music-wise. Might take us into some legit creative shit — huh, Marcus?"

Marcus nodded.

"The fucker wants fame and glory. He'll do want I want. Just keep an eye on him and watch his coke intake. If it gets out of hand, we could have trouble if he gets stupid, and make sure he understands you are one mean motherfucker, out to bust his head if he fucks up."

"I ain't got to do that for a long time." Marcus slowly rubbed his hands together.

Lewis laughed. "That's because shit has been going good. Everybody is productive, no pushback, and even the legit enterprises are making money. Shit, it seems contentment has spread across the land." Lewis laughed again, louder. He then said, "I'm not totally positive on this, though. Too many unknowns."

"What do you mean?" Marcus asked.

"This Mike guy at the club. He ain't afraid. He's thinking on an out, but I don't know if that just means for him to try and boogie or if he's got another hand to play."

Marcus looked puzzled. "You want me to do some convincing? I don't like the motherfucker no way."

"No. Let it be until it flushes out more. I think he wants the place to jump more, but I don't feel he's in it for any long-term activity. We might have to pull him in more to alter any plans he thinks he has.

"But this Corey, the doorman, that's got me thinking. How tight is he with Mike? And I don't like it he went looking for the job to Russell. See what you can find out. Send someone into the neighborhood, or do we have anyone in that part of town?"

"The girls in the massage house next to the club."

"Naw. I want to keep that operation low profile. Brings in good bread. Don't want the bitches thinking they're doin' more than they are. Shit, they be asking for a raise." Lewis covered his mouth and snickered, his body shaking as he thought more about what he said. Marcus grinned in approval.

Holding up one finger as if it helped to calm himself, Lewis said, "Why don't you just follow him? Stay back, don't get noticed, and see where he goes and does, who he hangs with, where his cribs at. If necessary, I might even get Michelle to rub up against him a little if it looks like we need more to know."

"You think that honkey is a pig?" Marcus asked.

"It doesn't quite feel that way, but this arrangement ain't solid yet. The whole point is to take this dope into white-bread land where the real money is. Step on the shit once or twice, jack the price, and cruise for a while. Let whitey and these yuppies make us some money while we keep our distance."

"I can dig it."

Lewis looked over at Marcus. "Give me five, man." The two slap their hands together. "See what you can find out about this Corey dude. I need to get more comfortable ... figure out another test. These are Caucasians, after all."

Marcus nodded, got out of the chair, and left. Lewis sat alone in Michelle's apartment. He thought of his kids and wife. He hoped she didn't ask where he'd been. "Time to leave the ghetto soon," he said to himself, looking at his Phenix Revue watch.

CHAPTER 19

Corey really didn't expect Mike to be at the club on Sunday, but he decided to drive by anyway. He wanted to check his work schedule and talk with Mike. Mike had a short fuse and wouldn't tolerate a bunch of questions, but maybe Corey could empty himself a little of this feeling that things might get out of whack at the Repartee.

He wanted to keep the doorman's job. The music, the people — the club seemed like it was catching on, though there wasn't too much competition when it came to live music venues. DJs and lighted dance floors remained the norm. Corey wanted to think his prestige would rise in manning the door at Repartee. Plus, it was a scene that could give him ideas to write about. He just didn't want to get caught up in a bunch of dope dealing that he could better avoid if he knew more, just a little more.

Corey turned off 39th Street at Clark and then made a quick left turn down the alley that ran parallel to 39th. The alley would take him behind the club and into Nichelson's parking lot. If Mike was at the club, his Pontiac Trans Am was parked there.

Corey didn't spot Mike's car and was just about to head back to his house when he spotted the Trans Am near the restaurant's front door.

Mike was getting a late breakfast. Corey pulled into a parking spot and then sat in his van for a moment. He wondered if it was a good idea to bother Mike now. Maybe just a phone call later would do. Corey lit a cigarette. He watched the erratic rhythm of cars stopping and going at the light at 39th and the trafficway. He flipped his cigarette out the window and walked into Nichelson's, glancing over at the front counter to see if Donni was working. She was off, probably recouping from a tough Saturday night. Corey found Mike in a back-room booth reading the Sunday newspaper with his coffee.

"Hi, Mike. Can I talk to you for a minute?"

Mike pulled the newspaper down and looked up at Corey. He was tired, and this was a face he didn't want to see right now.

"I'm trying to relax here, Corey. Can't this wait?"

Corey stepped back. Irritation was all over Mike's face. "Sorry, Mike. I'll just give you a call later. Will you be at the club today?"

Corey gave Mike a weak smile and started to turn away. Mike decided he needed to know what was on Corey's mind. He needed no surprises. He had a plan to follow through on. "Sit down," he said. "Want some coffee?"

"Yeah, that's good."

Mike waved over a waitress, and Corey had his coffee. Mike folded the newspaper. Corey took a sip and then asked, "Have you got the schedule worked out for when I'm working the door this coming week?"

"Haven't thought about it much, but figure at least on Saturday night when Island Sound plays. Maybe Wednesday when that country band plays, and Thursday with that metal band."

"Sounds good, Mike. Not keen on metal but, yeah, any night. There should be a big crowd on Saturday. Reggae is catching on in town."

Mike smiled. "Anything pro-ganja is popular."

"Right on."

Mike took a sip from his coffee, intently looking at Corey. "You're not bothering me on a Sunday morning to only ask about the schedule and voice a pro-marijuana position. What's up with you?"

Corey shifted his position in the booth. "Mike ... about that sack thing the other night, I was wondering if ..." Corey stopped for a moment. "If it's an ongoing thing or what?"

The muscles in Mike's jaw tightened, and his eyes narrowed. He then lowered his head. "There's no 'what' to it," he said forcefully as he looked up. He then leaned forward, his elbows down on the table, his hands across his forearms. He figured, on the one hand, asking about the sack is natural. It's not within the normal doorman duties. On the other, asking about something a doorman should just do is wrong since it's none of the doorman's business. Mike wasn't sure yet.

"What do you think is going on with the sack, Corey?"

Corey leaned back, taking his eyes off Mike. He didn't expect the question and didn't want to speculate on it. "I'm sorry, Mike. I didn't mean to ask something that was your business. I just like the job, like the club, think it's a good thing for the city, for the musicians ... for me. I guess it's none of my business, is it?"

"It's none of your fucking business, Corey," said Mike. He continued to stare at Corey. Corey looked down and took a sip of his coffee. The men sat in silence; Corey felt Mike's eyes still on him.

"What are you doing these days, Corey? Still driving for that delivery service?"

"Yeah," said Corey, looking up.

"How's that going?" Corey took it as a sincere question.

"Slowing down. Carter's economy, Iran hostage shit, the Republicans gathering around Reagan. I don't know where it's going, but I don't think it's going up. The van's high maintenance, and I need long and heavy hauls to make a buck. I'm thinking of other things to do."

Mike nodded. "Other things, huh? How's the writing?"

Corey was surprised at the question and pleased. "I've got some ideas out to a couple of editors; might get an assignment."

"Really. You've been published before, right?"

"Yeah, a couple of arts quarterlies—one essay, a short story, and a couple of poems. But I'd like to get something published that's a little higher profile, you know. Something that's a kick, something that's got some journalism to it. My goal is to have a full-time writing job, and only newspapers and magazines offer that." Corey was smiling. He liked when someone asked about his ambitions, even if he wasn't really working that hard at fulfilling them.

Mike wasn't smiling. "Journalism. Ideas to editors. That's why you asked about the sack?"

An anguish look of surprise formed on Corey's face. "No, Mike. Has nothing to do with it. That's done. I'm not asking anything anymore. I would never ..."

"Never what?"

"I just want to keep the doorman's job. Please, Mike, it has nothing to do with it ... selling an idea to an editor." Desperation rang in Corey's voice.

"What ideas do you have out?" Mike was calm. He liked the feeling of pressuring someone showing fear.

Corey sighed. "No ideas, Mike. I'm just talking. I haven't put together a query letter in almost a year. I was just talking. Really."

Mike kept his eyes on Corey. Corey took another sip of coffee, staring into the cup. *If something is going on, this idiot surely wouldn't be stupid enough to mention journalism.* "Part of your bullshit pickup line, huh. Just talk?"

Corey's shoulders dropped. "Yeah, Mike, you could say that." He wanted to believe that Mike believed him.

And Mike did, for the most part. He also realized that Corey might be too damn inquisitive for his own good — and Mike's. Mike reached for his newspaper. "See you Saturday, Corey, and forget about it. Now, let me go back to my Sunday time."

Corey nodded and got up. As he walked away, he turned to look back at Mike. He waved. Mike didn't wave back.

Mike wondered if he should have just told Corey some of what was going on. *He might have seen it as easy access to some coke and more partying or as a way to make some money on the side. Or not. Corey could flap his jaws, and Marcus would leave him in a ditch somewhere. The journalism thing is bothersome. Would he see this as an opportunity to make a name for himself? How hungry is he? Enough to be careless with his mouth? Yet, having Lewis put in a doorman isn't really a good option now. Control of the club shifts, and my plans to book with a stash become more problematic. Maybe I need my own stack test with Corey, something that will involve Russell, so it gets back to Lewis. But maybe that ain't worth it.* "Fuckin' bullshit," Mike mumbled to himself.

For a minute or so, Mike lost himself in a long, blank stare. If he had been closer to the front window, he might have seen Marcus' Seville parked a row back from the front of the diner. Corey missed the Seville also.

Corey felt queasy as he shuffled to his van. He didn't know what Mike thought about his question, but it could mean he wasn't going to be the doorman for long. Or that he could be getting a visit from people he didn't know. Or both. He didn't want to know all the details. All he wanted to do was be the doorman of a happening club in a non-happening city. That's all. *Fuck the writing, fuck the ideas-out-to-editors shit. Maybe it's better to just quit. But how would that look?*

"Fuck!" Corey said aloud as he slammed his hand on the steering wheel. *And what happens if they try to pull me in more? I don't want the drug-dealer scene. It was enough of a hassle when I dealt pot, and with coke, there's even more paranoia. Shit. I had to talk about journalism, and now Mike thinks I want to be Bernstein and Woodward. Fuck. Can't quit the Repartee now — looks too suspicious. I'm just going to have to show up on Saturday and see what comes down.*

Corey sunk deeper into his own thoughts as he opened the front door to his house. He didn't notice the Seville pulling up to park across the street. *This was dip-shit easy*, Marcus told himself. Finding Mike's suburban apartment meant tagging him from the club. Then he meets doorman Corey the next morning, and now he finds out where this yahoo lives. Good morning, following clowns. Marcus smiled. Lewis will want to know that the white boys got together outside the club. But it's Sunday, his day with family. No business on Sunday. I'll tell him when he calls me in the morning at Milken's.

CHAPTER 20

Milkin's Barber and Beauty had been on Truman Road at Brooklyn Street since the early '60s. Rupert and his son Robert operated the two-room shop. The father and son worked the barber side, and Rupert's sister Evelyn had three chairs on the beauty shop side.

The shop was neat and tidy. KJAM 106.5 FM, "The Urban Sound" was always on the radio. Photos of Martin Luther King, Malcolm X, and Aretha Franklin hung on the walls. Milken's was a gathering place for the neighborhood and for some who had left the neighborhood.

Lewis Richardson had known the Milkin family since boyhood. His grandmother had brought him to the shop to get his haircut when she had her hair done. Little Lewis got to know Rupert as he sat and waited for his grandmother. Rupert liked the boy and encouraged him to stay in school and stay out of trouble. The advice appeared taken; Lewis studied business at a local community college and developed a profile as an up-and-comer.

Marcus Rudd also knew the Milkin family. His Aunt Eve, who raised him, knew Evelyn from church. Marcus, a few years older than Lewis, first met him at the barbershop as he waited for Eve to have her hair done. Marcus was big for his age, Lewis bookish and quiet. Eve and Evelyn didn't live that far apart, and when either visited the other, the boys got together.

As they grew, Lewis helped Marcus with his school studies enough so Aunt Eve even felt Marcus would get through high school. In turn, he made sure bigger neighborhood boys didn't push Lewis around. Marcus' high school days ended when he severely beat up the school's football coach, who ridiculed Marcus in front of his teammates for not knowing offensive schemes.

"You're as dumb as they come, Marcus," said the White coach, a holdover from before the white flight took hold in the neighborhood. "Are you even smart enough to plow a field behind a mule?"

Eve and Evelyn both pleaded to have the charges dropped, promising to pay for the coach's medical bills and asking to have Marcus transferred to another school. But the system wanted to punish Marcus. He got six months at the Boonville Training School for Boys, the state's largest and most violent juvenile facility. His sentence was extended twice for fighting and concealing shanks in his bunk area.

When Lewis drove to pick him up after a year and a half, Marcus said, "Shit, I was close to running the joint. Now let's get out of this cracker town."

"Well now, man, you can help me run what I've got," said Lewis.

While Marcus was gone, Lewis' grandmother passed. He inherited her house and car, sold both, and used the money to go beyond reselling dime bags of pot. With added bulk, he expanded his sales to local college campuses, sometimes making deliveries himself. With eyeglasses and a business-like appearance, Lewis didn't intimidate the White kids.

Lewis took his profits and bought into legitimate businesses, starting with repair garages and small grocery outlets. He kept that money in the neighborhood, pleasing local people and ensuring some measure of respect and related protection. He upped the size of his drug purchases but limiting the heroin areas just to accommodate connections on the West Coast, letting the street-level dealers be more independent while promising protection for his cut, and getting more into cocaine distribution, particularly into the local disco clubs. Lewis also started making contributions to local political campaigns and charities. He became an example to the local White establishment of what a Black man could achieve, an image he wanted to cultivate.

Out of respect, Lewis and Marcus stayed away from Milkins as they built their enterprise. As Lewis branched into legitimate businesses, he gradually reacquainted himself with Rupert. During a hard time when younger Robert was sick and medical bills piled up, Lewis stepped in to help. Rupert was grateful.

Needing a place to conduct business, Lewis offered to give Rupert the money to buy the building where the shop was located. Rupert agreed, telling Lewis he didn't want to know anything about Lewis or Marcus' business. Lewis was relieved at that request.

Marcus ran Lewis' street operation from the back room of the barbershop. Lewis rarely appeared at the shop, and when he did, it was to get a haircut and to see what Rupert knew about the goings-on in the community. Strictly social. He'd then slip into the back room if need be.

Phone calls came and went out on a second phone line under the shop's name. A drop safe was located behind the lone desk, hidden underneath a two-drawer file cabinet filled with paperwork from some of Lewis' legitimate businesses. Lewis had two accountants, one for his businesses and another for the other operations. Marcus watched over both with the one ledger kept in the safe with cash; the books for the businesses that Lewis openly declared himself as the owner were handled by a small firm that Marcus periodically visited — something the accountant in charge of Lewis' account didn't relish. To tone down his nervousness, Marcus often reminded him he had gotten an associate degree in business at a local community college.

"Where?" the accountant asked. "Boonville," Marcus would answer.

Only a few of street lieutenants knew about the barbershop. Marcus usually went out on the street to collect money and solve problems. Little was done in the open. Junk had always been an in-the-shadows activity, but with pot there was a tendency to display one's high. Lewis moved heroin reluctantly, only to pacify other organizations with more of a history and clout than he had. Marcus pushed his pot dealers to deal in quantity and to move it quickly that way. "Don't act small fry," he would say, knowing that Lewis didn't like the bulkiness of marijuana or any hassles with storage and moving it.

Some of the White pot dealers also pushed along powder cocaine. Lewis felt that with coke, there was future expansion and more money, especially in hip, middle-class White circles. With talk of a smokeable form of cocaine drifting in from California, Lewis figured demand would increase.

There were drop sites for the drugs scattered about the city, and some business was conducted in noisy restaurants or fast-food outlets. If there was a serious problem where someone had to be convinced to do something or be punished, there was a soundproof basement room — with a floor drain — in the massage house next to the Repartee.

Use of the barbershop office was discreet enough that even the police didn't know of its exact location. They only knew that an office used by Marcus, as Lewis' main man, was located somewhere east of downtown. To the cops — the ones that suspected — Lewis was untouchable; Marcus wasn't.

When Marcus felt his day was over, he headed to his apartment off Paseo Boulevard on 31st Street in a building owned by Lewis. Unlike his boss, Marcus had stayed close to where he grew up. He lived alone. Aunt Eve had passed, having never had a conversation with Marcus about his birth parents. Marcus had pushed the question away his entire life. What company he got came from an occasional hooker and from the stray cats that came to his first-floor patio apartment. Marcus would leave out food and occasionally let one or two in on a cold night.

Poverty clung to the neighborhood as it had for decades: burglary and car break-ins frequent occurrences, and here and there, a shooting. Cops were an after-the-fact occurrence.

Marcus' apartment building was pretty much left alone when it came to street crime. Lewis' dealers knew to keep the dealing away; other criminals wanted to avoid the wrath of Lewis and Marcus. That made the building and block around it an oasis of sorts, quiet and clean, with Marcus always getting a respectful nod from other tenants and an occasional home-cooked meal from some of the older ladies in the building.

Marcus accepted his life. He was grateful for Lewis, whose smarts and connections had kept him away from prison. With Lewis, Marcus had learned self-control. He had yet to kill anyone — Lewis thought it mostly unnecessary — but he had hurt some people, hurt them bad, tortured them. It didn't bother him, though the screams and pleading sometimes got unsettling. Marcus was good, very good at bringing terror to people and a permanent memory of it. People were convinced Marcus killed people. Marcus was perplexed at times as to why he got annoyed with that assumption. Still, he knew his reputation — so much so that it didn't bother him when he'd forget to carry his Beretta .380 when he went out.

Russell hunched over a small black notebook, slowly turning pages as he read the names and phone numbers. Most names were of musicians, some he knew personally, others just a name and number of a band transferred from a bar napkin. It was a quiet morning, with a slight breeze sweeping through his tiny apartment balcony. He ignored the view, what there was of it. His apartment was part of a three-story complex up the hill from the Plaza shopping district. All the south side balconies peered over the rear loading and delivery docks of a Sears store. The docks were quiet on Sunday; the din started at 7 a.m. the next morning. The stereo was on. Paul Butterfield's harp was urging on Michael Bloomfield, his Gibson Les Paul responding with roaring licks on the band's extended jam "East-West." Russell looked up from the notebook. He slowly moved his head left and right, marveling at Bloomfield's guitar licks. The Paul Butterfield Band was no more, and it wasn't long before Bloomfield would be found dead in San Francisco. But Russell didn't know that as he read down the list of musicians and bands. He needed the right match to satisfy Lewis.

Some of the phone numbers were duds; musicians come and go,

leave town, come back, bands break up, re-form. Musicians are funny people, Russell often told himself, funny in the way of being different, special. They seemed always exposed to the vagaries of those who had lost their innocence long before them. In Russell's mind it took someone like him to both shield and reveal the truly creative ones, a task that always meant getting and holding their attention. That's what a good promoter does to make money for his artist and himself. Dealing with gangsters who own clubs and move dope — once the big time opens — those guys, like Lewis, can be eventually ignored.

"He isn't nationwide," said Russell aloud.

He turned to the back of the notebook where the listings were more recent. For the last few years, Russell had regularly booked six to eight bands. Island Sound, the reggae band, and the Good Riddance band got weekly attention. Four or five others—three rock bands, one country, and a ten-piece soul band — not so much, mainly because most of those band members had day jobs or families or were fighting among themselves, and Russell wasn't always sure who was available.

But if Lewis opens up connections to out-of-town clubs, I could attract more bands to book and manage. I might have to have an assistant, an office. Things could be real good. His eyes stopped at Greg Zurkee's name.

This could be the right guy to handle the chore. Zurkee was more grounded than the usual working musician. But he hustled and took any gig Russell lined up. He looked for out-of-town dates, wanted a name, and had a hot girlfriend to impress, a chick who saw herself riding higher with him. Russell figured if he called their apartment and Becky answered, he was going to get Greg's ear on the proposition, especially if it meant the potential for bigger and better gigs. She wanted Greg to succeed, and he wanted to please her. Russell reached for the phone and dialed Greg's number. Becky answered.

"Hey, it's Russell, pretty lady. How's it goin'?"

Becky had been cleaning up after cooking Greg breakfast. He was in the spare bedroom of the couple's apartment near the Art Institute. It was the music room where Greg played around with arrangements for the band on a Logan electronic keyboard and listened to jazz on a reel-to-reel tape player. He had stumbled across hours of recorded jazz from the 1950s and '60s on tapes at a flea market in the Westport entertainment district.

Russell and Becky continued their small talk. "Things good at the Repartee?" Russell asked.

"No real complaints," Becky answered. "Tips could be better, but Mike's a pretty good guy to work for."

"The band sounded good on Thursday."

Becky beamed a smile. "Oh, yes. I love the way Greg plays."

"His trumpet?"

Becky giggled. "Stop, Russell," she teased back. "Of course, the trumpet."

Russell let out a laugh. "Maybe I should take up an instrument. Could attract somebody as pretty as you."

"I'm sure you have no trouble in that department," Becky said, getting uncomfortable with where the conversation seemed to be heading. "Want me to get Greg?"

Russell could sense Becky wasn't up for flirting. "Yeah, get him, babe. Might have some new opportunities opening up for him."

"Super!" said Becky. "I'll get him."

Becky called out Greg's name. He didn't hear her. He had the headphones on listening to the reel-to-reel. Becky quickly got impatient when Greg didn't answer back. She scurried into the music room, shaking Greg's shoulder from behind to get his attention.

"Russell's on the phone."

Greg thought it a little weird Russell would be calling on a Sunday. They usually worked out play schedules in person over coffee — tea for Russell — at Nichelson's once a month, usually on the first Friday of the month. In Greg's mind, Russell was a precise guy, liking a regular routine and having the usual attitude that most musicians lack any sort of discipline. But maybe it was just that a band fell through somewhere, and this was a last-minute gig.

"Hey, man. What's up?" Becky stood close to Greg.

"Some opportunities might be opening up," said Russell. "Likely involve some travel and possibly some dates at clubs you haven't played in ... maybe in bigger towns."

"So, you've lined up some gigs in Chicago, New York, and LA, right?" Becky's eyes brightened as Greg turned to look at her.

"Not quite, horn man. But I'll get some details this week then we'll talk."

"At our regularly scheduled sit-down?"

Russell could detect the subtle sarcasm. "Yes, Greg, I will deviate from the normal protocol."

Greg grinned. "Okay, man, I hear ya. Just let me know." And he hung up the phone, nudging Becky aside to do it.

"Tell me, tell me," Becky asked as she began to tickle Greg's ribs.

He pushed her away gently. "It's nothing! He wants to get together about new play dates and different clubs. That's all."

"When? Where?" Becky said, bouncing up and down on her toes. "Oh, Greg, we could really start to get things going. Maybe going to California!"

"Easy now," said Greg. "Might be a good thing comin' about or might be just Russell talkin'. But, yeah, he usually doesn't call on a Sunday to talk business."

"When are you going to meet? When, when, when?" Becky said, spinning around, her arms held out from her body.

Greg laughed. "Get a grip, Becky. He's going to get back to me."

Russell was satisfied, and he could picture Becky badgering Greg for details. She spurred Greg's ambition along. She wanted big things to happen in their lives, and to happen as quickly as they could. He took her longing in stride, reasonably content to view his growth as a musician as a long-term thing. To friends and observers, Greg seemed as if he could play his horn on a street corner and be happy with coins being dropped into his instrument case.

Russell wondered whether he should contact Lewis and find out what out-of-town places he had in mind to set up play dates. That probably meant dealing with Marcus. No, he'd wait for Lewis to contact him. He took a sip of his tea. It was cold. Russell didn't know how much legwork Lewis expected from him, but probably a lot. Russell didn't like that thought. The last thing he wanted was to be known as someone who could point someone to where he or she could score. He was a music promoter; it was about the music. That's what he was about. This thing with Lewis, that was just to open some doors with club owners in bigger cities, get his name out. Set it up, and it would take care of itself. Just pick a few of the right people to carry it along.

CHAPTER 22

Monday was the day of the week Mike had to figure out what to do with himself. The club opened back up on Wednesday, starting off four nights of music, but other than that, he kept it closed. He put the word out about renting the space to community groups during those off nights to pick up a few dollars, but there were few takers. The stairs were a problem, and without a kitchen and tables and chairs, instead of mostly benches, it was hard to attract events like wedding receptions or private parties.

With nothing going on, Mike tried to stay away from the club — to clear his head, he would tell himself — but found it hard to do. He thought about joining a gym or taking up golf, but such an effort was, to him, like wearing a hair shirt — wanting style and knowing he'd be irritated with the result. He had asked himself more than once why he didn't have a woman in his life, someone beyond some short-term thing that ended when the sex got stale. He considered himself not that bad looking — a little overweight, okay, but he had his hair and didn't mind shaving. He liked women but was not all that intrigued by them. They were either pretty or not, nice body or not. Such was the result of Mike's world of drink, woozy come-ons, faithless laughter, and next day afternoon wakeups. Only the occasional soft and wonderful touch broke the predictability.

Mike didn't figure they liked to talk much about things with men. To him, they wanted to be complimented, have things bought for them, entertained if need be by taking them here or there. If he knew what love was, it was what he felt toward his mother, something a decent guy was supposed to do. As a club owner, Mike had little trouble getting a woman interested, and that generally led to sex. Owning a club and knowing musicians does that. *What else was there?* Mike had asked himself many times. Everybody was doing everybody, so it didn't mean much.

Couples like Greg and Becky seemed outside the norm. Most everyone was solo, on the make, man or woman, briefly entangled, and nobody seemed all that depressed by it. Committed relationships were counted in weeks or maybe months; being with someone for a year or more meant something was happening more than just good sex. When that occurred, some people seemed taken back by the mystery of it.

With the deal with Lewis happening, Mike found it even more difficult to relax in his apartment. Thoughts of putting away money and moving on transformed the club into more of a home than his apartment, a feeling Mike didn't worry about. So, it was Monday, mid-morning, and Mike was behind his desk at the Repartee. He picked up the phone.

"Hey, Russell, it's Mike. You busy?"

"In a relaxed frame of mind, having a cup of tea on my balcony while contemplating where I have to be today, but there's some time," answered Russell. "What's on your mind, Mike?"

Already, Mike was irritated by Russell.

"Look ... without getting too much into it, I would like to talk, and you know what I want to talk about."

"Not sure if that's a good idea," said Russell, sitting up. "Need to keep everything as uncomplicated as possible, considering."

"Yeah, I know what 'considering' means, and that's why I think we need to talk."

"Please give me a better reason, Mike," said Russell, then taking a sip from his tea.

"Corey."

Russell stiffened and then put down the teacup. He wasn't expecting that answer. *What does the doorman have to do with it?* "Okay. Where?"

"Keep it simple. Come by the club around 5."

Russell agreed. Mike was relieved. He looked around his office. Now, his apartment seemed more appealing. Maybe he'd goof off some before meeting Russell. Clean up the place a little, take a long shower, and then go down to the Plaza for a late lunch. Who knows, might get lucky, find a lady, and line something up for later.

CHAPTER 23

Marcus parked the Seville in the alley behind Milken's and went in through the back door. He had made some stops earlier, collecting the weekend take from street sales. Things seemed good. The black trash bag felt full. The barber/beauty shop was closed on Monday.

No one had gotten popped over the weekend, so he didn't need to check with his city or county jail contacts. The street crew was telling him that products were getting low. Marcus would bring it up with Lewis and then plan on taking a trip out of town for a day or so — St. Louis or maybe Chicago.

He threw the bag upon the desk and then emptied it. The money made a mound about a foot high, covering half the desk. Most of the bills were in small bundles with a rubber band around them. Marcus began arranging the bundles in stacks on one corner of the desk. He unlocked a metal storage cabinet by the door and got out the cash-counting machine. He could only run the machine on Sunday or Monday when Milken's was closed. No need to have customers in the shop wondering about the noise. On other days, he had to count by hand.

He got out a ledger book from the drop safe. Marcus would note the amount taken in, recalling from memory a rough amount from each of his dealers listed under their street names. Anyone Marcus deemed half-steppin' got a quick talking to before he left the block. He also had to watch for anyone getting ambitious, so he had contacts with some users who could keep reasonably straight in their habit and let him know if someone was branching out.

Lewis never questioned Marcus about the amount. He just called in the number, and Lewis would call back a few minutes later with his percentage. Marcus had no complaints.

When the count was done, Marcus waited for the call.

"What's up, nigga?"

"Same o'. Around ten and fifteen."

"Things cool?"

"Nothing on the surface. Tribe's mellow."

Lewis hung up. Five minutes later, he called back.

"Figure a two-one for take-home."

"Okay. Other things on the front page, man?" said Marcus.

"Call me from the corner in a half-hour."

The pay phone was up the street outside a liquor store Lewis had an interest in. He wasn't listed as the owner but had fronted the money to a relative who wouldn't have trouble getting a liquor license. It was one of his many businesses in which to launder money when needed.

Marcus put away the cash-counting machine and counted out his percentage, shoveling the rest of the money into the safe for Lewis to pick up later. Getting in his car, he slid the new Sugarhill Gang cassette into the dash-mounted player. Marcus then eased out onto Truman Road. He had some time to kill. He reached to turn up the volume on the album's third cut, "Bad News Don't Bother Me."

Twenty minutes later, Marcus had Lewis on the phone.

"Thought you should know that the comedian and that young blood at the door got together over breakfast."

"When?" said Lewis.

"Yesterday ... at that diner around the corner from the club."

"What you tellin' me? That things are getting heavy?" asked Lewis, irritated.

"Don't know. Thought you should know."

"Fucking white motherfuckers! Stay on it." Lewis hung up.

Back in the Seville, Marcus checked the time on the car's dashboard clock, then hit the play button on the Sugarhill tape. He'll swing by his apartment, shower, make sure there was food out for the cats, then later go park his ass in front of the Repartee to see if Mike showed up. Give it a couple of hours. If he didn't show, then he'd cruise. But somewhere in there, he'd go visit the massage house next to the club and drop a fifty on one of the girls to visit him later that night. But if things looked weird, like another get-together, he'd call Lewis again.

Sometime after 5 p.m., Jensen and Frederick's plain Ford turned west on 39th. Both men immediately recognized Marcus' Cadillac parked across the street from the Repartee.

"We got to get something goin' here, need to figure this out," said Jensen. Frederick nodded in agreement. Marcus hadn't noticed the Ford drive by.

By that afternoon, Pinky was toasted. The half-print was long gone, as was the six-pack. He found a half-full fifth of bourbon in his closet under a pile of clothes and hit that, too. He thought about picking through Corey's stash to roll a joint but quickly put that thought aside. He wanted a booze edge, and dope slowed him down. He'd chill a while and then head up to Bain's. *Maybe that fucker had some work for him to do.*

Gary had opened at 6 a.m. and would close at 9. Mondays were long and slow days; time spent dusting the shelves, straightening the cooler, and thumbing through magazines. Just before 6, the front door buzzed, and Pinky walked in. His collar was turned up, and he was hunched over. People who knew Pinky would recognize it as his drunk walking stance.

"Bain, my man," Pinky called out as he turned toward the counter, focusing his bloodshot eyes upon the storekeeper.

Gary leaned back. "Little early for that, huh, Pinky?" he said. There was disappointment in his voice.

Pinky moved over to the cooler, scanning the beer selection. "Early for what?" he called out mockingly. Just then, feeling a little queasy, Pinky fell forward, catching himself with one hand against the cooler door. He leaned his head in against his outstretched arm for a moment and then stood straight up, leaving a big handprint on the glass.

Gary, watching Pinky, frowned. "Pinky, you okay?"

"Fuckin' A," Pinky said as he moved back to the front counter. "Look, man, yeah, I had a couple ... You said the other day something about work ... or some such shit."

"Not the time to talk about it, Pinky. Maybe you should think about heading home."

"Been there, done that," Pinky answered back. "Give me something to do, man. I need the bucks. Need a routine, man."

Gary let out a long breath and then rubbed the back of his neck. "Yes, I figure you do, Pinky." There was a longing to the way he said it. "Maybe we can work something out," and Gary reached out to touch Pinky's hand. Pinky didn't flinch. Then he said, "Back off, man, ain't in the mood. Just want some work, money to drink."

"I could help you out, make things a little calmer," said Gary.

"Yeah ... help yourself out too. Look, get me drunk enough, and you can suck my dick, okay? But I want work and money first."

Gary was taken aback by his directness, but he didn't want the opportunity to get by. He could help Pinky, mend his heart, maybe love him. "How about we talk on Wednesday? I could show you some things, get you acquainted with the store, the register. But we'd have to do it when you're sober."

Pinky smiled. "Yeah, that's what everyone says. Okay, man. Wednesday, and I'll be bone dry."

Before Gary could tell Pinky what time to show, the front door again buzzed. Kim Cuc walked in with her teenage son William. Pinky stood straight up upon seeing the Vietnamese woman and boy.

"Hi, Miss Kim," Gary called out.

Kim smiled weakly and bowed her head. William ignored Gary and Pinky, and the two moved down one aisle of the small store. She took hesitant steps, scanning the items on the shelves. William walked behind her in a more confident gait, glancing back over his shoulder at

Pinky. When she found what she wanted, a box of powdered detergent, the pair walked to the counter. Pinky stepped aside, staring at her. Kim opened a small purse as Gary punched the price into the register.

"That will be one ninety-nine," Gary said, looking at William.

As Kim began to unfold a few bills from her purse, Pinky said, "How long have you been in the US, mama *san?*"

A worried look came over Gary's face. William stepped toward the counter and turned toward Pinky, partly shielding his mother.

"How long, mama *san?*" Pinky asked again louder.

"Pinky, I don't think…" Gary began.

"*Khong biet. Khong biet*," Kim said quickly, interrupting Gary.

"Oh, you know, don't you, gook?" Pinky yelled. "I bet you understand. What part of Vietnam are you from?" Pinky's voice now was low and threatening.

"She doesn't have to answer," William said. "Leave her alone."

"Leave her alone, GI, that what you mean? Well, me GI, you dink," said Pinky, pointing his finger at William's chest.

With that, William moved his legs apart and clenched his fists. Pinky then turned his body sideways, weaving a little as he put his hands up. Before he could steady himself, William shoved Pinky, pushing him into the candy display on the front counter. Pinky spun to the floor.

"*Dien cai dau*, him *dien cai dau*," cried out Kim as she pulled William away from Pinky. Holding on to him with one hand, Kim dropped three dollars on the counter and pulled William out the door.

Gary stood stiff behind the counter.

"Yeah, I'm *dinky dau*, for sure," Pinky said as he slowly raised himself off the floor. "Fuckin' crazy for sure." As he stood, Pinky looked at the candy bars and bags of chips scattered on the floor. He laughed. "And the fuckin' dinks got the best of me again."

Pinky looked around the store, weaving a bit. He saw a broom in the corner to one side of the counter.

"Pinky, come on, help me straighten this up, please," Gary said as he came out from behind the counter. When he saw Pinky pick up the broom, fear took hold, and he thought of the gun he kept under the counter. But Pinky turned away from Gary, took the broom, turned the handle out and away from him, and began walking down the closest aisle, holding the broom handle horizontally against items stacked on the top shelve. With each step, soup cans, sugar bags, detergent, pickle jars, and all manner of store items came crashing to the floor. Pinky smiled broadly with each step he took.

Gary dialed 911. A few blocks away, Jensen and Frederick heard the call from dispatch sending a patrol car to Bain's Liquor. The detectives decided to see what was going on.

When they arrived, Pinky was handcuffed and sitting in the back seat of the patrol car with a cop behind the wheel. Gary was talking to the other police officer. "This could be our opportunity," said Jensen, turning off the Ford.

Jensen walked up to the officer talking to Gary, showed him his badge, and said, "Let me handle this. Just put him in the back seat of our car." The police officer shrugged and didn't question Jensen's reason. He then motioned to his partner to put Pinky in the detective's car. Pinky had his head down as Frederick took Pinky from the uniform cop.

"You're going to handle the report?" the cop asked.

"Yeah, we'll take care of it," answered Frederick, turning to Gary.

Jensen walked into the store with Gary. It was a mess. "He did this?" Jensen asked.

"Yes," said Gary. "Some Vietnam vet stuff kicked in when a Vietnamese woman came in with her son."

"What'd he do? Hassle her?"

"Yes," Gary answered, his hands on hips as he looked around at what Pinky had done. "Nothing's really broken that bad. Looks worse than it is."

"He threaten you?"

"No, not really. He was drunk, and we were talking about a job."

"You were talking to him about a job, and he was drunk?" Jensen asked.

"I know, it sounds weird. But I want to help him. I thought giving him something steady would help with the healing. I think Vietnam vets have been pushed aside. Nobody's really helping them."

Jensen nodded, not really believing Gary's reason for helping.

"I don't know if I want to press charges," Gary said as he stepped away from Jensen and began picking up the items scattered about.

"That's your choice but think about it. You could be helping him or setting yourself up for more problems. Obviously, the guy's got problems, and booze ain't the answer. Think about it." Jensen waited for a response from Gary, who was looking at Pinky in the back of the detective's car through the store's front door window. *So, this is homo love,* thought Jensen, then he said, "Either me or Frederick will drop by later to talk again. We'll need to know what you're going to do."

"What are you going to do? Take him downtown?" Gary asked, turning back to face Jensen.

"Yeah. He needs to sober up and think about what he did. We can't hold him forever without some sort of charge. One of us will get back to you by the end of the day. You here all day?"

"I'm here," said Gary.

In the car, Jensen smiled at Frederick. He then turned back to Pinky. "Pinky, yo Pinky. We're detectives. Going to take you downtown, put you in a holding cell, let you get your act together. Got it?"

Pinky nodded. *The shit never leaves.*

At the downtown police station, Jensen put Pinky in a holding cell just inside the detective division office. The two detectives then sat down at their adjoining desks and began to strategize.

"Gary the fag doesn't want to press charges," said Jensen.

"What the fuck?" Frederick said in surprise.

"Yeah, can you dig it? Must be love." Both men laughed.

Frederick pulled the knot of his tie away from his neck. "That works in our favor," he said. "Listen ... we can tell Pinky we've worked out a deal with Gary not to press charges, but he must fly right and in return, he tells us what he can about what's going on at the Repartee while keeping his mouth shut about it."

"You think he'd go for it?" asked Jensen.

"I think the guy's tired and fucked up. But I don't think he wants to do jail time, and I don't think he wants to burn his bridges in the neighborhood. He might think Gary is out to fuck him — I mean literally — but he wants a job too. The guy ain't dumb."

Jensen sat still for a minute and then nodded. "I'll go talk with Bain, make sure he doesn't want to press charges and see where he's at about giving the guy a job even with what happened. He's got a thing for him, anyway."

"Yeah, you know that's right," said Frederick.

"While I'm gone, talk with Pinky. Tell him Gary called down here and wanted to talk with us. Tell him I decided to see him in person, so I'm on my way there."

"Think he's sober enough to talk with?" asked Frederick.

"Yeah, he is, but offer some coffee, too. Do the good cop routine; he's in that remorse stage."

After Jensen left, Frederick walked over to the holding cell. Pinky was sitting on the metal bench, his head down. He was still handcuffed.

"Mr. Grayson, how you doin'?"

Pinky looked up. "Okay, I guess." The booze was wearing off.

"I'll take those cuffs off. You going to be mellow?" Frederick asked.

Pinky nodded, and Frederick motioned for him to come to the cell rail. Pinky turned around without being asked, and Frederick reached in and took off the cuffs. "Want some coffee?" he asked.

"Yeah," said Pinky.

Frederick brought over a cup of coffee and said, "My partner has gone down to talk with Mr. Bain about your little stunt. Maybe we can help you out."

Pinky looked at Frederick as he took a sip of the coffee. Nothing is given out for free when it comes to cops. He thought about how he never really liked Black guys until he was in the Army. Then in Vietnam, he saw how they got the shit details yet still fought hard while not buying into the system. Pinky wondered if Frederick was ever in the military. "I don't know what got into me, man. That gook chick walked in, and the shit started. Memories always hangin' on me."

"Yeah, I hear you, man. Still, it ain't pretty what you did. You taking anything to control your anger, any counseling, you know, through the VA?"

"Fuck the VA," said Pinky.

Frederick nodded. "Yeah, I hear a lot of guys complain about the VA." He watched Pinky take another sip from his coffee. "A job could help ... Understand Bain can put you to work at times, even told my partner he was considering giving you a job."

"Well, I bet that's history," said Pinky.

"Maybe not. Let's see what my partner says when he gets back."

Pinky didn't look up from his coffee and turned away to sit back down on the bench. Frederick walked back to his desk.

Corey sat in front of the TV, flipping through channels, not really paying attention to what was on the screen. He wondered where Pinky was, not because he cared that much but because it was something other to think about than the club. *If Pinky was reasonably sober, maybe he could talk to him about the Repartee.* Corey wanted to keep the doorman job as long as he could play dumb. *Carolyn probably wants me to leave it — too many temptations. Pinky didn't give a shit, maybe; that's why it could be worth it to talk to him about it. Talking with Mike didn't do much to ease the apprehension. Maybe it was just time to boogie.*

CHAPTER 24

Near 5:30 p.m., Marcus saw Russell pulling up at the Repartee's front door. He watched as Russell stepped back onto the sidewalk and looked up to the building's second floor. A minute later, Russell stepped in through the open door. Lewis would want to know about this. Marcus decided to sit tight to see how long Russell was there and if anyone else showed up.

"You're a little late," Mike said as the two walked up the stairs.

"I wasn't sure about talking about this, and I'm still not," Russell said.

"You got me into this with this Lewis investor shit, and I need to know what's going down. Not all the details, but enough to protect my ass. And Russell, I know you know what's up."

Russell didn't respond until they were in Mike's office, with Russell sitting in the chair in front of Mike's desk. "You want me to get a beer from the bar?" Mike asked, knowing he didn't want one.

"No, I'm good," said Russell.

"Okay then. Tell me what's going down."

Russell cleared his throat. "Lewis — through Marcus — is going to distribute coke through some bands that will be playing here. That's it."

"So, the coke comes in here, and you — or whomever — pass it along to the band, and they take it wherever they play next."

"Something like that."

"Who picks the bands?" Mike asked. Russell didn't respond. "You?" Russell still said nothing. "So, you pick them. I get it. A little deal with the devil, huh, Russell? You help the gangster push some coke, and in return, you get your name out there as a music promoter via some help from Lewis. So, I think he's ambitious. We're looking at a Midwest network ... or beyond."

"Don't overthink it, Mike," Russell said.

"Fuck you." Mike ran his fingers through his hair. "Okay, that's all I need to know ... except who's going to be the doorman? Considering the sack trick that went down earlier, the doorman will know which band is getting the stuff and when it's coming in, right?"

"I supposed, yeah."

"This brings me back to Corey. Does he stay, or does he go? And what do you know about him? Considering he's a writer or whatever, is he lookin' to get a name, write about this little escapade? You brought him in. He's your friend."

Russell shifted his body in the chair as Mike looked at him intently. "Got any tea?" Russell asked.

"Tea? I haven't got any tea, Russell." Mike was getting angry. "This is a bar, a nightclub. You want a beer, a shot, I've got that. No fuckin' tea. Now, what's with Corey?"

Russell thought about getting up and leaving, but he knew Mike wouldn't let that happen yet. Russell started in about Corey.

"The guy helped me distribute flyers for some of my earlier bookings. We have some mutual friends from high school. That's it. He writes, though I don't know when considering he's always chasing tail."

"Yeah, I know that's right." Mike relaxed a bit. "Okay, let's assume he's not going to play Bernstein and Woodward. Can he keep his mouth shut?"

Both men studied the question. "I don't know," Russell said. "He's a talker — that's mainly how it works with the ladies."

"Okay. If I let him go, say after Wednesday night, who's going to step in? Knowing Lewis, I don't get to choose. I may be stuck with that gorilla Marcus, who's about as friendly as a rabid dog ... unless you work the door."

Russell sat up. "I don't want the door. I figure I'll know where the stuff is stashed, do what's necessary after the show, and that's it. I'm not sitting on a stool at the door, sorry."

"Okay. I know, not your style, bad for your music promoter image — too working class," Mike said sarcastically. Russell didn't seem offended. "Maybe we just keep an eye on him for the first couple of runs. See how it goes."

"Or you could talk with Lewis about it," said Russell. "I think he's got some doubts about him also."

"Great. I might as well ask for that behemoth Marcus to work the door," Mike said with disgust.

Russell shrugged. "I don't know. Talk with him if you can."

"I will," Mike said, looking directly at Russell. He realized that he never really liked the guy. "And you and I never had this conversation, dig?"

"Yes, I understand, Mike," said Russell.

Marcus checked the dashboard clock when he saw Russell walk out. About fifteen minutes inside. He wondered what they had talked about. He watched as Russell got into his car parked in front of The Pink Slip. *Maybe they were just suckin' each other's dicks. Musta not taken them long to come.* Marcus chuckled. *White guys do that shit.*

He started the car. He'd talk with Lewis tomorrow; nothing really pressing that he should know right now. Marcus drove up the street, turned down the alley by Nichelson's, and parked behind the massage house. *Line up some White pussy*, he told himself, then pick up some ribs for dinner and head home.

Russell sat in his car for a moment. He never noticed Marcus' Seville. He got out of his car and went into The Pink Slip.

CHAPTER 25

By the time Jensen got back into the store, Gary had finished cleaning up the damage Pinky had done and was even more convinced that pressing charges against Pinky would just make it worse for him.

"You work fast," Jensen said.

"Have to. Got customers and don't want the place looking like... err, well ..."

"Like a crazy Vietnam vet trashed it?" Jensen said, finishing Gary's sentence.

Gary didn't smile. "Maybe something like that."

Two teenage girls came into the store. Jensen gave them the head-to-toe look and moved over to the magazine section. Gary went behind the counter. The girls giggled as they picked through the candy rack, occasionally glancing up at the pints and half-pints of liquor lined up behind the counter.

Don't even think about it, girlies, Jensen thought as he looked over at them, keeping his eyes on their backside longer than he should. They turned back away from the candy and looked at Jensen. One pulled the other back around. With their candy and chips, they left the store quickly after paying Gary.

"I like to leer," Jensen said, guessing what Gary was thinking. Gary nodded back, hiding the disgust he felt.

"Okay. You won't press charges, but we could, Gary. Drunk and disorderly, maybe even resisting arrest."

Gary looked stunned. "Why would you do that?"

"Just hypothetical," Jensen said. "Doesn't mean we'd do it. But what's Pinky's job prospects so that thought doesn't enter my thinking again?"

Gary walked over to one of the cooler doors. It was slightly ajar. Jensen studied the man. *He didn't walk like a fag*, Jensen told himself. Nothing effeminate about the guy, just an average-looking man stepping into middle age, much the same as Jensen.

Gary closed the cooler door. He didn't like the way this was going. Jensen was now a bully, one of many he had dealt with in the past. These cops wanted something, and Gary wasn't sure if it was from him or Pinky, or both. Gary knew it was a matter of enduring, like always. Not agreeing meant making enemies, particularly with the cops. He couldn't afford that, not as a small businessman. He had to survive. He needed them to show up when there was trouble. Funny, though, Pinky probably wouldn't hold it against him if he let the charges stand. Gary knew about being on the outside, and he knew Pinky did, too. Blaming yourself almost always overshadows blaming others. Gary gave Jensen a look the detective had never seen from the shopkeeper, a mixture of anger and superiority that Jensen couldn't totally read. It made him instinctively brush his hand across the left side of his suit coat to feel the bulge of his gun. Gary softened his gaze and said, "He can come back in, and we can talk again about it. Assuming he's not going off again, I think we can handle it."

"Think he could handle it with all those half-pints lined up behind him at the counter?" Jensen asked, pushing Gary to make sure he knew what he was agreeing to.

"I had thought about that. But it would be part-time, working the deliveries in the mornings, cleaning up, that sort of thing. I'm not at the point of letting him run the store while I'm not here."

"Good policy," Jensen said. "I'll pass that along to him and encourage him to see you real quick."

"So, he won't get charged?"

"No problem," Jensen said as he glanced at the door. "Got to get back. I'll tell Pinky about your generosity." Jensen half smirked.

"I still have some cleaning to do," Gary said as he turned away.

Never quite can figure these queers out, Jensen told himself as he walked to his car. *Either they're like college girls anxious to get fucked or overeducated smartasses so smug that they think everyone is dumber than them.* Jensen satisfied himself that Gary fell somewhere in between.

Pinky didn't say anything when Jensen and Frederick took him out of the holding cell and into a side conference room. Pinky couldn't remember when he didn't feel like a pawn in some big game. This was no different. Frederick directed Pinky to sit down. The two detectives remained standing. Pinky sat slumped over, his arms on his lap, hands clenched under the table.

"Good news, Pinky. Mr. Bain has decided not to press charges," said Jensen.

Pinky didn't react and kept silent.

"No charges, man," Jensen continued, raising his voice. "He's even willing to talk to you about a part-time job. Could be a path to you getting your shit together."

Pinky continued to remain still. Jensen took a step toward him and leaned over. "You listening, Pinky? No charges from Bain ... but that doesn't mean we can't file something to keep your ass here a while."

Pinky looked up at Jensen, then over to Frederick. "Can I get a drink of water?"

Jensen put his hand on the table and leaned in closer to Pinky. "You can get a drink later, maybe when you walk out of here or when we send you over to county. It's going to be your choice. Understand this, Pinky, this is a trade-off, a deal between you and us. You walk out of here agreeing to help us a little on the street — eyes and ears — or you're in lock-up, and Frederick and I get creative with what you did at Bain's, and any job you got from Bain goes permanently bye-bye along with your freedom for a while. Can you dig, or are you too shell-shocked to understand you have a choice?"

Pinky unlocked his hands and grabbed his kneecaps. He thought about slowly sliding a M7 between Jensen's fifth and sixth ribs, turning the bayonet upward to make sure the lung was punctured, and one rib cracked. Pinky smiled. Jensen and Frederick looked at each other.

Frederick gently moved Jensen away from the table and said, "Pinky, what do you know about the club Repartee on West 39th?"

Pinky looked up at Frederick. *Between these two assholes*, he told himself, *I'd rather deal with the Black one*. "Not much, except my roommate works the door there."

Jensen and Frederick smiled at one another. "Really," said Frederick. "What's his name?"

"Corey Edwards."

"He got another job beside the door?" asked Frederick.

"Drives a van for himself but tied to some delivery company."

"Where?"

"Some company in midtown. I don't know the name."

"Does he go out of town with his van or just city delivery?"

Pinky frowned. "I don't know. I'm his roommate, not his mother?"

"Look, dickhead ..." Jensen started before being interrupted by Frederick.

"Yeah, Pinky, we understand. We just want you to pay attention to anything he says about working at the club. That's all. You're just passing along any information about the club and what Corey does there, or the people he hangs with or anything like that."

"So, I'm a spy for you guys."

"We prefer the word 'informant,'" said Frederick.

"So, you got me straight with Bain, drop any charges, and as payback is snitch on my roomy? What else do I get down the line?" Pinky felt empowered.

"Like what?" Frederick asked, perturbed.

"Money. A few bucks here and there."

Anger rose in Jensen and Frederick. "We need to confer," said Frederick, and the two men stepped out of the conference room.'

"The little shit is trying to play us," said Jensen.

"Let him," answered Frederick. "So, it costs us some jack, big deal. He could work well for us, for a lot of things we're looking at. No one would suspect an alcoholic vet as an informant."

"That's the point," said Jensen. "Can the guy keep clean? A few drinks, some smoke or whatever, and he's off the deep end, and we're screwed."

Frederick thought about what Jensen had said. "I don't know, but he knows how to be disciplined. The military does that. Have him think he's doing something, a cause, something bigger than himself, and he could steer straight for us."

"You got a hell of a lot more faith in humanity than I do, Frederick. The guy's a fuck-up."

"Maybe so, but it's the only thing we've got now." Jensen nodded, and the two stepped back into the conference room.

"I'm sure you'll need cab fare home," said Frederick, sliding a $20 bill to Pinky. "And here's my card with mine and Jensen's phone number on it. We expect to hear from you by the end of the week, Pinky. Understand?"

Pinky looked down at the twenty and the business card. *What else have I got going for myself?* he asked himself. "Okay. Is that it?" Pinky took the money and the card.

"That's it, Pinky," said Frederick. "There's the door. We'll talk with you in a few days."

Outside, Pinky gauged the weather. It was brisk but clear. It would take him an hour or so to walk back to 39th Street from downtown. He didn't want to waste the twenty on a cab.

CHAPTER 26

Corey was in his kitchen. He sat at the table. The electric typewriter was on. Empty house, not in the mood to go out, might as well try to write. But, as usual, what he did put down sounded cheesy. The wadded-up balls of paper on the floor reinforced that feeling. Could he do anything beyond this dribble? Corey smiled. He was a bug-eyed character in an R. Crumb comic, hands on his chin, stoned into stupidity, trying to be Mr. Natural, frozen in the moment as if slowing peeing in his pants. Corey dropped his head to his chest, looked up, and then typed:

"One can read books, take in films, get high, have women, and still not know a thing about life."

Corey read the sentence, then again. It seemed more like the end of a story than the beginning of one. Self-indulgent, he told himself, and he read the sentence again. "I suck," Corey said aloud.

He pulled the paper out from the typewriter, wadded it up, and turned off the machine. He went into the living room and pointed the remote at the television. Might as well accept what I am right now ... until I get totally disgusted with myself, and then maybe I'll be something else. He thought of Carolyn. *Could being with her more, her alone, help me figure it out? Just fall into it, maybe. She wants that. But what the fuck do I want? What the fuck, I don't even know ... other than to be some famous dickhead writer, burning out, burning in. How pathetic a want.*

The front door banged against the wall as Pinky walked in. He saw Corey slumped in a chair in front of the TV, holding a beer. He then noticed the typewriter on the kitchen table.

"Don't say it," Corey spoke up. "I already know. I'm watching TV, and the typewriter sits on the kitchen table. Draw your own conclusions but keep them to yourself."

Pinky shrugged, then walked into the kitchen and opened the refrigerator. "Can I have a beer?" he asked.

"Yeah, sure," Corey answered back.

Pinky came back in and sat on the sofa. Corey looked over at him. "You look kinda haggard, man. Where have you been?" It was more of a statement than a question.

The two sat in silence, watching a game show on the television. The sound was barely audible.

Pinky took another drink and asked, "How's it going at the club?"

"It's going ... sometimes a little weird, though," Corey answered while keeping his eyes on the TV."

"Oh, how so?"

Corey looked over at Pinky. Pinky wasn't usually one for casual conversation. "Just weird, as usual. Mike's a grump, Becky's a fox, the music is good, and I get free drinks. Like nirvana, man." Pinky nodded, picking up on the sarcasm. "And I might not be there long."

"What would you do then?" Pinky asked, a little surprised that Corey was thinking of leaving the club.

"Drive my van and become just a patron of the Re-par-tee."

"Seriously, man?" Pinky asked.

"Yeah, maybe. Why you askin'? You want to take my place at the door?"

"Maybe," Pinky said.

"Wouldn't that be counter to your philosophy that 'Life sucks and then you die'?"

Pinky squinted at Corey. "How so?"

"It might be fun!"

Pinky let out a laugh. Corey smiled at him. Both men took a drink from their beers. Then Corey said, "We need to shoot some pool together." Pinky nodded as he took another drink from his beer.

"How about tomorrow night at Lou's? Carolyn's working — we'll get a discount."

"Sounds good," Pinky said as he got up from the sofa.

"Okay, figure on eight or so if I don't see you before then."

"Will do." Pinky began to walk up the stairs to his room. "Don't strain yourself writing."

Corey raised his arm and gave Pinky the finger. Pinky let out a quick, loud laugh. Corey heard him shut the door.

Corey sat, the television the only light in his eyes. *Pinky's fucked up but a good guy,* he said to himself. *Vietnam shit can stink up a guy's life. Hopefully, he moves out of it.* Corey took a drink from his beer. *If I do anything, I seem to attract interesting people into my life. Isn't a writer supposed to do that? But anyone who pays attention to their own life does that. It's all around ... even the stuff that's missed. How much have I missed?*

Upstairs, Pinky was searching through his room for a bottle. He found a half-pint of Beam in a shoe in the closet. It was three-quarters full. Pinky took a long drink, chased it with what remained of his beer, and sat on the bed. He reached into his back pocket and looked at the business card Frederick had given him. "This shit sucks," he said aloud and threw the card onto the bedside table. He thought about what he needed to leave town. The disability check would be in sometime next week. He could cash it and hitchhike up to Des Moines. Hang there a few days, do some day labor, take the bus to Fort Madison, and then catch the train to Chicago. Disappear in that city. *Corey, the cops, Bain — they can stay here and go fuck themselves. This puppy needs to leave. Till then, I could stall the fuzz or, at the very least, make shit up.*

Corey turned off the TV and was sitting in the darkened room when the phone rang in the kitchen. He debated about answering it, then thought of Carolyn. Out of the chair, he picked up the phone from the wall.

"Lu Wong's pizzeria."

"Joke's getting old, babe." It was Carolyn.

"Yeah, you're right. What's up with you? Comin' by?"

"Not tonight. Just got through studying, and I'm going to relax, light some candles, pour myself a glass of wine, and take a long bubby bath ... just for me."

"You could do that here, and I could be waiting on you with the candles and wine."

Carolyn smiled. "Then you'd want to get in with me, and my relaxing would be over."

Corey laughed. "What's wrong with that?"

"It isn't relaxing, Corey — though fun, depending upon your speed."

"My speed works fine," Corey protested without being harsh.

Carolyn's eyes widened. "Let me finish, please ... it's about me being with me, a girl's time to herself."

Corey ended his smile and darkened his tone. "Yeah, I get it. You need your time and some space. I understand."

"Corey, honey, you don't. Yes, I need time to myself. I work hard, and I need to wind down, but I don't see you enough so it isn't about 'space.' You drive the van and work two or three nights at Repartee, while I'm working four or five nights at Lou's and in school, too. I think we need to do more than just meet up after midnight. I would like to have dinner some night, a nice restaurant, the whole night to us."

"Okay, okay, there you go about me quitting the Repartee. You always go back to that," Corey said, his voice louder. "I like the gig. Nothing goes on there — just people and music."

Carolyn didn't speak. She felt heavy. Her silence made Corey go back over what she had said.

"All right, sorry. I'm just worked up — frustrated, I guess. Can I see you tomorrow at the bar? I invited Pinky to shoot some pool. If it's slow, we could talk too ... check our work schedules and see if we can coordinate a Saturday when we're both off. What do you say?"

By now, the conversation felt familiar to Carolyn. She listened to herself breathe. "Come up tomorrow. We'll talk some more. Now, I need to run my water."

Corey heard her resignation. He told himself he needed to figure this out. If he didn't, he would lose her. And he didn't want her to be gone ... not right now. "Have a good night, sweetheart; I'll see you tomorrow," he said as cheerily as he could.

"Bye." Carolyn hung up.

Corey held the phone to his ear for a few more seconds before hanging it up. Whatever was going on at the club was affecting his relationship with Carolyn, he decided. Maybe he should quit the club ... maybe he should do a lot of things. Maybe he should just go over to her apartment right now. Get some wine, her favorite ice cream, roll a doob, bring some reggae tapes — get deep into talking just like when they'd first met.

Corey chuckled softy. He hadn't really noticed her at first back then, the new girl waiting tables at Lou's. Corey either started or ended his nights at Lou's, depending upon what or whom he ran into on that particular excursion.

After a few weeks of hitting the bars without discovering anything new, Corey stopped in Lou's near closing time before heading home. It was slow. Carolyn was chatting it up with a couple of guys at the near-empty bar. Corey gave her a slight smile and headed back to the pool-room to see if anyone was on the pool tables. He had the room to himself, so he fished for some quarters and settled into the pinball machine, thinking about what drink to order.

Carolyn came up behind him. "Need something?" she asked in a soft voice. Corey acted as if he was startled. "Whoa." He turned to her. Her long black hair was pinned up. Whatever sadness there was in her life was absent from her eyes, a dark brown set into her olive-colored skin, her face tapered just a little as if God ran the lower part of his palms over her cheekbones and then pushed up slightly, smoothing out sharp angles. She seemed somewhat exotic, southern European or, maybe south of the border, like a woman familiar with drink, faraway dishes, and comely looks from men. Corey wondered if she was part Italian or maybe Greek or Spanish.

"I'll have a beer, a Bud," he said, keeping his eyes on her face. Carolyn cocked her head slightly without looking directly at him, nodded, and smiled back. Corey watched her walk to the bar. Lou was working that night. He looked at Corey with a blank expression. As she waited for Lou to pour the beer, she glanced down one side of the bar and then the other. Corey figured she knew he was watching her. He liked her figure, a fullness that gave off the sexiness like that of a darker-toned Marilyn Monroe — or better yet, Corey thought, *Sophia Loren.* Corey thought of Carolyn in bed with him, her long hair down, brushing his across his face, her large breasts gently swaying across his chest, the nipples hard, a distant smile, eyes closed, all meant for the pleasure of it.

"Here you are, stranger," Carolyn said while putting the beer atop the pinball machine.

Corey reached into his pocket for money. "No stranger here. Been coming in for a while. You new?"

"Just started a week or so ago," Carolyn said as she counted out change.

"Keep it," Corey said. "How often do you work?"

"Four nights or so, sometimes a day shift. I work around going to school."

"Oh yeah? Where?"

"JoCo. All I can afford right now."

Corey stayed on her face, but he gave himself a quick glance down. Carolyn wore an oversized dark blouse, the bottom tied at the front, and over a light-colored sleeveless T-shirt. A gold cross holding a tiny diamond hung around her neck, accenting her cleavage. Her look was different, Corey thought, but far from slutty. "When do you work next?" he asked.

Carolyn looked up at Corey's eyes. There wasn't anything there to push her away. She had watched him before he noticed her. She knew she would take a chance. She wrote her phone number across a blank order ticket. "Here's my phone number. Call me and find out."

She walked back to the bar. Corey sipped on his beer. He was a little surprised. *Had he missed something at some time?* he wondered. The question passed quickly. Nothing more to say here, he told himself — next conversation coming soon. Corey downed his beer. He walked up behind Carolyn as she was wiping the bar. "Talk you to soon," he whispered. Carolyn froze for a moment without turning around. Corey walked out of the bar without looking back. Lou caught it all. He pushed a rag across the bar top and looked at the bar clock. "You're not in a hurry to leave, are you, hon?" he asked Carolyn.

Carolyn saw his look of concern. "No, Mr. Levin. I'm not in a hurry."

"Good. Still, things to do before we close." Carolyn nodded as she wiped and stacked ashtrays. "And 'Lou' is fine. I like to hear my first name, especially from young women." Lou waited for a response, unsure if he stepped over the line. "I mean, I just prefer not to be so formal here. My wife always wanted everything on a first-name basis. If you were not doing so good and I was thinking of letting you go, then, 'Mr. Levin' might get me thinking longer. But you're doing fine, and Lou is ..."

"I understand, Lou," Carolyn interrupted. "I appreciate the job. Thank you."

Lou nodded and turned to the register to begin counting the money. "The keys are on the bar, Carolyn. Check the back room and johns. I think we're empty. If so, then lock the front and back doors. Still, some cleaning to do."

By now, Carolyn knew the closing routine. But she still liked it when Lou reminded her of it. He reminded her of her grandpa, who always told her to "Never let what you don't like stay with you."

The sun shining through the curtain-less window got Marcus stirring; next, he heard the soft meowing of cats. He opened his eyes and looked up at the ceiling fan above his bed. He then turned to the window and squinted. *Need to get one of those bitches from the massage house over here to ask about curtains,* he told himself. He looked at the clock on the nightstand. It was 7:30. About his usual time to awake when he wasn't drinking the night before.

Marcus went into the kitchen. At the sliding patio door a half-dozen cats milled about. "Damn ... the word is out. It's a mother-fucking menagerie," he said aloud, liking the scene.

He got a big bowl and filled it with dry cat food. As he opened the glass door and stepped out onto the patio, the cats swarmed at his feet. "Okay, kitties, here's some chow for you all." He moved away and watched the cats go for the food. He scratched his head with both hands as he looked down at them with a smile of satisfaction. Aunt Eve always liked cats, he remembered again, and cats liked her. She'd be happy he was feeding them.

Marcus lined out his day in his head. Get some breakfast, work out some in the room he had set up with weights and a punching bag, make the rounds on the street, then head to Milken's with the money and eventually call Lewis. It was a usual workday.

The street brought nothing new. Marcus noted which dealers needed dope and planned for delivery. By midday, he was at Milken's, coming into the back room through the back door. He counted the money collected, placed it in the safe, and left, walking down to Stop 'n' Go to call Lewis. It was Tuesday. Marcus knew he would be at the Swope Country Club in the south part of the city, likely in the lounge after playing a round of golf.

"What's up, my brother?" Lewis answered after being told he had a call. He was in a good mood. Marcus figured he had a good morning home, shot at a decent round, or both.

"Same O — no disturbances out there. Still, been watchin' the chuckleheads. Seems they had a small powwow."

Lewis' mood changed. "All this intrigue ... can't get shit off the ground with all this intrigue. Maybe I should have you convince these White guys we ain't jackin' around, get their white asses in line."

"Don't bother me none to do that," Marcus said.

"Yeah, I know, brother ... let me think." Lewis scanned the club's lounge as he stood at the end of the bar with the phone to his ear. He nodded and smiled at another man walking up to the bar. "Can't think here — got to play the role. Go by Russell's pad or call him and tell him to come to Michelle's place around 4. Make it convincing; he's got to show."

"Want me to bust him up some?"

"No, keep it in mind, though, but make your point still."

Marcus hung up the phone. He thought for a minute if he needed something from the Stop 'n' Go before walking back to Milken's. He went in and bought a pint of chocolate milk and a couple of cans of moist cat food. At the desk in the back room, he found Russell's number on the Rolodex in the safe. Since Lewis hadn't insisted he visit Russell personally, Marcus would just call. Marcus was satisfied with that, not sure why he didn't feel like telling Lewis he'd rather make a visit.

Russell picked up on the sixth ring. "Hello." His voice was groggy.

"Damn man, you crashed?" Marcus asked. His tone was forceful. Russell knew right away that it was Marcus.

"Ah, no, not really."

"Good, motherfucker, 'cause your ass is being summoned by Mr. Lewis today. And you better show, or I'd be poppin' your head like a pimple on your ass." Marcus smiled at his remark. *I'm getting downright poetic,* he thought to himself. "Don't want to do that, Russell, messin' up your personal presentation and such. 'Course, wouldn't mind it either."

Russell rubbed his forehead as he held the phone to his ear. He wanted to go back to bed and start the day over.

"You there, White boy?" Marcus asked, turning the phone around to his face and holding it close to his mouth.

Russell sighed. "I understand. What time?"

"Four, motherfucker, on the dot, where you came before," Marcus barked. He then waited to see if Russell had more to say. He didn't, and Marcus hung up the phone.

Russell went into his kitchen to heat some water for tea. "Everything all right?" a voice called from the bedroom. "Yes, fine, thank you," Russell answered. A young man, in his late teens walked into the kitchen a moment later. "Want some tea before you go?" Russell asked.

"You're sweet, but no, thank you. I must go, working tonight. We need to do this again." Russell nodded without looking at the man. They stood close to one another. Russell wrapped the teabag string around a cup handle. The man touched Russell's hand and leaned in to kiss him. The men held each other tightly, then broke apart.

"I want to see you again," Russell said as the man moved toward the door.

"That would be nice," he answered as he went out.

Russell took his tea and sat down at the kitchen table. He didn't want to think too much about meeting Lewis. He just wanted to think about the young man who had just left his apartment. But he couldn't. Seeing Lewis again so soon after the first meeting meant he wanted to know which band had been lined up. Other than talking to Greg the other day, Russell hadn't contacted any other band. He needed to have an answer for Lewis. Russell dialed Greg's number.

"Hello."

"Greg, it's Russell. How ya doin'?"

"Good, man. Good. What's up?"

"Can we meet today, maybe in an hour or two?"

"Wow, man. Quick. Has to be today? Had lined up some rehearsal time with the guys for a few hours before going to my bartending gig."

Russell knew he had to have some answers for Lewis. "Can you cancel? It's important."

"Jez, I hate to cancel. The guys get pissy about canceling. Juggling schedules with everyone having a day job."

"Your next gig is Thursday. You got tomorrow, don't you?"

Greg sighed. "All right, man. Let me make some calls. Where do you want to meet?"

"How about at your pad?"

"Sure," Greg said. "Becky's out for a while. What time?"

Russell looked at his watch. It was 1:30. He couldn't be late to meet Lewis. "I'll be there in an hour."

Greg wondered why the push. Maybe something's coming through. Becky would be excited.

As Russell drove over to Greg's, he thought of how he was going to put the deal in front of him. Russell liked Greg, even respected him, or at least his talent. Of the bands Russell promoted, Greg's band was the least trouble. They showed up on time, were consistent in their playing, didn't get wasted on free drinks, and if they got high, it was after the show, not during. The guy deserved — and could — move on out of this city. Russell decided that was his approach in getting him to carry out Lewis' plan.

"Hey, man," Greg said as he opened the door. He gave Russell a relaxed smile. The sentiment went well with his baggy shorts, sandals, and T-shirt depicting a silhouette of "Bird" playing his sax.

"My man," Russell said, giving him a loose embrace before sitting down.

"Got some water brewing for tea, but I'm limited on choices."

Russell was surprised. "Ahhh, a man of tastes. I appreciate it. What's my choice?"

"Got some green tea, some Earl Grey, and your basic Lipton. Sorry, that's it."

"I'll take some Earl Grey. Thanks, man."

Russell looked around Greg and Becky's apartment. The few other times he had come by he thought the place was very tidy for a musician's crib. It remained so. And nothing hinted at drug use — no roaches in an ashtray, no rolling papers lying about, no tray or mirror with a single-side razor blade. There was even a flowery smell in the room.

"Who's the dedicated homemaker? You?" Russell asked.

"Yeah, right," Greg said from the kitchen with a laugh. "Becky has her rules, and I follow them. The only thing she stays out of and doesn't gripe about is my instrument room, where my music resides, my refuge from domesticity."

"You're an artist, after all."

Greg didn't respond. The sound of clanging dishes came from the kitchen. Russell went over his approach to bringing Greg into the deal with Lewis. He decided to be reasonably straightforward, steering away from any information about Lewis or mentioning Marcus. Russell heard the teapot whistling. A few minutes later, Greg came out of the kitchen with a small teakettle and two cups. He put the tea on the coffee table in front of Russell. "Help yourself."

Russell poured some tea into a cup. Greg sat down in a chair across from him.

"I didn't think you liked tea," said Russell.

"Every once in a while. Helps give me an air of sophistication — more Russell-like if you dig."

Russell smiled at the remark, accepting it as a validation of him.

Greg cleared his throat. "Okay, man ... now that we've sorta jerked each other off with compliments, are you here to tell me that what you talked about the other day isn't going to happen?"

Russell held up one hand as he took a sip of tea. He liked the fact that Greg was turning a little testy, believing Russell's come-on was just jive. It made convincing him to go along a little easier. "No, no, man. Not even."

Greg smiled and nodded. "Good, man, good. Now, what gives? What's the details?"

Russell looked directly at Greg. "What we're going to talk about is between us, just us. No one, not even Becky, should know what I'm going to bring up. Do I have your word on this?"

"No problem."

"I think I can start getting you and the band more frequent, and likely better, out-of-town gigs, maybe eventually Chicago dates, and who knows beyond that."

"Really? Who do I have to kill?" said Greg jokingly.

"Nobody. But you would have to carry a package to where you're going to play."

"Package ... package of what?"

Russell thought of how to say what it was about. "Let's just say it would be something getting very popular these days."

"Okay, Russell, quit the dance. What are we talking about? Me movin' weed for you ... or coke?"

"It would be coke, a kilo or less," Russell said, knowing that he had no idea what amount Lewis wanted the band the carry.

"That's a lot of coke, a lot of jack." Greg felt uncomfortable. "This isn't coming out of you. You frontin' for someone?"

"I have an associate, an influential associate who has connections in the music world. He would help me get you known play dates where you would be noticed — you're good enough to be noticed outside of this city — in front of larger crowds in bigger towns that appreciate jazz, appreciate the excellence you and the band bring to an audience."

"Quit blowin' smoke up my ass, Russell." Greg got up and walked to the window to look outside. Russell took a sip of tea. He thought about what he'd say — if anything — to Lewis if Greg decided not to do it.

Greg turned back to Russell. "Look, man, I'm not against coke or anything. Becky and I do a line or two every once and a while, stuff someone gives me 'cause he liked the sound we make. It doesn't bother me that people do it. They want to shove money up their nose; that's their problem — and right. Music, jazz, that's my drug. I get high on that. But I don't like the risk. It's tough enough trying to make it as a musician in this jerk-water town."

"I hear ya," said Russell. "But this isn't about dealing — just carrying a package, that's all. Drop it off; it's gone, do your gig. That's all. You'll have deniability. You can play dumb if it's discovered. Only one or two people will know about it."

"Who do I get it from? You?"

"Maybe, probably," Russell said. "Might be you just pick it up somewhere, left with your gear by your horn, maybe."

"This doesn't sound too together ... kinda flaky. And who's this associate of yours?"

"It is together, Greg. Believe me. Obviously, I'm not going to fill you in with details until I get a commitment from you. And, for your own protection — and mine — my associate and anyone else involved in this enterprise won't be known to you."

Greg sat back down. He gave Russell a look of disgust. "Cloak and dagger shit, and if I got popped holding, I could face some real time, not to mention maybe losing Becky. 'Course, the only thing I would know about all this is you, Russell, giving you up."

Russell stood up. "Come on, man. If that's where you're comin' from, I'm gone. This is about bettering you and the band. I don't see it long-term. And if I've got to hear you talk about 'giving' me up, I'm out of here and think about getting another agent. Not like I'm making a killing off this." Russell started for the door.

Greg watched him walk to the door. "Hold on, man. We're friends — you've helped the band. Maybe I was talking about stuff that isn't going to happen." Russell turned around. "Let me think on it," said Greg. "I'll get back to you tomorrow or by week's end."

Russell nodded. "Let me know." In the hallway, Russell knew that Greg would go along.

CHAPTER 28

orey sat in his van listening to delivery calls coming over the radio. He had two calls so far this day, and it didn't look like it would get much better. He thought about signing out and going home. Nothing seemed right — the delivery job, his relationship with Carolyn, his writing ... when he did it. Nothing.

With a break in radio chatter, Corey called in. "347."

"Go head, 347," responded the dispatcher.

"10-7."

"You're signing out? It's not even noon. Might be some big calls this afternoon."

"Headin' home, Phil. Not feeling well."

"10-4."

With Corey at work, Pinky had the house to himself. Since it had been a few days since his dealings with Gary and the cops, Pinky figured it was today when Jensen and Frederick would come looking for him. Pinky had to have something to say or, at least, appear like he'd been working at finding out what was going on at the Repartee. The two were pricks to Pinky, like most cops, but Pinky knew he had to play along until he got some money together to leave town. Whatever was going on at the club, he didn't care. As for Corey ... he was a friend but a big boy too. *I ain't his dad,* Pinky told himself.

In Corey's bedroom, amid the books and clothes, Pinky didn't know what he was looking for. Whatever the cops suspected was going on wouldn't be plastered on the wall.... *Maybe Corey is writing about the Repartee.* Pinky looked around, kicking at clothes piled on the floor and picking up books to read their titles. On the bedside stand, he saw what looked like a journal. Pinky opened it and thumbed through the pages, words and sentences in longhand tumbling before his eyes. Pinky put it down without reading any of it.

Corey's electric typewriter sat on a chair in one corner with a sheet of paper still in it. Pinky lifted the paper up to read what was typed on it. The words "The day I started was the day I stopped" were centered at the top of the page. Pinky nodded. He knew he could relate to that sentence.

It didn't look like he was hiding what he'd written. The sheet left in the typewriter could be to show Carolyn he was working on something. Who knows? Privacy is privacy. *Fuck the cops.* He'll just say he didn't find anything in Corey's bedroom but make it sound like he really looked. Pinky walked out and went into the kitchen. Time for some coffee and a cigarette. Then go up to Bain's and act nice.

Corey didn't notice the four-door Ford parked across the street when he pulled into the driveway. The front door was unlocked. Corey called out for Pinky as he stepped in.

Pinky was upstairs in his room, having spent the last half-hour staring out his bedroom window at the Ford. He knew once he stepped out into the street, the detectives would have him in the car asking what he'd had found out. *Motherfuckers.*

"Hey, Pinky. What's up?" Corey called out again. Pinky stuffed his cigarette out and walked downstairs.

"Hey, man, you ain't delivering today?" Pinky asked.

"Naw, I took myself out. Right now, I'm kinda fed up with it — got things on my mind."

Pinky looked at Corey. "Working the Repartee tonight?"

"No, tomorrow, a country band. The shit-kickers will be in full force."

Pinky smiled at the comment. He liked country music; good to drink with. "Gunna make some more coffee — want some?" he asked as he walked into the kitchen.

"Yeah, sure. Too early for a beer."

"Yeah, maybe so," Pinky said.

"Okay, coffee," Corey said, and he sat down on the couch as he kicked off his boots. Pinky stayed in the kitchen, listening to the coffeemaker belch out its brew. Corey stretched out; his eyes closed. Neither man said anything. Pinky wondered if he should ask Corey if he noticed the Ford parked across the street. He decided not to.

The coffeemaker fell silent. "You take it black, right?" Pinky asked.

"Yeah," answered Corey. A minute later, Pinky walked into the living room and handed Corey his cup. Pinky sat in the overstuffed chair next to the couch. Both men took a sip while staring at the dark TV screen. "Probably nothing on but soap opera shit," Corey said. "But you're probably into that, huh, Pink?"

Pinky looked over at Corey. "When it comes to soap operas, you should talk."

"Yeah, you're right," said Corey. "Carolyn's on my case about making more of a commitment, and then there's the weirdness up at the Repartee. Then there's my bullshit want to write that doesn't seem to be nothing but ... a bullshit want to write!"

"Takes discipline."

"Discipline?" Corey said, turning to look at Pinky. "You should talk about discipline."

"I'm drinking coffee, ain't I."

"So, I see," Corey said, lifting his cup. "You're right. I can't get off the dime anywhere."

"Hey, man, I'm the one who's supposed to feel sorry for himself — 'nam shit and all. You got a girl, a job, some strange if you hustle a little. Me? I'll be pissed forever for doin' my time in the swamp."

Corey sat still, his hands cupped around the coffee mug. "Yeah, you're right. The woman's good for me — no pretense, no games with her. I'm not looking around."

"Famous last words," Pinky said.

"Hey, fuck you, Pinky," Corey said half-seriously. He got up and went into the kitchen to get a refill.

"Bring the pot out here," Pinky called out. Corey did.

The men sat a while in silence. "Ain't this fun?" Pinky said. "Couple of old fucks drinkin' coffee."

Corey rocked his head back and smiled, then looked around the living room. A typewriter is in his room, he told himself. "I'm going to my room, maybe spend some time writing ... something. What are you up to?"

"Maybe got some work at Bain's."

"That's good," Corey said as he got up.

"Got any ideas," Pinky asked, "for writing?"

"Not really."

"Hey, maybe you could write about the Repartee, the music, bands, you know."

Corey turned and looked at Pinky. For a second, he wondered if Pinky knew something about what was going on. "Naw, too close to home. Maybe sometime down the line." Corey turned away and then turned back to Pinky. "What about something on vets, their struggles, hassles with the VA, all that? I could feature you, and maybe you could give some leads for other interviews."

The idea surprised Pinky. "I don't know, man. A lot of guys won't talk. Too much hurt and bullshit. Plus, it's been written about before, and nothing really changes. People still think we're fuck-ups, baby killers ... I don't know, man. And why do you even care?"

"I care, man. We're friends." Corey waited for a response. Pinky looked down at his coffee cup. "We could talk about this more, maybe?" Corey asked.

Pinky looked up and nodded. "Yeah, it's possible. Let me think about it, but I got to be in the mood."

"Okay. I'll catch you later," Corey said as he went into his room.

Pinky finished his coffee. He showered and changed clothes,

hoping the Ford had left by then. He again peeked out his bedroom window. The Ford was still there. "Now I've got to deal with those two dildos," he said aloud.

As soon as Pinky touched the sidewalk, the Ford dud a U-turn and the passenger side window rolled down. "Get in," Frederick said.

Pinky pulled out a cigarette. "How about pulling down the block so my roommate doesn't notice I'm getting into a car with a couple of cops."

Frederick looked over at Jensen. The Ford eased down the street. Pinky lit his cigarette and walked that way.

In the car, both Jensen and Frederick turned back around to Pinky in the back seat. "So, Pinky, what have you found out?" asked Frederick.

Pinky took another drag on his cigarette. "Something's going on at the Repartee."

Jensen and Frederick looked at each other. "We know that Einstein, but what?" said Jensen.

"I haven't found out yet. Give me a break; it's only been a few days."

"Have to keep you on point," Frederick said. "Don't want to feel like we're being jerked around, Pinky. We want some information, or we're going to be like stink on shit with you."

"You already are," Pinky mumbled as he stuffed his cigarette out in the ashtray on the armrest.

"What'd you say?" Jensen asked.

"I said it's a very apt metaphor." Pinky reached into his jacket pocket and slowly pulled another cigarette from a pack. Jensen and Frederick watched intently. Jensen had his hand on the .357, laying on the car seat. "There's a country band at the Repartee tomorrow," Pinky said. "Corey's workin' the door. I could go, hang out, see if anything looked, you know, suspicious."

"A country band," Jensen repeated. "Are you gonna get shitfaced and forget what you saw?"

"No," Pinky answered back. "I want you assholes off my case, and the best way is to find shit out."

"Don't like being called assholes, Pinky. Remember who you're talking to," Jensen said. "But you got the right idea. We'll catch up with you on Thursday and see if you saw anything. Now go."

Pinky opened the car door but remained seated in the back seat. "I'll need a few bucks for the cover."

Jensen grabbed the steering wheel with both hands, turned, and reached for Pinky, but Frederick blocked his arm. "All right, Pinky," Frederick said. He kept his hand on Jensen's arm as he reached around to get his wallet. Jensen pulled his arm back when Frederick opened his wallet. "Here's five. Find something out, or my partner will play a tune on your head, and I won't stop him."

Pinky took the five dollars and got out of the car. He pulled the collar up on his field jacket and stood on the sidewalk as the Ford pulled away. He knew he couldn't play the two detectives for long. He had to have something on Thursday. Pinky felt a little shaky. Should have put a little Beam in that morning coffee he had with Corey. Now, on to deal with Bain. Work a few hours there, pick up some bucks, and, with the five, and what was left over from the twenty the other day, hell, he almost felt flush.

Corey sat staring at the sheet of paper in the typewriter. "The day I started was the day I stopped" was centered at the top of the page. Corey liked the sentence, but he wasn't sure what he meant by it. He thought about pulling the paper out and putting in a new blank sheet. But maybe it's a line in a poem. He liked what it meant for sure — change. That's all he knew right then. He propped his head up with his hands, trying to let something come into his mind. Oh shit, I need a key, he said to himself. Then the phone rang in the kitchen.

"Hi, how ... are ... you?" Carolyn asked in a singsong way. Corey smiled.

"Hey, babe. Feel fine. How'd you know I was home?"

"Drove down your street on my way to Lou's to get my check. I saw your van."

"Why didn't you stop?"

"Well, I was going to on my way back. That's why I'm calling, to see if it's okay."

"Why are you asking? Of course, it's okay."

Carolyn thought for a moment. "I saw Pinky in a car with two men down the street from your house. Seemed a little strange. They were older, in suits. I had to wonder if they were cops or something."

Corey didn't know what to think. Cops? And with him asking about the Repartee. "I don't know what's going on, honey. I'll ask Pinky. Maybe just a couple of his friends." Corey knew Pinky didn't have friends who wore suits.

Carolyn felt a little more at ease. "I guess maybe you're right. I'll be by in a few minutes."

"That's great! But give me a few minutes ... let me jump in the shower."

"I could jump in the shower with you," Carolyn cooed.

Corey grimaced. "That would be great, but I've got to run an errand too."

"Have you got someone over there?" Carolyn asked, her voice unsteady. "Corey Edwards, are you screwing someone? If so, I'll never, ever ..."

Corey cut her off. "I forgot to get you a key made. I'm sorry. That's all. I wanted to surprise you." He heard Carolyn sigh. "We're going to do this. I just have a lot on my mind, and I just forgot," he said.

"All right," Carolyn said in a whisper. "I wondered about that. Didn't want to bring it up, didn't want another fight. I'm sorry I assumed something else just now." Neither spoke for a moment. "I'll be there in a few minutes. Want me to bring you a sandwich?"

"Corned beef would be good," said Corey. "But take your time; I'm going to run up to Johnson's Hardware to get my key copied."

"Okay, sailor," Carolyn said, feeling as if her whole body was one big goosebump. "If they're slow with the sandwich, don't take that shower until I get there."

Corey smiled. "And I'll scrub your back, too."

CHAPTER 30

As Russell climbed the stairs to Michelle's third-floor apartment, he felt confident this meeting with Lewis would be short and to the point. Lewis would want to know which band was lined up. He'd be satisfied, and all the machismo stuff would be dialed down a bit. Russell gave two quick knocks on Michelle's door. Marcus opened it. He had an uncharacteristic smile on his face. "Come in, motherfucker."

Lewis was sitting in one of the overstuffed chairs. He was running the blade of a small knife under his fingernails, cleaning them. Lewis put the knife on the table and motioned for Russell to sit down opposite him in another chair. But instead of Marcus sitting down next to Lewis, he came around and stood behind Russell.

"So, Russell, my man, what have you lined up for me?"

Any calmness Russell had left him. "I think I've got it covered, Mr. Richardson. Talked with the leader of a band, and I think he'll come on board."

"Come on board? Come on board?" said Lewis. "What the fuck does that mean? Is that a nautical term, Russell?"

Russell swallowed and felt Marcus move behind him. "Just a phrase,

Mr. Richardson. A term. What I mean is I've got someone who'll cooperate, who's in — however you want to term it."

"And you trust this boy, Russell? And you filled him in with all the details?"

"Oh no — I mean, yes, I trust him, and no, he got no details. Just to deal with me, that's all. I offered no other information about anything. I just said if he does this — carry the stuff — I'll, or you, I mean you through me — he won't know you — he and his band will get some good dates outside of KC, some recognition. His band is that good. That's all I said. He knows nothing but that, Mr. Richardson."

Lewis was enjoying Russell's nervousness. "How can I believe you, Russell?"

Russell struggled for an answer. "I don't know, Mr. Richardson. You know me. I can be trusted."

"How about I let Marcus bust you up some to see how well I know you."

Marcus smiled. Russell shot up from the chair. Marcus pushed him back down.

"I wouldn't be any good to you if you did that, Mr. Richardson," said Russell, spitting out the words. "I do have the band connections you need."

Lewis picked up the small knife on the coffee table in front of him. He ran the blade under the fingernail of his left thumb. He then held the thumb up in front of him, lining it up in front of Russell's face. He then pointed the forefinger out, keeping the three other fingers in against his palm. He snapped the thumb down against the forefinger. "Bang," he said. Then bringing his hand down, Lewis said, "Get my drift, Russell, if you fuck this up."

Russell nodded in an exaggerated way. His underwear felt a little wet.

"Now, what were you and Big Mike talking about the other day?"

Russell sat rigid, staring at Lewis. He could feel Marcus standing close to him. Even before Russell finished saying, "What do you mean, Mr. Richardson?" he felt an open palm blow to the left side of his head.

Lewis chuckled. "And that was one of Marcus' love taps. You should worry if he picks up his ball-peen hammer. With a couple of taps from that, you really would be a dumb-ass White boy.

"Now listen. I know you met with Mike. I want to know — and I don't want no jive bullshit — what you two fuckers were talking about. You dig? Or do I have to dump your crumpled ass in an alley and find someone else who understands this shit?"

"Mike called me wanting to talk about Corey," Russell yelled.

Lewis looked up at Marcus. "The doorman," Marcus said.

"What about this, Corey?" said Lewis.

"Mike wanted to know more about him."

"Why?"

"Because I kinda hooked up Corey to the job as a doorman, and Mike wanted to know if the guy was okay, not someone who would talk about stuff."

"You said he asked for the job."

"Yeah, yeah, he did." Russell was squirming in his seat.

Marcus put his hand on Russell's shoulder and pressed down. "Settle down, motherfucker."

"Why would Mike worry about this, Corey?" asked Lewis.

"He writes ... that he might think it's a story he could sell ... write about."

Lewis looked perplexed. "What do you mean? Like he's a newspaperman? A fuckin' reporter?"

"Something like that," Russell said. "He's a freelancer. Sells an idea to an editor, writes about it, and if it's published, gets money for it."

Lewis leaned back in his chair. Killing Russell along with this, Corey would send a message to Mike for sure, maybe driving him out of town or getting him in tow. But Russell was right: It was Russell who had the connections to the bands, and eliminating Corey could bring questions from the cops, something this plan didn't need. And Mike can run a club, something Marcus couldn't do. *How does a simple plan gather all this shit?* Lewis wondered.

Lewis picked the pocketknife off the table and folded the blade shut. He then got up and went into the kitchen. Russell watched him.

He thought about the young man who had left his apartment earlier in the day. He wondered if he would ever see the man again. Lewis came back with a glass of wine and sat down.

"So, Russell, I figure Mike wouldn't be asking about this Corey dude unless you told Mike about how we would be bringing shit in the club and moving it out. Am I right, Russell?"

Russell put his head down and nodded.

"So big Mike knows the routine. Well, good. We'll just help the motherfucker out, get him real involved." Lewis took a sip of wine, then motioned to Marcus to get Russell up on his feet. Marcus lifted Russell up by the armpits and pushed him away from the chair.

"You're gone, Russell. Your lucky ass can still take you out of here. But you listen. You sit tight, make yourself available, particularly tomorrow night. Your friend Marcus will be getting a hold of you. Now farewell, Russell, and I don't have to tell you that you ain't talkin' to no one about this or, Russell, you will be rendered permanently unavailable. Got that, sucka?"

Russell said nothing, walked slowly to the door, and left. His hands were shaking, and his head hurt.

Lewis eased back into the chair. He spread his arms and legs out, and he rested his head on the top of the chair. His eyes were fixed on the ceiling. Marcus still stood behind the chair Russell had sat in. He knew Lewis was upset. "What's weighing you down, my brother?"

Lewis sat up. "These jive turkeys ... all my life, all your life, brother, we been dealin' with these jive turkeys. Always got to turn the dime faster, always got to play the role. Fuckin' shit. I get tired of it. Just trying to have a little enterprise, give the masses what they want, add to the pile, get comfortable, and I got to deal with this shit. Blabbermouth motherfuckers."

"What do you want me to do, bro? Waste them?"

Lewis looked at Marcus. "You trippin'? No. Not now ... maybe down the line, but not now." Lewis got up and walked to the balcony. He looked out over the park. "That bitch out there spendin' my money. Need some poontang in return," Lewis said to himself. He turned to Marcus. "I'm going to hang here, wait for the bitch to return.

I want you to go get an ounce of blow from our warehouse. Then, drop by Russell's crib and tell him that tomorrow night he goes to the Repartee around ten and drops the stuff off at the door with that Corey mother. Put the shit in a brown paper bag like before."

Marcus smiled. "I get it, man. Drop the shit off at the door, using Russell. The Mike dude don't know it's comin', and he gets confused."

"He'll also get the message; he ain't a dummy," Lewis said. "We're going to store shit at his club. That way, he's real into the fold, and he'll know that one anonymous call to the pigs, and he's toast for having the shit on-premises. He'll understand what's up, so expect him to squawk and call you. Lean back on him. He either runs or plays along. We're putting the fucker in a box."

Marcus put his hand out, palm up. Lewis slapped it. "Head out. I need to relax with Michelle."

CHAPTER 31

Becky heard the Yamaha keyboard as she walked in the door. She listened as she put her purse on the couch. A melody began, stopped, then began again as Greg played with variations. Becky smiled and went into the kitchen.

The music stopped sometime after Becky got out of the shower. She was in her robe on the couch when Greg came out of his music room. "Whoa, babe, didn't hear you come in." She reached behind to touch him as she watched TV. "No sound?" Greg said as he stood behind the couch, looking at the screen.

"Didn't want to disturb you," said Becky.

He leaned over her from behind and kissed her, sliding his hand down her robe to cup one breast as he did. "Mmmm."

"Yes, mmmm," Becky said as she pulled him to her for another kiss.

He came around to her front. He stepped out of his sweatpants and got in front of her. She opened her robe. Her legs were apart. He stepped up onto the couch, knelt, and put some pillows under his knees to bring his crotch to the same level as her head. She parted her lips, and he pulled her head forward. He watched her move up and back on his penis. He pulled away to give himself more time, then pulled her in again. She looked up at him while flicking her tongue on the head. The longer they were together, the better she got, he told himself. He rubbed her vagina, sliding two fingers in and out of her. He then got off the couch and got back in front of her. "Come on, baby, put that big boy in here," she said. He held one leg high and plunged in as far as he could. Her head went back, and he began to rub the outside of her thigh. He positioned her more comfortably so he could ease down to bring the lower part of his body against hers. They began to move in a slow motion. Soon, she stopped, lifting her hips letting Greg increase his thrust. In a few minutes, he jerked hard into her and then fell onto her. She moaned and bit his earlobe. They breathed into each other's necks, and she stroked the back of his head. Greg moved off her when she felt the tingle in her arm and said, "Greg, honey, my arm, please." He got up, put on his sweats, then flopped down next to her. Looking at her, he said, "I love you." She pulled the robe over her and reached out her hand. "You are my man — always my love, always." Greg knew she meant it.

Greg got up then extended his hand to help her off the couch. They embraced again while standing. She felt him hard again. "Say, mister, you're ready again so soon?"

"It's you. Can't get enough."

She laughed and pushed away from him. "Got to get some clothes on," she said.

Greg watched her walk to their bedroom. "Russell came by today."

Becky stopped and smiled. "Tell me in a minute," she said. "Tell me all."

Greg went to the window. It was a sunny, blue-sky midwestern day, a day where the shadows of other days didn't exist. He knew he shouldn't tell her; Russell had asked him not to. But she was part of him, part of the ride they were on together. He wanted to tell her.

CHAPTER 32

Corey and Carolyn lay on his bed, bath towels over both, their arms outstretched above their heads, holding hands, eyes fixed on the ceiling.

"Corey, look at the cobwebs. Do you ever clean?"

"Hey, I'm a guy."

"Yeah, I know . . . you reminded me in the shower," Carolyn said, giggling.

Corey turned to her, his face touching her cheek. "And we'd still be there if we hadn't run out of hot water."

"We ran out of hot water?"

Corey laughed. "Yeah, I didn't notice either, considering you're so hot."

He propped himself up on one elbow and kissed Carolyn. Pulling away, he put his hand on her forehead and then moved it back to stroke her hair once and then again. Reaching under her neck, he turned, pulling her on top of him. She lifted herself up off him, her legs straddling his body. "Won't run out of hot water here," she said.

"We never will, beautiful." He started to kiss her when she moved off him, looking at his clock on the nightstand. "Corey, I got to go," she said.

Corey turned and looked at the clock. "You've got a couple of hours or so."

"No, silly. Lou's going to the doctor — need to get in there early." She was off the bed looking for her clothes.

"And I was just getting started," Corey said as she slid her arms into her bra, pulling each cup down over each breast, adjusting, and then reaching behind to hook the strap. "Close your mouth, Corey," Carolyn said as she wiggled the bra for one more adjustment. He moved his eyes up to her face and, touching his fingers to his lips, blew her a kiss. She cocked her head with a smile. "Same to ya."

As Carolyn went into the bathroom, Corey reminded her he would stop by Lou's that night before she left. "Bring Pinky," she said. She was gone in five minutes, giving him a quick kiss as he lay on the bed.

He stayed there a while thinking of her. The first time he had ever gotten a woman a key to his place. *Yeah, she was better than anyone he'd ever had. Maybe it was about time.*

CHAPTER 33

"Hey, Gary," Corey said as he came through the door. "How ya doin'?"

"Not bad," Gary said. "Looking for Pinky? He's in the cooler restocking the beer."

Corey opened the cooler doors, stuck his head in, and yelled, "Hey, man!" Pinky put down a case of beer and came out. Taking off his gloves, he told Gary he was going outside for a smoke and to talk to Corey.

Corey watched Pinky light a cigarette. After glancing over his shoulder, Corey asked, "Does that guy always look at a guy like a guy looks at a chick?"

Pinky smiled and nodded as he took a drag off his cigarette. "Yeah, you kinda got to keep him at bay."

"You could always cross over, might perk up your sex life."

Pinky squinted and took another drag on his cigarette. "Bain checks out your ass too. Maybe we could do it together."

"Okay, man," Corey said, waving his hand. "Let's stop. I wanted to remind you that we've got a pool date up at Lou's tonight. You got the time?"

"Sure, man."

Corey looked around the parking lot as Pinky continued to smoke. "Ya know when Carolyn came by, she said she saw you talking to two guys in a car."

Pinky flipped his cigarette up against the trash dumpster by the side of a building. Corey waited for Pinky to say something. "Just a couple of guys from the VA checking up on me, you know, after I spent some time in counseling."

"Yeah, I figured it was nothing."

"Why the interest?" Pinky said.

"Man, the weird shit up at the Repartee just got me spooked a little."

"Give it up if you're trippin' on it," Pinky said.

"Yeah, I'm thinkin' — oh, by the way, Carolyn's got a key to the place. Just wanted to let you know that."

Pinky grinned. "Wow, man. What a step. Maybe I better be looking for my own crib."

"Maybe so, man. No rush, just be aware it could happen."

Pinky placed his hand on Corey's shoulder. "Hundreds of women across town will go into mourning."

"Eat it. You know, people do retire from things or just change."

"More power to you, man." Pinky was sincere.

"Thanks, man."

Pinky watched Corey walk to his van. He said he was going to pick up a few hours making deliveries. Pinky thought about lighting another cigarette but figured Gary would be poking his head out the door any second. He felt a little jealous. Carolyn was a good woman, the kind who could clear the fog in a man, even someone like himself.

Across the street, Marcus sat in his Seville. He had driven down West 39th on the way to pick up some barbecue and spotted Corey's van. Pinky was now a face he knew.

Carolyn had gotten to the bar just in time to take over for Lou. "I would have hoped you could have gotten here a little earlier," he said as she stepped behind the bar. "You know I like to give myself time to drive to the doctor — it's the traffic gets heavy later in the day." Lou took off his apron and headed for the back door.

"I'm sorry, Lou," Carolyn said. "I just kinda got hung up, really. Anything I should know? When are you coming back?"

Lou waved his hand. "Don't worry, I'll be back ... as long as the doctor finds me still breathing." He turned at the door. "I know you're young. Time can be wasted at your age." He wanted to say more, to tell her what he just said wasn't true. He looked beyond her, out the window. The day was bright. "Watch the place; do your usual fine job, young lady," he called out. Lou stared at Carolyn for a moment. She was Marge from forty years ago. He wanted to say, "Be back soon, honey."

Carolyn watched the door close behind Lou. *Was he angry or sad when he left?* she wondered. Oh well, didn't matter. She was happy. She reached around and felt the key in her back pocket. It was all going to be great, she told herself. Corey was the man she wanted. Things were good.

Everything seemed in order at the bar. Tubs were filled, glasses cleaned and stacked. She checked the work schedule taped inside one of the cabinet doors. She had one waitress and the cook tonight. They should be coming in soon. One customer nursed a beer down the bar, watching a talk show on the TV. The sound was off. The place was quiet. Carolyn grabbed some quarters from the register and went to the jukebox. She started to read the song list when she heard the crack of pool balls in the back room. She reached over the bar, grabbed a bar rag and walked that way.

Steve Lawton was at one of the pool tables by himself. "Hey, darlin'," he called out after seeing Carolyn. "Glad the scenery changed from old man to pretty young thing."

"Knock it off, Steve," Carolyn said as she began to wipe tables. Lawton stood there holding the pool cue, watching her. "Want to play? Pool, that is."

"Got to work the bar, Steve." Carolyn stopped wiping a table for a moment, determined not to get angry. She tried to gauge how much drinking he had done so far. "No work today?" Carolyn asked.

"Naw. Took off the day. Thought Pinky might be up here since the prick doesn't really work. You know, play him again to get my money back. Seen him around?"

"Not his keeper," Carolyn said. She moved to one side of the pool table opposite him. "Don't need any trouble, Steve, unless you want to drink somewhere else."

"Yeah, I know," Lawton said as he put down the pool cue. "Only come here because of you." He stepped around the pool table toward Carolyn. She shifted her body and stood square to him. "Don't get any ideas, Steve," she said. He stopped and stood in front of her.

"You're a tough bitch ... tough and pretty. I like that." He looked over her shoulder at the person sitting at the bar, then back at Carolyn. She thought about throwing the wet bar rag in his face if he stepped any closer. He looked away. "I'll be back," he said and headed for the door.

Carolyn relaxed. She was getting tired of the guy. She thought about talking with Lou about him, but Lou thought he was just fine. Lawton played up to Lou, talking about sports and construction work, guy stuff. Lawton was one of the few men in the place who really talked with Lou beyond just a barroom greeting. Still, Lawton was a snake as far as she was concerned. Carolyn decided she would just have to handle him as best she could. Maybe a swift kick in the crotch would be in order. Carolyn smiled at the thought. She looked at the clock at the back of the bar. It would be a few more hours before Corey and Pinky would be up to see her. She finished wiping the tables in the back room, then again went to the jukebox. She dropped in some quarters. The first song she chose was "Nobody Does It Better" by Carly Simon.

The bar was quiet and empty for another hour or so. Around four people getting off their shift from the hospital a few blocks away started coming in. It was burgers and beer time. As she scurried back and forth behind the bar, Carolyn kept watching the door, front and back, for Lou to return. She hoped nothing medical was keeping him. A little after five, Lou called the bar.

"They're keeping me overnight," he said, "for observation."

"Oh, Lou," Carolyn cried out loud enough that people seated at the bar paused in their own conservations.

"Now, now, young lady, don't worry. It's just that they want to do a few more tests tomorrow."

"What is it, Lou?"

"At my age, Carolyn, it's always the heart, and mine, as you know, is still a little bruised from Marge leaving."

Carolyn felt tears coming. She reached for a tissue by the cash register. "My nephew Walt is coming by the hospital. I'm going to tell him you know everything, and he doesn't have to worry about the business."

"Can he run the place, Lou?"

Lou laughed. "Lord no, the boy is a good man, but he has trouble figuring out how to open the refrigerator."

Carolyn let out a little laugh. The people at the bar seemed all to take a drink in unison and the bar's noise level raised back up.

"I need you to open tomorrow," Lou continued. "I'm pretty sure I'll be let out after the tests. I'll be just fine. Besides, I got pretty nurses to look at."

"What about me?" Carolyn said in mock concern.

"Next to Marge, you're the prettiest woman I've ever known," Lou said with a chuckle. "Remember, open at ten, but be there by eight because we're getting a beer delivery. You should have enough food to carry us through for another day. I'll be in as soon as I can. Kind of gives Walt a quick lesson in the bar business when, and if, he comes in … not that he'll grasp anything."

"Okay, Lou," Carolyn said in an even voice. "Call me tomorrow morning if you get a chance, and God bless you."

"God has blessed me my whole life, young woman. I'm not worried. I'll talk with you tomorrow."

Carolyn held the phone for a few moments after Lou hung up. She loved the old guy. What would she do if he died?

After Lou's call, Carolyn didn't feel like talking with customers. She busied herself with drink and food orders. Regulars who tried to keep the conversation going with her noticed that she had something on her mind. She mentioned to no one that Lou was in the hospital. Word would get around soon enough. Around eight, Corey and Pinky came into the bar. Corey noticed right away something was bothering Carolyn.

"What's up, babe?" he asked.

Carolyn walked down the bar toward the storage room near the back door and motioned for Corey to come with her. Pinky knew to stay at the bar.

In the storage room, she reached for his hand. "Lou's in the hospital," Carolyn said. Her hand tightened around his, and she felt tears welling up.

"Hey, what did he say?"

"He said that they're keeping him for observation. It's about his heart."

Corey kept his eyes on Carolyn. He smiled. "Lou's a straight-up guy. That's probably not all that bad. Don't worry, he'll be back."

Carolyn let out a breath and pulled Corey's shirt to her face to dab her eyes. "Thank you," she said as she hugged Corey, thinking how Lou didn't think much of him.

They held each other for a moment. Corey felt good comforting her. He stepped away and said, "Come on, babe. I need a beer." He kept holding her hand and led her back to the bar.

As Corey sat down next to Pinky, he said, "The lady's smile has returned."

"Yeah, she was upset."

"What'd you do, man?" Pinky asked.

Corey turned and looked at Pinky. "Hey, it's not always me. In fact, it had nothing to do with me. Get over it."

"Okay, sorry, man. I forgot you're reformed."

"Fuck you."

When Carolyn brought the two men their beers, Pinky held up his mug and motioned toward Carolyn, then Corey. "Here's to you two," he said. Corey nodded in thanks.

Lawton walked into the bar around eleven. Corey and Pinky were in the back playing pool, finishing up their last game after deciding it was time to head out. As Lawton came to the bar, he gave Carolyn a toothy smile. "Give me a draw, honey," he said.

When Carolyn brought back the beer, she warned, "No trouble, Steve, or I'm calling the cops." He smiled again at her as he took a sip and walked away.

Pinky was zeroing in on the eight ball for a side pocket shot when Lawton took a seat near the pool table. "Looks like you have trouble beating him, too," Lawton said to Corey.

"I let him win," Corey said as he heard the eight-ball hit the bottom of the pocket.

"Yeah, that's what I tell myself," Lawton said, putting two quarters on the pool table.

Pinky picked up his cue and walked over to the wall cue rack. "We're leaving," he said.

"I show up, and you're leaving? What are you, a chickenshit, to play me again?"

Corey laid the cue on the table. "No, man. We really are leaving. It was decided before you showed." Corey stood straight, looking directly at Lawton.

"All right, maybe next time," Lawton said, looking at Pinky. He watched them walk to the bar, then picked up his two quarters. "Next time, I'll show up earlier," he yelled.

"You got some shit going with this guy?" Corey asked Pinky as they sat down at the bar.

"Yeah, I guess. Took some money from him the other night, and he's pissed about it."

Corey tried to pick up on any fear in Pinky's voice. There was none. Carolyn came up to them. She read the concern on Corey's face. It gave her a good feeling. Corey said he was leaving with Pinky. She asked if he was going home. "Sure," he said. She believed him. Corey then asked if she was upset.

"No, I'm not ... it's just that Steve, the guy in the back room.

Corey turned around. Lawton was playing the pinball machine. "What's the guy doin' to you?" Corey turned completely around at the bar and continued staring at Lawton. He was too into the game to notice.

"Really nothing...being a jerk. Really nothing more than six other stray guys in here on a Saturday night." Carolyn pulled at Corey's arm to get him to turn around.

"What time are you closing down?" said Corey.

"Midnight if it's slow," said Carolyn.

Corey glanced at the clock behind the bar. It was ten after eleven. "I'll be back up a little before midnight, okay?"

Carolyn reached over the bar and pulled Corey to her. She kissed him, then keeping her face close to his, said "okay" while looking directly into his eyes.

Corey smiled at her, not quite sure what she was thinking. He then glanced back at Lawton once more before he and Pinky left.

Carolyn already had the front door locked when Corey returned to the bar. She was at the register counting the night's receipts. He tapped on the glass to get her attention. "Everything okay?" he asked as she let him in.

"Yeah, he left soon after you guys left."

"What's his problem, anyway?" Corey asked.

"I don't know. He's not a bad-looking guy but has an attitude, and he drinks too much. He could be nicer."

"Sometimes that just doesn't happen with some people," Corey said. "No girlfriend? No women he hangs with?"

"Never seen him with someone, but he's hit on a few in here. Doesn't seem to go anywhere. I don't think he has much of a come-on line."

Corey smiled at her. He loved the way she was both all-knowing and full of questions. "My come-on line must have worked ... or maybe you were just horny."

She punched his stomach softly, and he quickly grabbed her. They embraced and kissed, and she broke away. "Let's clean up and get out of here."

He helped her ready Lou for the next day's business, vacuuming the rug in the dining area and stacking the chairs on the tables. She wiped the bar and drained the tubs. They were out of there by 12:45. Corey didn't ask if she was coming to his place. He knew she would, and he was glad about it.

Pinky heard them come in. They were quiet and went quickly to his bedroom. Pinky sat on his bed drinking a beer, an ashtray next to him with a roach and clip. *All this domesticity*, he said to himself. He couldn't help but shake his head and yell, "Ha!"

"What was that?" Carolyn asked as she lay next to Corey.

"Pinky. Lots of nights, I can hear him talking or screaming in his sleep. Gotta be that Vietnam shit."

"I didn't know," said Carolyn.

CHAPTER 34

Corey left his house early on Wednesday. Carolyn stayed in bed. He kissed her lightly goodbye. She didn't stir. He wanted to get on the road and make it a full day. Work hard and long, hope for some good tips and maybe he'd have enough money by the end of the month for a ring. He could hardly believe what he was thinking — a ring? *Jesus, I'm in love. Fuck, such a deal.* Corey laughed out loud as he got into his van. He was almost giggly when he called into the dispatcher.

Becky didn't sleep well. She didn't like what Greg was going to do. She wished he hadn't told her; she wanted to believe that when he started getting dates in big cities, it was just because of his music and that carrying coke for Russell had nothing to do with it. She started breakfast for Greg, bacon, and eggs. She had class soon and then later a shift at the Repartee.

Mike was at the club before nine. He had a beer delivery. It took two guys to bring the kegs up the stairs. "When are you moving to ground level?" one would usually ask. But this time, the only thing said was, "Got to catch up Mike, on the bill, or we can't deliver anymore."

Russell swung his legs off the couch and sat up. He held his head with both hands and didn't want to open his eyes. He could feel himself swaying and knew if he fell back down on the couch, he would puke. A baggie of coke lay on the coffee table, along with three empty bottles of wine. He hadn't touched the coke. Marcus had made that clear. "Listen, White boy," he'd said. "Touch the shit before delivery, and I'll break both your arms, so he'll have to hire someone to wipe your ass. Understand, motherfucker?"

It was almost eleven when Pinky got up. Carolyn was gone, and the house was quiet. He went down to the kitchen and made coffee. He walked outside onto the porch to get the newspaper. Parked in the front of the house were Jensen and Malcolm. Both men turned and waved at Pinky. Picky froze for a moment as he bent down to get the newspaper. He did not wave back.

Lewis was in his office at his home. He had put in a call to Florida. An order had been placed. He called Marcus. "Get your beach threads out, bro. You're going to Florida next week."

"I got time to lay on the beach a day or two, go clubbin', and get some Latin pussy?"

"Shit ya," said Lewis. "All this threatenin' of people probably tires you out. You need a break."

Both men laughed.

CHAPTER 35

Corey got to the Repartee a little before seven. "Hey, Mike," he called out as he walked to the bar. Mike was checking the beer coolers, mentally noting what brand needed to be restocked. He didn't look up. Corey waited until it seemed Mike had completed his count.

"Anything I could do, Mike?"

Mike grabbed a rag and began wiping the bar. He didn't answer; he just moved down the bar, making big circular motions, occasionally flipping the rag over as he wiped. When he finished, he threw the rag into one of the stainless steel sinks.

"Beer's okay," he said. "Check the johns for TP and backstage for any bottle or glasses, then sweep around the door and down the stairs to the sidewalk." Mike kept his eyes on Corey. "The cover is three bucks for this band, and their shit-kickin' following likes to drink, so keep an eye on the crowd."

"We expect a big crowd?"

"I hope so," Mike said as he turned away. "Becky should be here any minute. I'll be up in the office."

"Say, Mike ... everything's normal, right?" Corey said as Mike came out from behind the bar. "There's nothing I should expect at the door?"

Mike walked back to where Corey stood. "Nothing's happening; everything is normal." His voice was low and relaxed. Then he added, "You want to keep working the door, Corey, then don't ask any more questions. Just do the job, drink your free beer, and help keep things in order. In other words, everything's normal. Any more things like the other night then I'll let you know. But remember, don't ask about anything."

Corey felt he soon needed to leave the Repartee. Things were not normal.

"I'll be in the office," Mike said as he put his hand on Corey's shoulder. "Have Becky buzz me when the band starts bringing in their equipment. Nobody gets in other than the band until seven-thirty."

Corey nodded. Mike walked away and up the stairs to this office. Corey looked around the room. It was quiet. The stage was empty except for the mic stands. The benches, tables, and chairs were lined in order, nothing askew. The lighting was subtle, but the glass ashtrays still glittered here and there. Corey did a slow 360-degree turn, lifting his arms as he did, stretching out as much as he could. Mike was upstairs; no one would see him. He felt good, glad he knew of this place. He stopped his slow twirl and stood still. He thought of Carolyn working the bar at Lou's; he thought of the future, one with her. He felt afraid. He tried shedding the feeling — time for the john patrol. He started to walk to the restrooms but stopped. The floor creaked at a spot near where he stood. It was a new sound to the place, one he had never heard. He found the spot again and pushed in and out. He decided the sound was like one of those spooky noises from a Scooby-Doo cartoon when Shaggy and the gang walked through a haunted house. Maybe the Repartee was haunted now — it could be with all the shit going on. He kept on pushing that spot on the floor.

"What are you doing with your foot?" Becky asked, surprising Corey while looking down at the floor. A slight perfume smell hung with her like she had just gotten out of the shower. *Don't go there,* he told himself. He kept his foot on the floor, pressing down. "Kinda sounds like those creepy sounds from a Scooby-Doo cartoon, doesn't it?"

Becky squinted at Corey. "The floor? Maybe … yes. But shouldn't you be doing something else? Or are you just stoned?"

"Uh-oh, bad mood, and maybe I am, or maybe I just never knew the floor creaked. It's always too noisy to notice. Now it's quiet. See how quiet it is."

Becky swung her purse off her shoulder and walked behind the bar. "Okay, Corey, that's all cute, but people will be coming in soon. Where's Mike?"

Corey pressed on the floor one more time. "He's in the office. He said to call him when the band comes in. I'm going to check the johns."

By the time the band started, a hundred people or so were in the club. Cowboy hats, boots, tight jeans, and big belt buckles made for the norm. Corey made a note of the number of single guys in the bar compared to the few women who didn't seem paired. *Maybe it will balance out?* Parity made for less of a chance for trouble.

Back Country played traditional country mixed with rockabilly. The band members were the expected good 'ol boys save for the drummer, who mirrored a sullen biker type. By ten, another hundred or so people had arrived. Mike worked the bar, keeping a steady eye on the guys milling around in front of him. Becky serviced the benches and tables without much banter with the patrons. Occasionally some guy slapped her butt when she walked by, and she would smile politely and then tell him if he did it again, "that big guy behind the bar" would make sure he was barred from the Repartee for good.

As the band finished their second set, Becky walked up to Corey. "Not drinking much tonight. A little weird, don't you think?" she said.

"Yeah," Corey said. "No fights, no woman coming up to me to complain about some guy buggin' her; it's almost boring."

Becky smiled. "Don't worry, Corey, there's another set." She turned and looked back at Mike at the bar. "You know what's going on here, do you, Corey?"

Corey didn't answer right away. He looked at Becky directly. "If you're asking me about what I think you're asking me, we probably shouldn't talk about it right now."

Becky frowned and started to say something when she heard the band members returning to the stage. She began to walk away, turned, and mouthed, "Can we talk later?"

Corey nodded. Maybe she knew something he didn't.

The band started its third set with "Chevy Van," a song keeping to the somewhat mellow mood of the night. Expecting something looser and louder, Corey caught Becky's eye and opened his hands in a gesture of surprise. She smiled back and then turned away. Corey kept his eyes on her. *Could have been something between us,* he told himself, *but now I've got Carolyn, you got Greg.*

Corey planted himself on the stool. He didn't expect many more people coming through the door, thinking the rest of the night would just be making sure nothing got out of hand. Sensing the band was well into its last set, Corey followed Mike, working behind the bar, trying to catch his attention to get another beer. That's when Russell walked in. He looked disheveled and in a hurry.

"Hey, Russell," Corey said. "Didn't expect to see you. You represent this band?"

Russell didn't answer. He glanced up to the bar. Mike hadn't noticed him walk in. He then handed Corey a brown paper bag. Corey looked down at the bag. "This again?"

Russell then turned and walked back down the stairs. Halfway down the stairs, he met Pinky coming up. "Hey, how you doin'?" Pinky said as he flattened against the wall to let Russell pass by. Pinky had seen Russell around but couldn't quite remember his name or what he did. Russell didn't respond. At the top of the stairs, Pinky saw Corey looking around the room while fumbling with the bag.

"Hey, Cor, a bag of shit too hot to handle?" said Pinky with a grin.

"What the fuck you doin' here?" Corey said, still holding the bag.

"Whoa, man. Just here to listen to the music, that's all. Chill out." Pinky reached into his front pocket and pulled out some bills. "What's the cover?"

Corey waved Pinky on. "Forget about it. On me."

Pinky didn't argue and started walking toward the bar. He stopped and turned toward the stage. Back Country shifted into Marshall Tucker's "Can't You See," and most everyone in the Repartee began singing along, moving to the dance floor, or watching the band get to a higher gear, everyone except Mike. He stood frozen at the bar, staring at Corey. Corey started a step toward the bar. Mike held up his hand and shook his head. Corey turned and looked around his stool. He dropped the bag on the floor and pushed it with his foot into a dark corner.

Outside the Repartee, Marcus watched Russell leave the bar. In and out, the sack had been delivered. He would head home and call Lewis. They both would laugh at the surprise that had been delivered. Soon, Mike would be calling Lewis or Russell to find out why there was another sack. Marcus liked all this scheming. He bellowed a laugh and started up the Seville. Time to chill at the crib.

Down the block, Russell stepped into The Pink Slip. Maybe his young friend was there, or maybe a new young friend could be found. Right now, he didn't care much about anything but that.

Mike debated whether to have Becky tell the band no encore even if the crowd wanted and expected it. He didn't know what was in the sack but suspected it wasn't a rolled-up T-shirt. Cutting the band short could lead to complaints and questions. He decided to let the night play out as usual.

Sometime after 1 a.m., as the crowd was clapping and whistling for an encore, Mike motioned for Becky to come to the bar. "When the band comes out and starts again, go around and start picking up the empties and the ashtrays," he told her.

"No last call, Mike?" Becky asked.

"Yeah, no last call. Tell people the bar is closed. But before doing that, go tell Corey to stay put by the door. After everyone clears out — including the band — he can come up here and get his last free beer."

Becky could see that Mike was agitated. He squinted into the crowd, scanning clumps of people, stopping here and there to focus on an individual. "What's wrong, Mike?" she asked.

Mike turned back toward her and then slammed his hand down on the bar. "Do what I'm telling you, Becky. Just do it!"

Becky leaned back and away from the bar. She stood glaring at Mike and then turned away and walked across the room to Corey. Mike saw them stand close. Becky talking into Corey's ear. The band was starting its final song. Corey ran his fingers through his hair, listening to what Becky was saying. After she walked off, Corey looked toward Mike and nodded.

Since coming in, Pinky had alternated his attention from the band to Corey. *A lot of whispering and glaring among the three people working,* he told himself, *and earlier, Corey was dancing around with a sack in his hand. It's something to do with dope, no doubt.* Pinky downed his beer and walked over to Corey.

"Oh man, completely forgot about you, sorry," Corey said. "Were you getting into the band?"

"Yeah, sorta. Good band, some of my kind of music," said Pinky.

"Find a lady to dance with?"

"Shit. Looked like most of them were paired up."

Corey nodded. "Hey, do me a favor and tell Carolyn — if she's up — I'm going to be a little late getting home."

"Okay," Pinky said. He looked back at the bar to where Becky stood.

"Look, man, it's not what you think. So please, will you cut me some slack?"

"Your business," Pinky said as he reached for a cigarette. "I'll see you later."

Outside, Pinky looked up and down the street. He walked a few steps toward Southwest Trafficway and could see that the "Open" sign was still on at The Pink Slip. Maybe time for one more. As he stepped into the bar, he saw Russell sitting in a booth with another man. *The guy from the Repartee,* Pinky, said to himself.

The crowd was gone from the Repartee within twenty minutes of the last song. Mike refused any quick for-the-road drinks and word got around that the bar was closed to drinks, no exceptions made. Corey stayed by the door, making sure no one carried out any half-empty bottles. It was a familiar routine. A few people grumbled about the bar closing so abruptly after the band's last song. Corey stayed polite, glancing over his shoulder often as he watched people file out.

As band members occupied themselves with putting away their instruments and amplifiers, Mike motioned Corey to come up to the bar. He brought the cash box and sack. Mike grabbed the sack and put it behind the bar. As he did, he saw Becky watching him as she was wiping tables. Mike was about to talk with Corey when a member of the band came up to the bar. He asked for the band's cut from the door. Mike counted out their share, complimenting them on their music. Corey couldn't tell whether Mike was being sincere or not. With their money in hand, the musicians began stacking their gear at the top of the stairs.

"Go down and hold the front door open for them. Offer to help if you want," said Mike.

Corey didn't respond. As he walked away, he looked at Becky still wiping tables. As Mike watched Corey disappear out the front, he called Becky to the bar.

"Don't worry about finishing up. I can do it in the morning tomorrow. Give me your starting cash, and I'll see you tomorrow. Okay?"

"Okay, Mike. Can I at least count my tips and freshen up a bit before I go?"

"Okay sure, but I'm kinda in a hurry tonight, Becky."

"Obviously," Becky said, pointing down one end of the bar. "Let me get my purse?"

With Becky in the ladies' room and Corey downstairs, Mike took out the sack. He felt the bottom of it and squeezed. The softness told him it was what he thought it was. "Motherfuckin' Black asshole," he mumbled to himself. Mike knew Lewis had him. *One anonymous call to the cops, and I'm done. Coke on the premises means I lose everything, rack up lawyer bills, and maybe spend a good stretch in prison. Fuckin' prick has me, and I've got to play the shit his way.* Mike thought about calling Lewis. It was nearly two. No. He'd be expecting that. *I'll just sit tight, making him think either the coke wasn't delivered or I'm doing something with it. Make the asshole wonder.* Mike walked upstairs to his office. The coke would go into the safe. *Tomorrow, I'll go by Russell's apartment before calling Lewis and be prepared to know his boy Marcus probably will be getting into my face.*

When Mike came back to the bar, Corey was there with Becky. "Nothing to talk about," Mike said, sensing their anticipation.

Corey reached for Becky's arm to walk away then he turned back around to Mike. "What do you want us to do, Mike? It's a little confusing about what's going on here."

Mike leaned toward them, his big arms outstretched on the top of the bar. "I don't need to explain anything, understand? Want to keep your job? Then, just do the job and don't say anything or ask any questions. I'm getting tired of telling you this. This shit is out of both of your leagues."

Becky shook Corey's hand away from her arm and then reached to hold his hand. Mike came out from behind the bar. They stepped back away from him. "Relax, just be cool about everything." His voice was a normal tone. "Now, I'll lock the door behind you. Have a good night." As Mike motioned them toward the door, Corey said, "Mike, how about my fifteen dollars for working the door tonight? And I never got my last beer."

Mike reached for his wallet and handed Corey the money. "So sue me on the beer," he said sarcastically. Corey folded the bills and shoved them in his front pocket, and he and Becky walked down the stairs onto the sidewalk and out into the early morning air.

CHAPTER 36

Carolyn rolled over and looked at the clock's lighted numbers on the nightstand. A sliver of anxiety hit her. Corey should have been home by now. Maybe he was talking with Mike, maybe he was giving someone a ride home, maybe something was wrong with his van. Maybe he's just being a jerk. She crunched the pillow, flipping it over. She lay on her back, looking at the ceiling. The cobwebs were still there. Back on her side, she curled up, bringing her legs close against her body, and closed her eyes. She pictured him coming in close to dawn smelling of alcohol and dope, babbling on about how great the band was, how great the afterparty was, clueless to her feelings, making her wonder how many women were there and if they gave out party favors. She brought her hands up to her face and tried not to cry. She lay there a minute more, then got up and put on her jeans, pulled over a T-shirt, and looked for her car keys.

"I think we need to talk," said Corey. Becky nodded. "Let's go around the corner to Nichelson's and get a bite, okay?" Corey looked back at his van parked on the street. "Where you parked?"

"In the side lot by Nichelson's," said Becky.

"Okay, let's walk."

Corey didn't move as he thought about Carolyn. "I don't know, Becky. How about tomorrow? I need to get home."

"I don't want to wait, Corey. I saw Russell come in. Please, let's talk now."

Donni saw them walk in. *He won't sit at the counter,* she told herself.

Corey held Becky's arm and steered her to a booth against the front window. The diner was still crowded with people, young men finishing up breakfast food, stretching out the time to get a little more sober or sitting with a woman, animated in their conversation in the hopes the pairing would go into the daylight, and the single men surveying the room, gauging their chances for possible pickup.

"Haven't been here in a while … late, after the bars close," said Becky. "It's still a meat market, isn't it?"

"Yep," Corey said, knowing he had lost count of the number of times he was a lone guy sitting at the counter eyeballing a woman or two with a pickup line going through his head.

A tired-looking waitress came over. Corey ordered black coffee, Becky a Coke, suggesting they split an order of fries. The waitress took the order without comment. They shared some small talk — how waitressing was tough work, and that Greg was in Lawrence playing a gig and wouldn't be home until early morning. Corey's eyes widened a little when Becky mentioned it.

"How about you, Corey? I heard a girl moved in," Becky said.

Corey was surprised at the question. Carolyn had only been there a few days. "Man, does everyone know my business?" Corey said. Becky laughed. "It was a guess, Corey. I just guessed, considering I hadn't seen you hit on anyone the last few times you worked the door. Congratulations."

Corey shifted his position in the booth. "Thanks. Her name is Carolyn, and I think she's great. I mean, man, it's about time, don't you think?"

Becky smiled big. "So, the stud doorman is out of circulation, my, my. Welcome to the real world, Corey, and be thankful for it."

"Please," Corey objected. "I wasn't that bad, now."

Becky didn't say anything back, but Corey could see in her eyes that maybe he didn't know himself as well as he thought.

They talked more about relationships, Becky expressing her hopes that Greg's ambition in music would be fulfilled and that they could leave the city and go to New York or California. Her dreams flowed out — big house, travel, kids — all kinds of things that Corey had heard before after too many dates with the same woman. Now, he thought of Carolyn as Becky continued. He wondered about her dreams with him. Would she give him what he needed to write so they could have dreams?

When Carolyn saw Corey's van still parked in front of the Repartee, she slowed her VW and came up behind it. She halfway expected him to be sitting in it, talking with some woman, sharing a beer and a joint. She knew she would create a scene, but where it went from there, she didn't know. She walked up to the passenger side and looked in. The van was empty. Now worry set in. Carolyn looked up and down the street. It was deserted, no traffic on the street or sidewalk, and she didn't recognize any of the cars parked near the van as belonging to anyone she knew. Pinky didn't have a car, and she had heard him come back to the house earlier. She slowly walked back to her car. *Maybe he's in Nichelson's,* she thought. She'd drive past the front and see if he was sitting at the counter.

As their conversation slowed, Becky picked through the last of the fries and asked, "Do you know what's going on at the Repartee?"

Corey leaned back in the booth. Becky waited for him to talk. He stared back at her. "I don't know, Becky. Mike's always kinda tough to deal with. Maybe it's the money flow — I don't know."

"What was in the sack tonight, Corey? I saw Russell bring it in and give it to you."

Corey thought of how he could lie about what was in the sack. Nothing sounded plausible. Corey looked around the diner; they were part of the décor, blended in. He leaned forward and reached for one of Becky's hands. "It was coke," he whispered.

Parked in front of Nichelson's, only a few yards down from where Becky and Corey sat, Carolyn felt herself melting into the seat when

Corey touched Becky's hand. She had the urge to smoke a cigarette, something she never did. But she wanted something to keep her from crying, anything other than crying. But she couldn't stop it from coming. She fell over into the passenger seat. It was a quiet cry.

"Is Mike selling it?" Becky asked.

"I don't know. I don't really want to know. My guess is it has something to do with that big Black guy who was in the club the other day, but I don't know. I'm thinking about getting out of there, but I don't know. I mean, I don't have anything against someone doing a line or two — shit, if it's set in front of me, I'll do it, and I buy a dime tab every once in a while. But this ... it kinda feels like heavyweight gangster stuff."

Becky thought of what Greg had said. *"But Russell, he's no gangster."*

They both sat there in their own thoughts, Corey wondering if he should tell Mike he was quitting and Becky deciding she wouldn't say anything about Greg's deal with Russell.

"I see the wheels turning, Corey. What are you going to do?"

"I don't know yet. But it just dawned on me — I'm touching the shit. I could get my ass hung. You, you're not. You could play dumb if the cops came rushing in."

Becky hadn't thought of that, but Corey was right — she was just a waitress. But what about Greg? "But maybe if it's done quietly ... no one talks about it and some other way of doing it besides handing over a sack," said Becky.

"I don't know. I need to decide after this weekend what I'm doing, whether to quit, move on, or whatever." Corey waved the waitress over.

Outside, in the VW, Carolyn continued to lay across the front seats. She thought about either leaving or waiting to confront Corey.

As Corey counted out the money for their coffee and fries, Becky thought about his word "whatever."

"Would make a good story, wouldn't it, Corey, all this stuff? I mean ... since you're a writer."

Corey pushed the meal receipt and money to the edge of the table. "Why is everyone always so concerned about my writing subjects?" he said, the words coming out quickly. "Shit, I get a few pieces published, no one reads it, comments on it, not a fuckin' response. But somehow, everyone's curiosity is up now."

Becky scooted over to the edge of the booth. "I'm sorry, Corey. I was just wondering if you would use the opportunity to…"

"Becky, forget it," Corey said, cutting off her sentence. "What I write is my business, but I'm bright enough to know how not to get my ass in a wringer."

In front of Nichelson's door, Corey had calmed down. "You going to get home, okay?" he asked Becky. She nodded, turned, and began to walk across the parking lot to her car. Corey watched her for a moment, now wondering if she knew more than he assumed. *I should have asked her what she knew,* he told himself. As he began to walk back to his van, he saw Carolyn's VW. He strolled slowly to her car. Just before he got there, Carolyn sat up. Her eyes were red, her lips tight together. For a moment, Corey was confused, then he knew why she looked upset.

"Hey, baby, why are you here?" He then looked back at the diner. "It's not what you think."

"Oh, yeah, fucker, what is it?" Carolyn got angrier and more hurt just saying those words. Crying alone seemed easier.

"She's Becky, the waitress. We needed to talk about something, that's all. She has a boyfriend and lives with him. There's nothing going on." There was anguish in Corey's voice.

Carolyn started the VW. "It's after two in the morning, Corey. Your favorite time, isn't it, to do your hustler shit." She backed the car out of the parking space, grinded the gears in trying to find first, and drove off. Corey stood on the sidewalk. He felt like he knew nothing and had nowhere to go.

Carolyn could barely see as she drove back to Corey's house. Thank God, she told herself, no one was on the road. By the time she pulled into the driveway, she had stopped crying. She did a mental inventory of what stuff she had in Corey's house. He found her in his bedroom, throwing clothes into a bag. "Please, Carolyn, let's talk, please."

She stopped what she was doing and came close to him. "You're the same Corey. I can't trust you. You want to write, but you don't. You just use it to get laid. I'm sure that's what you were talking about — your writing! That and getting fucked!" Carolyn hit Corey in the chest with both fists and turned away. "I could have helped you become that writer you want to be," she said, her back to him. The crying was starting to come back. "But I can't trust you ... I can't." She grabbed her bag. At the bedroom doorway, she turned and tossed his house keys on the bed.

He followed her to the door, not saying anything. He stood there watching her step off the porch and into the dim light of the early morning. He turned away when he heard her VW startup. He went into the kitchen and opened the refrigerator. Pinky walked in as he opened a beer. "You okay, man?" he asked.

"No," Corey said.

CHAPTER 37

Mike didn't leave the club until nearly 5 a.m. After Corey and Becky were out the door, he did three quick shots of bourbon and then spent the good part of an hour nursing beers at the bar, staring at the sack before deciding it really had to go into the safe in the office. Thoughts about stashing it under a loose floorboard or above a ceiling tile seemed ridiculous. *Then what? Hope the mice eat the coke?* Mike laughed. He pictured himself going to Lewis, explaining that mice or squirrels or some unidentified rodent had eaten the half-ounce of coke. He, Lewis, and Marcus would all laugh together ... then he likely would chew on the barrel of a gun while listening to threats from Lewis.

The scenario may have eased his worry, but it didn't make Mike feel any less like he was in a box. Any thoughts of grabbing some money and skipping out of town as Lewis got comfortable with him left. *The guy has my balls, and I've got to go with the deal all-in or do something like pull every cent I've got together and torch the place on my way out of town.* Mike was surprised at thinking those were his choices. "What the fuck happened?" he said aloud. This wasn't what he had in mind in opening the Repartee — as if anything you do that makes you feel good is what you have in mind. He felt tired, his brain washed out. It wasn't fear; it was fatigue. He walked upstairs to his office, bouncing the coke in the palm of his hand along the way. *Coke in brown paper sacks — could almost be lyrics Weird Al Yankovic would use in a song.*

With the coke in the safe, Mike flopped down behind his desk. *Any debate about what to do is over. I'll put up a stink about getting the sack of coke without notice, maybe give Lewis a little fun by getting in his face all excited like — making Marcus huff and puff — and then show him I've decided I'm part of it. I'll be contrite. What the fuck, I might make some real money. It could be cool until ... it isn't.*

Mike turned off the lights in his office and patted his front pocket, checking to see if he had his keys to lock the front door. Breakfast at Nichelson's sounded good. He walked across the club, glancing at the stage as he went. At the top of the stairs, he turned to look back at the bar. Only the neon beer lights behind the bar were on. Some clubs he worked as a comic had the same layout; he remembered focusing on the lights at the bar as he delivered his jokes instead of looking at the people's faces in the audience. Would they have laughed more if he had looked at them? Mike didn't know.

In Nichelson's, he took a stool at the counter instead of a booth. Donni was off work in twenty minutes and figured Mike was close to being her last customer. But she was glad he sat at the counter. Mike was known as a good tipper so every waitress in Nichelson's liked it when he sat down in her station.

"Mr. Mike, it's been a while," said Donni as she put down a cup of coffee. "Up early or out late?"

"In between ... yeah, other than Sundays, I don't come in much. You don't work Sundays, do you?"

Donni stood in front of Mike, one hand on her hip, the other holding the pot of coffee out away from her body. "No, I don't. Church obligations."

Mike chuckled and then took a sip of coffee. "Yeah, right. What's that? The church of lost souls?"

"Yes, Mike. Part of the same congregation you belong to."

Mike kept his smile as he watched Donni pin his food ticket on the wheel in front of the kitchen window. Physically, she had the sex appeal of a telephone pole. Still, Donni could make straight guys wonder how straight they were, and then not worry about it.

His breakfast went down quickly. When Donni came around to refill his coffee cup, she asked how the food was and then said, "Your doorman Corey was in here earlier but later than usual. You must have had a good crowd last night."

"Not bad," Mike said, looking at Donni as if she had more to say.

"He was in here with, I think, your waitperson, the frizzy-hair girl."

"They sit at the counter?"

"No, when that Corey boy has a girl, he sits at a booth. Gives him more room to maneuver his lines. That cutie likes the chase."

"So, you didn't hear what they were talking about?" Mike tried not to seem anxious to know.

Donni sensed the concern in Mike's question. She cocked her head to one side and smiled. "Didn't hear anything, Mike. Is something going on at the Repartee? My shrink shingle is out, you know."

"I can handle whatever happens at my club," said Mike, his voice having lost its easiness. "Where's my ticket?"

Donni turned her back to him and added up his food ticket. She placed it in front of him. "Thanks for coming in," she said in a flat tone and walked away.

Outside in front of Nichelson's, whatever energy the breakfast gave him was gone. He was sure Corey and Becky had talked about the coke. They both saw the sack ... *the stupid, fucking sack*. Mike looked up at the sky. There was a freshness to the coming light. He could go pound on Russell's door and get him up to talk, or he could just go home and crash. He was sure to be awoken by Lewis or Marcus. Maybe he could dream his way out of all this. The thought had a strange comfort to it. Mike decided to head home.

CHAPTER 38

"What's on the agenda today?" Jensen asked as he took the plastic lid off his coffee cup to take a sip.

"Why do you always ask me that same question about every day when you know the answer?" said Frederick.

Jensen looked over at Frederick, surprised at his remark. "Man, in a bad mood or what? I'm just asking like I always do." Jensen couldn't help but smile.

"Well, yeah, that's the point, Jensen. What do you think, some dumb-ass nigger gots to be programmed each day to the work?" Frederick had his hand on the car door handle. "I'm going back in to get some gum before I stab your honkey-ass, motherfucker."

"All right, I apologize, Malcolm," said Jensen out the window as Frederick walked away from the car to go into the 7-Eleven. *Gee must have had a bad night at home.* Jensen took another sip of coffee. *Can't figure these Black guys out. Everything is racial.*

When Frederick came back to the car, Jensen had a file folder open. "Anything new on Lewis or Marcus?" Frederick asked. He was calmer now. Jensen had seniority, and he was junior to the detective. Jensen could have him back in uniform if he wanted it.

"No, nothing new in the new surveillance reports. Same comings and goings except Marcus parked out front of the Repartee last night for about an hour."

Frederick watched Jensen turn the pages, some typed, others handwritten, stopping every so often to read a paragraph. "Anything about seeing Pinky showing up?"

"Yeah, here. He was observed entering the Repartee at 21:45."

"That's it?"

"Yeah, that's it. When Marcus left at 23:05, they broke off the surveillance and then had a patrol car go by and call in that he was back at his house at 23:30."

"So, we can assume Pinky stayed a while at the club."

"Yeah," Jensen said as he shut the file folder. "Let's go park in front of his house. Make our presence known."

Pinky was up by 9 a.m. Gary wanted him at the store that morning to stock the shelves for the weekend. Corey was already gone. When things seemed screwed up, Corey worked long hours — sixteen, eighteen hours — staying on the road making pickups and deliveries until the dispatcher told him to go home. It was his therapy — exhaustion. Pinky knew by the time he got back to the house, Corey would crash quickly and then wake up the next day and do it again. After a few days, he would be back to more sane hours, having thought out what to do concerning Carolyn — give it another try or let it go.

Pinky planned on going to Lou's later that night to see Carolyn. Maybe he could help patch things up between her and Corey. Or maybe if he had a shot at getting her interested in him. Pinky knew Corey usually didn't fight to keep a woman.

Pinky saw the Ford even before closing the front door. "Fuck!" he said to himself. Jensen had the passenger door open as Pinky did a slow stroll down the walkway in front of the house. "Want some company on your way to Bain's?" Jensen asked.

"I'll pass," said Pinky.

"Get in anyway," said Jensen, pointing to the back seat.

Pinky didn't know if they knew he was at the Repartee last night or not, or if they had sent in an undercover to the club. Did they know about the sack thing? Did they know anything? Pinky decided to let them talk as much as he could.

Jensen turned around to Pinky. Frederick watched Pinky's face in the rearview mirror. "Enjoy the band last night, Pink?" Jensen asked.

"Not bad."

"Yeah, those country bands, got to love 'em. Country folk are decent folk, huh, Pinky?" Frederick looked over at Jensen. "Well, they are," said Jensen responding more to Frederick's look than to Pinky. "So, tell us what went down."

"Went down," Pinky repeated back to Jensen. He couldn't tell if Jensen knew about the sack or was just using the phrase to get him talking. Pinky took the chance he didn't know. "Nothing went down that I could see. Just a bunch of shit-kickers having a good time." Frederick and Jensen glanced at each other.

"What did you see, Pinky?" Jensen's tone was serious.

Pinky looked over at Frederick, who was now turned around, one arm resting on the back of the seat.

"Look, I really didn't see anything, nothing. I'm not trained. I don't know what I'm supposed to look for." Pinky wondered how his voice sounded.

Jensen leaned over the seat like he was going to grab Pinky. "Did anyone seem high? Coming in and out of the john or a back room." Jensen smiled. "You know what high is, Pinky, don't you?"

Pinky frowned at the comment.

"How did your buddy roommate act?" asked Frederick. "Was he nervous? Did he give anything to anybody? Were people constantly coming up to him as if asking for something?"

"No, no. He was his usual self." Pinky knew if they knew about the sack, it would have come out by now.

"Anyone carry anything in or out of the bar?" asked Jensen. "Anyone act weird, nervous, in a hurry?"

Pinky looked out the car's back seat window at the house he shared with Corey. The porch gutter sagged a bit, and the paint on the trim around the front window was beginning to peel. He thought of one of his summer jobs before going into the Army, how he hated painting houses, sweating atop a ladder, worrying about wasps and hornets buzzing about, and tearing down birds' nests.

"Hey, hey," Jensen said, snapping his fingers. "You hear what we asked?"

Pinky thought of Russell coming down the stairs. "Yeah, one guy seemed nervous and in a hurry. He was dressed real classy, nice threads, neat."

"Coming or going?"

"He was leaving as I was coming in."

"What time was that?" asked Frederick.

"It was relatively early, before ten." Pinky then added, "I saw the same guy later in The Pink Slip."

"The Pink Slip," said a surprised Jensen. "A little AC/DC there, Pinky?"

"I went in there to get a last drink," Pinky said, irritated at the remark. "They closed the bar at the Repartee early. I wanted one more. The Slip will serve right up to closing."

Frederick and Jensen looked at each other; both were smiling.

"So, what was this guy doing — or should I ask?" Jensen was chuckling while looking at Frederick.

"He was hanging with other guys," said Pinky. "Slamming down shots. They were higher than kites. Not really drunk — high."

Both Frederick and Jensen turned back around. Jensen opened the file folder and wrote much of what Pinky had said on the yellow legal pad. Pinky took out a cigarette and asked Frederick for a light. He pointed to Jensen, who then tossed a lighter into the back seat.

"Tell me what the guy looked like," Jensen said, holding a pen to the yellow pad. Pinky described Russell as best he could. He embellished nothing, knowing he had seen the guy around and thought that Corey knew him. That thought didn't worry him.

"So, you don't have a name?" Jensen asked after taking down the description. "No," Pinky said. "But I've seen him around at other bars in Midtown."

"You better not be fuckin' with us, Pinky," Jensen said.

"I'm not, but I just thought maybe it was something you should know."

The three sat in the car in silence. Jensen doodled an image of a bird on the legal pad. Frederick watched a couple of squirrels chase each other around the trunk of a tree. Pinky decided he would stay with what he had said. The detectives knew nothing of the sack, so anything he said could satisfy them for a while.

Jensen looked up from the pad and said, "Go to work, Pinky. And remember, our deal is still on. We'll be in touch."

Pinky got out of the car. Jensen waved Pinky away. It was four blocks to Bain's. Pinky started a slow walk. Maybe it would be good that Corey got back with Carolyn. He needed to get out of the Repartee, and she could convince him to do that if they settled the romance problem. Save Corey's ass and get out of town. The thought stayed with Pinky all the way to Bain's. He hadn't felt this good about something in a while.

With Pinky well away from the car, Frederick asked Jensen, "You buying this?"

"Not in a million years. Either he's trying to deflect us away from anything coming down in the Repartee, or he's just making up this story about some well-dressed guy because he thinks he needs to give us something."

"What if he's not jiving us? What if it's The Pink Slip that's tied to Lewis, not the Repartee," said Frederick.

"Get real, Frederick. Lewis, and especially Marcus, isn't going to fuck around with a queer joint. You ought to know that. You're Black, aren't you?"

Frederick turned away from Jensen and stared out the car's front window. His mother had been so proud when he told her he had made detective. She told everyone on the block. "My boy could be chief someday," she told anyone who dropped by the house. He wanted to believe he was promoted because he had worked hard as a patrolman, that the brass recognized him as having the potential to be a good detective, not because he was Black. But he knew Jensen didn't believe that. To Jensen, it was just affirmative action in play, and he got the Black guy as a partner.

"Besides," Jensen continued. "Most queers are into poppers and uppers. It gets their dicks waggin' much better than coke or weed."

"How would you know, Jensen?" Frederick said. Jensen let the remark slide. "Let's get back to the office and talk with the DS." They talked about a plan as they drove on.

When Jensen walked out of the detective sergeant's office, he went straight to Frederick. "What did he say?" Frederick asked.

Jensen thought about being a smartass but decided against it. "He likes our ... err, your idea. They're going to send in a half-dozen uniforms tonight around eleven to shake the patrons down. Anyone holding will get pulled in. Make a lot of noise so the word gets around."

"Good," said Frederick. "And Jensen, it is our idea. We're a team, though I wouldn't call us salt and pepper brothers."

Jensen smiled. "I hear ya, and I can dig it — is that the way to say it?" Frederick's expression went blank. "Anyway," Jensen continued, "hopefully, the word should quickly get next door and into Marcus' face, and maybe loosen things up. Stir up some shit."

"Where are we going to be at, boss?" Frederick's blank expression remained.

Jensen moved some papers on his desk. "We'll hang back tonight, and tomorrow, we'll talk to the supervising officer to see what they got and if anyone they pulled in said anything."

"We going to stake out the Repartee tonight, too?"

"No," said Jensen. "We'll put some eyes on it on Friday."

"Well, hell. A night off, right?"

"Yeah, Malcolm, you got a night off. You can go play basketball at the Southeast Center."

"Fuck you, whitey," Frederick said, and then both men laughed.

CHAPTER 39

I t was well past noon when Mike awoke. He lay in bed staring at the window, a ray of sunlight catching one side of his face through an opening in the blind. He thought of the night before — the sack, Russell, Corey, and Lewis ... *Fucking Lewis. I'm caught in that nigger's grip. What's left?* Mike rubbed his eyes, then scratched his crotch. *Just make the best go of it and protect my ass as much as I can. Hello, new day. Yeah, right.*

After a couple cups of coffee and a shower, he was ready to visit Russell. There would be no dancing around the topic, just a simple, "What the fuck is going on?"

It took nearly three minutes of pounding on Russell's door to get him to open it. Mike knew he was there; his Volvo was parked out front. Russell didn't walk anywhere. In his world, walking was uncool.

"Man, what the fuck? You want to bust the door off its hinges?" Russell said after opening the door.

"Don't care, Russell. You know why I'm here," Mike said.

Russell shuffled to the living room and then flopped onto the couch. Mike followed, sitting in a chair across from Russell. Both men shared weariness. Before Mike could say anything, Russell stood up. "I'm not going to let you berate and interrogate me without some tea." He walked away and then turned and asked, "You want some?"

Mike shrugged his shoulders. "Yeah, I'll take some. What the fuck."

He leaned back in the chair, listening to Russell in the kitchen. He heard cabinets open and close, and it wasn't long before the teapot whistled. Russell filled a small teakettle and brought it out to the living room on a tray with two cups. "Earl Grey okay for you?" he asked Mike. "Here's some sugar and lemon if you want it."

"Yeah, whatever," said Mike.

After a few sips of tea, Mike put down his cup and said, "Okay, Russell, what's going on? Why the delivery?"

Russell wasn't going to hold back on Mike. "Lewis wanted it. He wanted to put pressure on you."

"Well, I know that. But why?"

Russell put down his cup and straightened up. "He knew we talked the other day. Marcus was watching the place, following me or something. Lewis figures you might be scamming on him, err, we're scamming — I think he's a little afraid of you, Mike."

"Yeah, I'm not particularly afraid, but that doesn't mean I won't do what he asks. And I'm glad you said 'we,' Russell, 'cause it was your ass that got me in this."

"I did the introductions, Mike. You took the leap."

Mike glared at Russell. He knew Russell was right. "So, bringing the coke on premises was to get me to toe the line because one phone call and I could be toast."

Russell nodded. Mike felt angry and a little sick to his stomach. For a second, he thought there might be something in the tea, but he shook off that thought. Do it or not do it; coke still makes you paranoid. Mike looked at Russell. He knew that to handle Lewis, Marcus, and the whole deal, he needed some sort of ally, someone like himself, who only cared about himself. Mike accepted that about himself and saw the same in Russell. Maybe together, there was shelter in that someway.

"Okay. The best thing to do right now is go along with this. Watch our ass, don't piss off Lewis as best we can, maybe even make some money and hope this shit settles somehow. That's what I think."

"I'm in agreement," said Russell. "And frankly, Mike, any other way, and I think Lewis would ... kill us, especially if we tried to push back." Russell had a dejected look. His fear had turned to resignation.

Mike wasn't surprised by Russell's remark. "Yeah, I don't doubt it. It's not something I want to think about too much. I'm sure you feel the same way." Mike looked around Russell's apartment. Neither man spoke. Finally, Mike said, "This shit is bizarre," and then he laughed.

"You got that right," Russell said, shaking off his dark mood, smiling as Mike continued to laugh.

The mood didn't last. Mike rubbed his hands together. "I think the thing is, is that we need to gain his trust and never be alone with his goon Marcus."

"I agree," said Russell.

"That means keeping what's going down as tight between us as possible. No leaking, nothing to get Lewis concerned about something going on that he doesn't know about. We do a lot of 'yes ums.' We get him to believe we're solely doing his bidding; get him to relax, and we can relax a little."

Then Mike thought of Corey. "Your friend Corey. He knows what's going on — or is close to figuring it out. We need him in with an understanding or out, and if so, then out quickly. But whatever we do, we got to do it with some finesse."

"I think we should keep him in the dark as much as possible," said Russell. "Right now, he only knows about the sack. He could get afraid and quit, then what? If he starts talking about it, it will get back to Lewis, and everything might blow up. Lewis would then leave us out to dry."

"I don't think he's a dummy. I don't think he'll make noise about it. He doesn't know about Lewis or Marcus, or who's doing what with the coke. I can continue to lean on him to just do the doorman's job and see if there's an alternative to him down the line — someone who's not so inquisitive and doesn't give a shit. Maybe a roadie, someone from one of the bands."

"I could probably find someone to take his place," Russell said.

"We'll see. The thing is, to try and control this as much as we can at the Repartee." Mike again thought of last night. "What about Becky?"

Russell raised his arms, moving his hands back and forth with palms out. "No worry. She's okay."

Mike looked at Russell intently. "So ... Greg's band is the first run, and she knows? You made the arrangements, a deal with Lewis, huh?"

Russell was surprised at how quickly Mike figured things out. "Yeah, I've got a deal with Lewis to line up the bands. In return, Lewis would help raise my profile as a promoter."

Mike leaned back on the couch. He kept his eyes on Russell. "No shit, so that's the hook. And you believe Lewis would follow through to help you?"

Russell shrugged. "Whatever he is, he didn't get where he got by not keeping his word on some things. You can't lie all the time and become somebody."

"Now you admire this guy?" said Mike. "The guy sucked you in because he could grease your way, simple as that. You got your deal, Greg's got his promises of bigger gigs, and I'm left holding the sack ... so to speak." Mike grunted at his feeling of sudden helplessness.

Russell shook his head. "Wait, you save the club, Mike. Money will flow your way, you'll see, and the music, all kinds of music, good music — will be heard in this town, again, at your club."

Mike thought over what Russell had said. He had to like it as much as it felt like he was greasing his ego. There didn't seem to be any other choice. There was no one to trust but himself. He knew that. He thought of Becky again. "So pretty Becky is okay knowing what's coming down?" Russell nodded. "She's an ambitious wench, always knew that," Mike said, more to himself than to Russell.

"I asked Greg not to tell her, but he couldn't not tell her, so she knows," said Russell.

"I guess good pussy does that," Mike said.

Both men fell back in their seats as if they had just shaken off any lie that they shared.

Marcus finished his rounds and called in the money count to Lewis. It was late afternoon. He was at the liquor store on Truman Road on the payphone. "Ain't heard shit," he said to Lewis. "Motherfucker does have my phone number, right?"

"I don't know, can't remember if I gave it to him. Don't matter. Swing by the club this evening before he opens the door. See what's coming down in how he acts, and let me know. Make sure the teaser we sent over is still there. Call me later tonight."

"Right on," Marcus said. "Before that, I'm going to cruise by some of our blocks, make sure our people aren't slackin', and then wash the ride before I head over there. That cool with you?"

"Yeah, no problem. But get me confident on this. I'm thinking we get this shit rollin' soon." Lewis hung up the phone before Marcus could ask about his Florida jaunt.

The morning dragged for Pinky, making him anxious and short-tempered. Other than a shot of bourbon in his coffee that morning, Pinky was riding a mini wagon. Between opening boxes to stock the shelves and listening to Gary rattle on about Dan White's sentencing and going to San Francisco to protest, then thinking of Jensen and Frederick and how long it would take to figure out his story about Russell and The Pink Slip was bogus, Pinky was close to busting something. He needed to drink and think.

"Hey, man, I've got to go," he told Gary around 1 p.m. "I appreciate it, man, but you can cover the rest of this."

Gary was surprised. "You could put in another two hours, Pinky. Plus, I was thinking maybe I could teach you the register; learn enough to give me some time off."

Pinky had his field jacket on. He lit a cigarette as he stood before Gary at the store's front counter. "Look, please, another time. I got stuff on my mind."

"Maybe I could help," Gary said.

Pinky gave him a thin smile and pushed open the door to leave.

"Tomorrow morning, same time, Pinky?" Gary said. Pinky waved back as if he was swatting at an annoying insect and yelled out into the parking lot, "Yeah."

As he walked back to the house, Pinky did a mental inventory of his booze stash. Maybe a couple of open half-pints in the bedroom, another under the couch downstairs, and a couple of beers in the fridge. Not much. With his mood, it would take more to get him as drunk as he felt he wanted to be.

Pinky thought of turning around and walking back to Bain's to ask for his pay for the day. Buy a fresh pint. But he would have to deal with Gary's bitchin' about his drinking and probably listen to another come-on. *Maybe I should just let the guy suck my dick and make some money that way.* Pinky flicked his cigarette butt into the street. He stopped a block from the house to scan the street to see if the two cops were there again. They weren't, but Corey's van was in the driveway.

"You're home at a different time," Pinky said as he stepped through the front door. Corey was on the couch eating a sandwich and drinking a beer. He looked up at Pinky and shrugged. "Takin' a break so I can work into the night."

"Lot of driving, man," Pinky said.

Corey didn't respond. The two men sat together in silence. Corey ate slowly, glancing every so often out the open front door. Pinky slouched in the chair, his head back, eyes closed.

"You want to talk about it, man?" Pinky said, wanting something else on his mind than finding a bottle in the house.

Corey turned to look at Pinky. "I don't know, man," he said before turning again to look out the front door. "She thinks I'm fuckin' someone else, and I'm not. Isn't that the way it always comes down to?"

"Yeah, maybe," Pinky said.

Corey waited to see if Pinky would say more. Pinky thought he should, but he didn't know what to say. Women, girls, they were great, and men always fucked it up somehow. But Pinky didn't want to say that. Corey already knew ... and when a guy gets blamed for something he didn't do, it's like payback for all the things he did but never got caught at.

"Can I have one of your beers?" Pinky said.

Corey gestured toward the kitchen without saying anything.

"Man, I don't know what to say," Pinky said as he walked back into the room. "She's a good woman, Corey. Maybe it will come around again."

"I don't know. Maybe it's just something to write about." Corey downed the rest of his beer and then perched the empty bottle on his knee.

Pinky sat back down. "Maybe if you left the club, got away from the temptations, so to speak. She would notice that."

Corey began rolling the beer bottle between his hands. He wondered how long it would be before he no longer felt this way, before Carolyn was just another woman he had for a while. "Something's going down there. I'm going to hang until it all plays out," he said. Corey then thought of Becky.

Pinky looked at Corey in surprise. He really didn't want to know what was going on. He wondered if he should tell Corey the cops were already sniffing the place out. But then, how would he explain he knew that?

Corey continued to stare out the front door.

Pinky knew Corey as a friend — he had to. The guy put up with him, with his drinking, his rants about the system and the Man, his screaming nightmares, and yet he never asked about the war. He knew not to ask, but then he listened when Pinky was so drunk, so angry he could talk of nothing else, until the pain and liquor made him go quiet.

"What kind of stuff is happening there?" Pinky asked.

Corey stood up. "Seen my van keys?" he asked.

"Saw them on the kitchen table," Pinky said.

Corey got his keys and then walked to the front door. "It's some kind of dope shit. I've got to stay alert — it could be a hell of a story."

"Man, you could get yourself hurt too. You're too close." Pinky's concern was real. "Get out of there, man, if that's what it is. It ain't worth it."

Corey stood at the door. He turned and smiled. "Think Carolyn would come back if I broke open a big story on movin' dope? *City* magazine would jump on it."

Pinky shook his head. "That ain't the way, man. Too much shit could come down on you." Corey shrugged. "Come on, Corey. Look out, man — please, get out of there. Not good."

Corey stepped out the door and walked to his van. "Ain't the way," Pinky called out. Corey didn't look back. He watched as Corey pulled out of the driveway. "Mother fucking idiot," Pinky said to himself. He stood at the door looking out into the street. He pictured Corey in the hospital, his body mangled, his face bloodied, softened and disfigured . . . like the gooks he'd help drag into a burial pile in the bush.

Pinky thought about Jensen and Frederick. Maybe he should talk to them about it. *No, I can't trust them. They don't give a shit about Corey or me or anybody. It's just about being the Man.* Pinky sat down and reached under the chair cushion and felt a half-pint.

CHAPTER 41

Marcus turned off Roanoke Boulevard onto 39th Street past the Repartee, then turned into Nichelson's parking lot. He saw Mike's car parked in a slot across the alley not far from the rear of the Repartee. Marcus parked his Seville close by and went to the payphone in front of Nichelson's. He dialed the Repartee. Mike answered the phone.

"Open the front door, motherfucker. We got to talk."

"Yeah," said Mike, and he slammed the phone down. He did a slow walk down the steps to the bar and then down to the front door. He was calm by the time he opened the door for Marcus. The entryway leading to the stairs was narrow. Both men brushed against each other as Marcus stepped inside. Mike re-locked the door and then stepped in front of Marcus, his back to him, and began walking up the stairs. He was in no hurry. Marcus followed a few steps behind. As the men reached the top, Marcus moved to the side of Mike.

"Want a beer, drink, soda, or something before we go up into the office?" Mike said as he stopped at the bar.

Marcus was surprised by the offer. Mike's calmness was beginning to irritate him. "This ain't all that friendly — you know that motherfucker."

Mike turned and walked up the stairs to the office. Marcus followed. There, Marcus sat down in the chair in front of Mike's desk. Mike moved behind his desk, sat down, and brought his hands together behind his head. He leaned back and waited for Marcus to talk.

"You got the shit last night, didn't you?" Marcus said.

Mike nodded. Marcus was getting more irritated. He had expected Mike to be agitated, nervous, fearful, and full of questions about why the coke was delivered without him knowing about it.

"Well, what you got to say?" Marcus demanded. "You do some of the shit? Where is it?"

"Take it easy," Mike said. "It's in the safe. Nobody touched it. You want it back?"

Marcus thought about it. Lewis hadn't said to pick it up. "No, keep it for now, but don't touch it."

Keeping it bothered Mike. It could be permanent leverage Lewis could exercise at any time.

Neither man said anything; both just looking at each other. Mike could tell Marcus wasn't happy that it wasn't going the way it usually did when he did Lewis' business. Mike decided he needed to keep it calm.

"Look," Mike began, "I get it. Tell Mr. Richardson I get it. He's in control; it's his thing. I'm in because I want to keep my club, so I get it. It was a test, and a show of who's in charge. You guys could hang me with a phone call, so I get it."

Marcus didn't expect this. *The white motherfucker understands. But he is White.*

"Good to hear," Marcus said. "Good to know we got your ass. You play, and you get what you want. You fuck us around, be stupid, and your ass will never walk again."

"I hear ya," Mike said.

Marcus stood up. He knew if he stayed longer, he might begin to think about wailing on the dude. Fucker didn't seem all that scared. That made Marcus angry, and this White fuck knew it. Still, Lewis would want him to stay professional.

"What's the plan coming up?" Mike asked. Marcus walked to the office door. "Keep the shit in the safe, and you'll know what you need to know soon," said Marcus. He walked out without shutting the door.

Mike sat at his desk. He exhaled, loud enough so that he knew that he wasn't as calm as he thought with Marcus in his face. *Dumb Black motherfucker will be back. I locked the front door. He'll be back here demanding I unlock the door.* Mike would apologize for the oversight, be contrite, keep things calm, and make Marcus think that his visit made him forget he locked the door back up.

After three minutes or so, Marcus hadn't returned. Mike began to wonder if he was downstairs waiting for him. Mike walked down the office stairs slowly, then across the club's main floor, turning to look in all directions, then down the stairs to the front door.

The door was open to the sidewalk, hanging crooked by one door hinge but still upright. The doorframe was splintered on both sides, with jagged pieces of wood sticking out. Mike wondered how many kicks it took for Marcus to get through the door. He pushed the door back a little and stepped out onto the sidewalk, looking both ways. The after-work traffic was getting heavier on 39th. People in cars going by or stopped at the traffic light gawked at the broken door.

It wasn't until after 7 p.m. that the new door, lock, and doorframe had been installed. The emergency repair had cost money Mike hadn't expected to spend. He decided that playing games with Marcus wasn't cost-effective, much less a smart thing to do.

It was open mic night, so Mike expected to work the place himself. He'd check IDs and fill the drink orders at the bar — no cover. There wouldn't be much of a crowd, and if there was one, well, tough, people would have to stand in line. He wasn't going to call Becky in. Fixing the door was expensive enough.

People started drifting in around 8:30, clustering around the bar and making conversation with Mike or others. Most were part-time musicians, some with girlfriends, talking about gigs and bands breaking up and who had left town. Mike was familiar with the din. After a few drinks, and lots of acknowledgments among those who knew each other, someone would saunter to the stage — maybe with a couple of other players in tow — and get the open-mic jam going. Mike kept only three microphones live to keep the music — or musical mistakes — at a tolerable noise level even though open mic stayed acoustic.

By then, a good crowd had gathered, not too many that Mike couldn't service them but steady enough that it seemed the night would be profitable even with the cost of a new front door. The music came at a regular pace with pauses for musician changes, a good mix of solo sets, and four or five musicians pulled in playing familiar songs known by most all. Much of the music was easy country or ballads with guitars, fiddles, and an occasional saxophone to up the tempo. A woman here or there would step up to sing a blues number or heartache love song. No one embarrassed themselves, and the audience — those not into talking among themselves — always gave the players a good hand.

The atmosphere had Mike relaxing. He didn't think of Marcus, Lewis or Corey. He even found himself being interested in what people were telling him. Being caught up in counting the cash as it came in wasn't there. He listened to the stories about this musician or that, wishing someone well who was leaving a day job behind and hitting the road, and eyeballed the women, though most everyone seemed to have come with someone. No woman flirted with him, though they always smiled. *Where are the bartender groupies?* Mike wondered, half-serious at one point.

Around 11:30, people began to wander out of the club. Everyone who wanted to play seemed to have played. When no one took the stage again after five minutes, Mike walked down the end of the bar and turned on the reel-to-reel player. "Hootie Blues" came on. It was music that would get the country crowd out the door. Mike was glad he had recorded *The Last of the Blue Devils.* Now, only if he could get Jay McShann to play the Repartee, the table would then be set. *Could Lewis get him in? Naw, McShann has class; Richardson is a gangster trying to get class.*

As Mike wiped the bar, still shaking off any thought of Marcus or Lewis or coke and got into McShann's piano, he noticed a few people coming back into the club. A group gathering at one end of the bar talked intently among themselves. Mike moved down that way, curious.

"What's going on, Sam?" he asked a musician he recognized.

"The cops raided The Pink Slip earlier. They're still everywhere. The street's blocked; people parked out front can't go anywhere. Looks like some of us will be hangin' around a while, Mike."

Mike put down the bar rag and walked back to the middle of the bar. *What the fuck is going on?* he asked himself.

CHAPTER 42

Pinky woke up on the living room couch a little after eleven. Had he turned on the TV, he could have seen the local news covering The Pink Slip raid. The house was dark. Corey was still out on the road. Pinky turned on the porch light, and then went to the bathroom. He took a piss and threw some water on his face. He wasn't hungry, but he could use a drink.

Carolyn was probably working, he figured. Pinky changed his shirt, brushed his teeth, and combed his hair. Maybe she would ask about Corey. Maybe she wouldn't and ask how he was doing. Either way, it was worth the walk.

Pinky could see that Lou's wasn't crowded as he walked up to the front door. But he paused before going in. Sitting at the bar was Lawton. Carolyn was looking at him, listening to whatever he was saying. She was smiling. He had his hand on top of hers at the bar.

The door clanked when Pinky stepped in. Carolyn pulled her hand away and waved at Pinky. He sat down at the end of the bar where it curved into the wall, his back to the front window. He could see Lawton had a shit-eating grin of a smile. Pinky looked away as Carolyn walked toward him.

"Hi, Pinky. How are you?" She was in a good mood. Not much grief that Pinky could see.

"Still got the gig at Bain's. Maybe I'm finally getting the hang of civilian life."

Carolyn ran her fingers through her hair at the temples and smiled big. "I'm impressed. The owner ... what's his name, Gary? He a vet?"

Pinky laughed loud enough so Lawton could hear. "Not even, but he tolerates me."

"Maybe he's taken a liking to you, Pink. I heard he especially likes his male customers." Carolyn held out her hand and flicked her wrist as she said it.

Pinky leaned back. "Ha, ha ... how about a beer?"

"Sure, Pinky," said Carolyn. Lowering her voice, she added, "No tabs, Pinky. I need the cash. Lou's rule, sorry."

"No problem. I got a few bucks. Bring me a big draw."

Carolyn smiled at Lawton as she walked by to pour Pinky a beer. When she came back, Pinky asked, "Awful friendly with Lawton. Got a thing going now?"

Carolyn was surprised at Pinky's directness. "He's not such a bad guy, Pinky. Besides, I'm free to do what I want with whom I want. What are you, my dad?"

"I'm sorry. Yeah, a little too direct. But maybe it ain't my place, but Corey and you ... he's hurting some. Maybe it isn't what it seemed to be."

"I don't want to talk about Corey. He's an asshole." Pinkies watched Carolyn's eyes half-close and go wet. She looked down and then back up to Pinky, her eyes now red and angry. "Pinky, you're my friend. Don't push this. It hurts, and I want to get over it. Don't come in here to talk about Corey ... please." She walked away, then stopped and turned back around. "No trouble with Lawton either, Pinky, please."

Pinky nodded and took a big drink of his beer. He had enough money for another one then he would leave.

With his back to the bar's front window, he couldn't see the tiny light from a cigarette across the street and the figure of someone leaning against the outside wall of the closed coffee shop. Not far, under a streetlight, sat Corey's van. By the time Pinky left Lou's, the van was gone.

Mike had kept the bar open until the legal closing time. He wanted to keep people around after learning about the raid. It's all people talked about at the bar, with suspicions flying about why the cops had gone in. Some thought it was nothing more than harassing the gays. Others, those who knew it was a place to score, be it straight or gay, thought it was about drugs. Mike just listened. When asked what he thought, he just shrugged and said, "I don't know, I don't go in there."

When the last person left, Mike took his time cleaning up. He thought about where his car was parked in Nichelson's lot by the alley. Mike thought of Marcus. Maybe it was best to coffee up at Nichelson's, and if Donni was working, she might know something.

Mike took a stool at the front counter. It was after 4 a.m. The place was pretty much empty except for a few cab drivers eating breakfast before checking out and a couple of cops drinking coffee. Mike was glad to see the cops. They were far enough away so as not to hear Mike when he asked Donni, "You know why the cops raided The Pink Slip?"

Donni didn't seem surprised at Mike's question. "Harassment," she said, "maybe boredom too." Donni smiled at her answer.

"That's it?" Mike said. "Come on, there's got to be more to it. You know more about what's going on in this neighborhood than anyone, Donni. Come on, does it take a big tip for a better answer?"

"Do I, Mike?" Donni said. "What's going on at your club, Mike?"

"Nothing," Mike snapped back. "Fuck it, I'm just curious because I don't know everything about everybody who comes into my place."

Donni smiled and looked over at the cops sitting at a booth near the back wall. "Looks like you're a little low on coffee, sweetie. Let me fill you up. Hold tight."

She came back with the pot, filling Mike's cup. "Someone said they were just really looking for someone, then decided to just have some fun and check out everyone. Those holding something they shouldn't have got arrested. Your place should pick up some business, Mike, since liquor control will shut them down for a while."

"The Repartee is a club, music club, not a bar, so likely no," said Mike, irritated, knowing that Donni liked to push people's buttons. "Looking for someone ... that's it? Who?"

"Don't know, sweetie. That's all I know." Donni stepped away as the dishwasher brought out clean silverware, cups, and plates from the kitchen. "Got things to do, sweetie, before the breakfast rush. Then, I'm out of here."

It could have nothing to do with the Repartee, Mike told himself. Nothing at all. But he knew Marcus and then Lewis would find out about it, and they might not think it had nothing to do with the Repartee. Mike figured Lewis would use his connections to find out the reason for the raid and then push him for what he knew. That's the game Mike told himself — ask the questions you already know the answers to. Lawyers and criminals play it all the time.

Early Friday afternoon, Marcus found out about the cops hitting The Pink Slip. One of the street dealers mentioned it when Lewis came by to pick up the proceeds from the day before. "What's ya think about that raid on 39th?" the dealer asked Marcus while leaning into his car.

"What you talkin' about, nigger?" Marcus said. "What shit on 39th?"

The dealer told Marcus about a couple of White dudes, regular customers, "cocksuckers," who drove by The Pink Slip, thinking about stopping in just as the cops were pulling up to the curb.

"Were the cops looking for anything or anybody?"

"Don't know," said the dealer. "Could have been the cops just having fun, fuckin' with the faggots. Shook up my two regulars, and they didn't stick around. In fact, they came to see me right after to get calm."

"Went down last night?"

The dealer nodded. Marcus stared out the windshield.

"Find out anything you know and let me know," Marcus said. "Your two regulars should know what went down when they come around again. Find out. Get on the good side of this, and maybe you in line for a bonus."

The dealer smiled and stepped away. Marcus made the rest of his collections and then headed to Truman Road. He stopped at the liquor store to call Lewis before doing the money count. After telling Lewis of the raid, Marcus asked, "Why didn't we know about this before it went down?"

"Because we go no interest in some queer joint, and why would we deal with those dick suckers?" said Lewis. "You want to start chasin' queer dealers? Dress up your image real good, huh."

"Ain't interested, Lewis."

"Yeah, I know, neither am I unless we keep it real down low. But that's for another day. How'd you find out about it?"

"One of my cats heard it from some of his White dude junkies who drove by when it was going down."

"What they say?"

"Nothing. My cat is checking it out."

"Good. Let me catch up with my bitches on the PD to find out. See if the stories jive when we know. Call me later, in a couple of hours, at Michelle's."

CHAPTER 43

Jensen came in early Friday morning to read the report. Frederick showed up around a half-hour later. "Anything worthwhile?" he asked after getting coffee.

"Not much," said Jensen. He was sitting at his desk, fingering through the report. "A couple of outstanding warrants, one guy holding some sherms, another with some bennies and coke, so it wasn't a total waste of time."

"What about the guy Pinky described? Was he one of them?"

"No one fits the description," said Jensen.

"Would it be worth it to talk to the derelicts who we're holding?"

"No, not yet. Need to be able to offer something, if there's any connection, and to know more. I'll get the names and rap sheets, but let's wait."

"What about sending Pinky back in tonight?" Frederick said.

"Not yet. He was just in there — too soon. Let's just let things stew and focus on what the sergeant will want to know. We'll ask him to make sure a patrol car cruises by regularly just to be seen."

Pinky was sprawled crosswise on his bed, arms out from his body, head hanging over one side of the bed, legs hanging over the other side. His brain was submerged in foggy over-indulgence, the only bodily rumblings coming from his intestines signaling that soon he would visit the toilet. Until then, a ringing was shaking apart Pinky's stillness.

Downstairs, the phone was ringing. Pinky stirred, trying to identify the noise. "Fuck," he said weakly. The phone kept ringing. Pinky rolled to his feet and stumbled downstairs, holding onto the railing with both hands. He answered, it was Gary.

"Can you work for a while?"

"Now?" Pinky said, feeling the bathroom visit coming on.

"Yes, I have to help a friend."

"Awww, man. I had a rough night."

"Your rough nights are every night, Pinky. I need your help. Please."

Pinky let the comment go. It was basically true. He didn't give a fuck.

"Okay, okay. I'll be there in a half-hour or so. Let me get it together." Pinky hung up and headed for the bathroom.

Gary was waiting outside the store when Pinky walked up. "Can you figure out how to run the register?" he asked.

Pinky waved his hand. "Yeah, don't worry, I got it. If not, I'll keep a running tab on paper. What's the emergency?"

"Well," Gary said hesitating, "he was arrested last night, and I have to bail him out. He's in the county jail, and he ... well, he won't admit he's gay — in the closet — so he might get hurt if I don't get him out."

"You mean he'll get burned at his job, right?"

"Pinky, he's a friend."

Pinkly looked at Gary. The guy was sincere, no bullshit. He thought of Vietnam, the string of guys in and out of the hooch. Some got close, some needed to be fragged, a bleeding heart in everything, be it death or joy. A shitstorm there, a shitstorm here. Everything.

"So, he's in the general population tank instead of a single cell. Yeah, some guys could have a field day with him if they pick up on it, and the COs won't give a shit."

"I have to go," said Gary, walking to his car. "Please, Pinky, no trouble."

"Yeah, yeah, I'll keep the place together and be real nice to the customers."

Pinky walked into the small store. He checked down each aisle to see if anyone was shopping. The store was empty. Pinky went to the cooler and grabbed a small bottle of tomato juice. He downed it quickly, stuffed the empty in the trashcan outside, and lit a cigarette. The sky was hazy. He blew smoke rings as he waited for a customer. He heard church bells in the distance. *A lot of good that does,* he said to himself.

Traffic at the store picked up throughout the afternoon. It was Friday, payday for many of the working people of the neighborhood needing something, be it a six-pack or box of laundry detergent. Some wanted to cash their payroll checks. Pinky had to decline. "Hey, I'm just fillin' in. Gary will be back before closing," he would say. Around four, Carolyn walked in the door, hesitating for a second when she saw Pinky behind the counter.

"Can you help me, sir?" she said in a mocking, high-pitched voice.

Pinky laughed. "So, I guess we're still on good terms, huh, sweetie?"

Carolyn kept her smile big, leaned over the counter, and kissed Pinky on the cheek. He blushed and felt a stirring in his pants. He wondered if her good mood had to do with sex, sex last night with Lawton. Pinky hoped not.

"More, more, please!" Pinky begged.

"Who knows, maybe someday," Carolyn said. She had one hand on her hip, with one leg cocked away from her body at the knee. She had painted her lips and wore big butterfly earrings. Her blouse was open low, the small, gold cross hanging between what she liked to show off. Pinky just stared. *She got laid,* he told himself. The two just looked at each other, and then Carolyn said, "Yeah, we're good, Pinky. Get me a pack of light 100s, will you?"

Pinky reached behind the counter and got the cigarettes. Carolyn put two dollars on the counter. She put the pack in her purse and then said, "How's Corey doing?"

Pinky was surprised at her question. Before he could answer, she added, "Did you hear about the big raid at the Slip last night?"

"Well, no. What happened?"

"The cops arrested a bunch of people. Lou's now worried that they'll hit his bar. He thinks they're looking for someone."

Pinky now understood why Gary had him work. "Apparently, Gary — the owner of this place — knew someone who got arrested ... thus, I'm here."

Carolyn didn't respond. She was at the front door, pushing it open. "Got to go to work, Pinky. Catch you later."

"Hey," Pinky called out, "you wanted to know about Corey."

Carolyn turned. The door was closed. Through the glass, she mouthed, "Maybe later," and she was gone.

Pinky wondered if Frederick and Jensen had called for the raid after his conversation in their car or if it was just a coincidence. Pinky decided they had taken his story seriously. He knew they would visit him again. He didn't want to go back into the Repartee to play informant. He hoped that by accident, the cops had found someone in the Slip who knew something. If not, they would be back in his face. He would stick to his story about the guy going into the Pink Slip. Their next target to lean on could be Corey. Pinky decided it was time to end the dance with the two cops. He was doing okay at Bain's, had a routine, and kept his serious drinking at home. *They could hassle me on the street, sure, but what else is new? I just have to make sure I'm not carrying any dope.*

Corey was in a real bind, and that worried Pinky. But worry was more a civilian luxury, something Pinky hadn't fully been tuned back into. The stink was still with him; the choice between dying for someone or killing someone hadn't left. In the bush, you didn't worry; you were just constantly scared or *dinky dau* — crazy. Corey put up with my shit, a guy who at times was fucked up like me, though in a different way, a dumb way ... like before I went in.

The good vibe in talking with Carolyn was gone. Pinky reached down to the bottom shelf where the cheap pints and half-pints were displayed. He picked up a pint of gin and slid it into his back pocket, then moved the bottles up to close the gap on the shelf. He would pay Gary later, he told himself.

CHAPTER 44

Corey was back at his house before Pinky. He had a few hours before he'd have to be at the Repartee. He got a beer from the fridge and sat on the couch. He stared out into the cluttered living room — piles of magazines and books, shirts hung over chairs, dirty glasses and dishes, albums propped up against the wall, ashtrays filled with cigarette butts and pot seeds, and dust on most everything but the plastic cover over the stereo's turntable. Such a picture usually didn't bother Corey or mean much. He always had somewhere to go and take what he wanted for another day. Working at the Repartee had been a big avoidance from the mess, from his place and his life. He always looked forward to working the door — the music, the banter with musicians, the women, the buzz from the beer, and the later anticipation that there might be some sort of after-gig party. It all got him up despite a long day delivering in the van. But not now.

Staring at the clutter before him, Corey could feel something was going to come down. Maybe he could ride it out, stay distant, play the cute party guy only interested in getting laid, getting high, and talking about his dreams. That seemed to bring on blind luck — others got busted, OD-ed, got the clap … whatever … and ol' Corey slid through it and on to the next job or next girl. Worked for years.

Then there was Carolyn. Saying his trouble with her was karma for all the selfish things he had done to other women didn't make his anger and hurt go away. *Karma was so much hippie shit,* and it didn't explain anything, and he didn't deserve it. *I love her, and that should be enough. Nothing happened with Becky because I love Carolyn.* "Fuck!" Corey screamed.

Pinky opened the front door. "Man, what's up? I heard you yell coming up the walk."

"Nothing. Just frustration."

"I can dig it," Pinky said, sitting down in the chair across from Corey. He then sat up and pulled the bottle of gin from his back pocket. He put it on the table next to him.

"Where you been, man?" Corey asked.

"Workin' the store. Gary called me this morning 'cause he had to bail some friend out of jail, so he asked me to work the store while he was gone. Fucker took most of the day, but he got him out."

"What did the guy get arrested for?"

"He got caught up in the raid on the Slip last night."

Corey looked puzzled for a moment. "The cops raided The Pink Slip?"

Pinky nodded as he broke the seal on the gin bottle. "Where you have been, man?"

"Working, like the rest of the world." Corey watched Pinky take a swig from the bottle. "Man, there's some OJ in the fridge — mix it with that. Watching you drink that stuff straight is going to get my ulcer going."

"You don't have an ulcer," Pinky said as he got up off the chair.

"I should with you living here."

Both men laughed. Corey took another drink from his beer.

Pinky came back into the living room with his drink and sat down in the chair. "You working the Repartee tonight?"

Corey nodded.

"Man, why don't you just give it up? I know you want to straighten things out with Carolyn. Give that a shot — fuck the club."

"A little direct, aren't you?"

"Well, I'm not known for my subtlety."

"You would think with a name like Pinky ... where'd you get that name, anyway?"

Pinky smiled at the question. "My mom, she always told me — from the time I could remember — 'You're in the pink.' She worried that I would get sick, so when I did as a kid, she would say, 'You'll be fine. You're in the pink.' Positive thinking or some sort of shit. I don't know. And when she would pick me up at school when I was a kid, I could hear her call, 'Here, Pinky, I'm over here.' The other kids heard her, so it kinda stuck."

"You don't tell too many people that story, do you."

"Not really. If someone asks, I usually say it comes from my first name, Peter."

"That's always what I thought."

Pinky took a drink of his gin. "We're getting all mushy here. Let's go back to your shit."

"Oh, Carolyn? Yeah, I miss her. Maybe in time, she'll believe me. I wasn't fucking anybody. But I got to shake it man, no different than before." Corey repeated the words *no different than before* back to himself in his head, trying to make them mean what he wanted them to mean. "But this raid on the Slip," he said to Pinky. "The shit keeps getting weirder around the Repartee. Hitting the Slip must have something to do with that place."

"Why?" asked Pinky. "They could be just fuckin' with the gays. Bustin' heads to prove a point."

"I don't know," said Corey. "As long as I've been in the neighborhood, the cops have never screwed around with that bar. It's still a neighborhood joint during the day, filled with old guys." Corey paused, watching Pinky screw and unscrew the lid to the gin bottle. "I'm going to work the door tonight. Maybe somebody will know something about what's going down."

"You're not still thinking of some big exposé on the bar, are you?" said Pinky. "Playing Joe detective?"

Corey stood up and downed his beer. He cocked his head and shrugged his shoulders. "I'm cool, Pinky, just curious. I'm going to shower."

"Yeah, right." Pinky took a small drink and looked around at the living room. "This place is a mess," he said aloud.

"What you say, Pinky?" Corey called out from behind his bedroom door.

"Nothing, man, just commenting on the living arrangements."

Corey didn't answer back. By the time he was out of the shower, Pinky had left. An empty glass and the gin bottle were on the table. Pinky was walking back to Bain's. Maybe Gary knew more. Gary had his head down, turning the pages of the daily newspaper, when Pinky walked in. "There's nothing in here about the police at the Slip, nothing."

"It's gay shit, Gary. They're not going to put in anything about the cops hitting a gay bar. Man, you should know that."

Gary looked up from the newspaper. He searched for emotion in Pinky's face. "It's anyone's bar!" There was irritation in his voice. "Why are you back? Need money?" His voice now had the added element of sarcasm. Pinky was a little taken aback. He had never heard Gary express anger or irritation or verbally jab at anyone.

"I'm sorry, man. But you know the newspaper in this town. Don't offend anyone, so don't print anything that will. The cops are never criticized, and the homosexuals are invisible."

Gary nodded and then hit a button to open the register. "How long were you here? Four hours?"

"Something like that," Pinky said. "Gary, I appreciate the quick bread, but I really came back up to see how your friend was doing and if you knew anything about why the cops raided the Slip."

Gary looked at Pinky directly while biting at his thumbnail. "I put up bail. He had some pills. Now he's afraid."

"Worried about people finding out about his job?"

Gary nodded. "My friend thinks it was more than harassment. He thinks the cops were looking for someone. Here." Gary pushed the money across the counter to Pinky. Pinky reached and took the money and folded the bills in his hand. "Who?"

Gary shrugged. "He's in there a few nights of the week and can't recall anyone new that hadn't been in there before." Gary then asked, "Why are you so interested? Been to the Slip?"

"Yeah, yeah, a few times. They serve late — quick drink before calling it a night."

Gary was smiling, a closed-mouth smile as if he was pleased with himself. *Great,* Pinky thought, *Now he thinks I dance both ways. What the fuck.* Pinky unfolded the bills and dropped four dollars on the counter.

"What's this for?" Gary said.

"I took a pint of gin earlier — didn't drink at your store. So now I'm covering it. Okay?"

Gary picked up the money. He held it for a moment, then said, "Please don't do it again, Pinky. I want to trust you."

"You can trust me. I came back up here, didn't I? Could have said nothing."

Gary sighed. "Might need you Saturday evening. I will show you how to close."

"What time do you close on Friday and Saturday?"

"Ten," Gary said. "You'll be out of here by ten-thirty. Come in at six."

"I'll see you tomorrow," Pinky said, and he walked out of Bain's. At the corner, he turned west toward Lou's.

Corey was out of the shower. He had time before heading to the Repartee and gave the thought about cleaning the living room a quick thought. *Would have,* he told himself, *if Carolyn was coming over after work. But she wasn't, so why? Maybe by Sunday; cleaning up as a means to move around and shake off a hangover.* He went to the kitchen and got a beer, sat down, and pointed the TV remote.

CHAPTER 45

Lou's was crowded when Pinky came in. Friday night, burger night. He found a stool open near the front door. Carolyn was hustling food orders and drinks. It took a few minutes before she saw Pinky. She brought him a draw without asking.

"Here, didn't think you were particular about your beer on me. I was kind of a bitch the other night."

Pinky smiled. "Thanks, sweetie."

Pinky watched her work. Smiling, throwing back her long black hair, putting her hands on her hips when someone made her laugh, making the men at the bar strain a little when they watched her lean over the bar sink to clean glasses, her breasts bouncing as she washed and rinsed, the gold necklace swaying, touching the side of each breast, making men's eyes dance. Pinky wondered if Corey had given her the necklace. She was a woman men could watch for hours, Pinky decided. Her whole body seemed to hold beauty. She wasn't spectacular in the sense of a model or airbrush magazine pinup, but total in her appeal. A woman to have kids with and never get tired of the sex. Pinky laughed at the thought, then said, "You're a jerk, Corey, for letting this go."

"Excuse me?" the guy next to Pinky asked.

"Sorry, man. Just talkin' to myself."

Carolyn brought over another beer. "Want to run a tab since you're a working man now?"

"Why not? Bring a shot of Crown also, and I'll even have that two-for-one burger, plain."

"Lordly, lordly, I do believe this will be the first time I've ever seen you eat."

"I'm trying to impress you with my normalcy."

Carolyn laughed. "That's definitely what I need in my life, normalcy."

"Maybe it will come back to you, sweetheart." Pinky was surprised at his sincerity.

Carolyn turned away, then turned back. She came in close to Pinky. "Tell him to call me, okay?"

Pinky's head snapped back. Carolyn went to put in his food order.

After two shots, four beers, and a burger, Pinky was content, almost mellow. That feeling had been long absent. It wasn't just an alcohol buzz, he decided, and the rush to be totally wasted hadn't appeared. He felt okay, almost a part of something that had nothing to do with Vietnam, ten years past. *Maybe it takes a decade to feel something else again*, he thought.

"How are we doing?" Carolyn said. "You look like you're in a daze. Maybe I need to cut you off."

"Feelin' normal, darlin'," Pinky said. "Tab me out, and can I have that second burger to go?"

"Not supposed to — you're supposed to eat it here. But I'll do it for you." Carolyn smiled at Pinky. He decided he wanted a woman like her.

Just as she placed the to-go burger on the bar in front of Pinky, Carolyn looked over his shoulder to the front door. Lawton walked in. "Must be the right place," he said. Pinky turned around. Lawton didn't look at him. He kept his eyes on Carolyn as he sat down a few stools away from Pinky.

"Tell me you're not still interested in him," Pinky said.

Carolyn turned back around after watching Lawton sit down. "No," she whispered. "I'm not. But he's a customer, and I have to be nice. And you need to be nice too, please, Pinky." Carolyn then walked over to Lawton.

The mellowness had left. Pinky half expected Lawton to come over and challenge him to a pool game. But his interest was in Carolyn. His eyes fixed on her body, on her every move when she turned away to pour a beer or cash someone out or walked down the bar to place a food order. It was a hungry look, a wanton look. Pinky had seen it before, guys out of the bush on R&R, a look without thought, an instinct seeking completion. Pinky thought about going down the bar and asking him if he wanted to play pool. But Carolyn wasn't looking Lawton's way and wouldn't likely unless he asked for another beer. She was tough and could handle things. Pinky tried to catch her eye. She didn't look his way. He downed the rest of his beer. Lawton was turned around on his stool, looking at the pool players in the next room. Finally, Pinky stepped off the stool and yelled, "See you later, Carolyn."

She stopped what she was doing and waved. "Remember what I asked you to do," she said.

Pinky smiled and mouthed the words "will do." He looked at Lawton before going out the door. He had turned around and sat with one hand holding his chin. He was looking into the mirror behind the bar. He had made his play, and nothing stuck. Carolyn was waiting for Corey to return. Pinky was sure of that.

Corey parked his van in front of the Repartee a little after seven. He was earlier than usual, but he wanted to see if Mike knew anything about the raid on the Slip. He figured he couldn't just ask straight out, but he knew he had to bring up the incident. Mike already was suspicious, and knowing about it without knowing anything more than anyone else in the neighborhood might take away some of that suspicion.

After the usual greetings and helping Becky wipe the tables and benches, and then bring beer to the bar to restock the coolers, Corey and Becky watched Mike count out the money for the night — both Becky's waitress bank and money for change at the door.

"Mike, did you hear about what happened at the Slip?" Corey said.

Mike handed Becky her bank and set the door money in front of Corey. "Yeah, I heard."

"What happened?" Becky asked.

Mike kept his eyes on Corey, but he didn't answer Becky. "The cops raided the place last night, and made some drug arrests," said Corey. "That's all I heard." Mike took his eyes off Corey. "That's it, isn't it, Mike?"

"Why would I know more? I don't live in this neighborhood. The cops made some drug arrests. With that, we've got to watch our Ps and Qs, got it? Liquor control might send someone in, so check IDs and don't tolerate any goof causing trouble. Now I'm going upstairs. Open the front door at eight."

"What about the band setting up?" Corey asked as he turned to look at the stage. The mics and monitors were in place.

"They came in this afternoon and set up," Mike said as he walked up the stairs to his office. "Open your eyes."

"He's in his usual bad mood, isn't he?" Becky said. Corey shrugged his shoulders. "Do you know who got arrested, Corey?"

Corey turned to Becky. "Why should I know? It's a gay bar at night. I don't drink there."

"Touchy, aren't we," Becky said. "Gee, everyone's in such a friendly mood." She then reached over the bar and grabbed a rag. She began wiping the waitress station. Corey took the door money and walked to his stool at the front. He picked up a Repartee monthly band schedule as he walked by one of the tables. Rotten to the Core was scheduled for tonight. "Great, a metal band," Corey said to himself. He checked his watch. Twenty minutes until showtime. It was going to be loud; better get a beer to begin to desensitize.

Mike sat at his desk. All day, he had expected Marcus would show up. Lewis had to know about the cops hitting the Slip, and Mike figured Marcus would come by and push to see what Mike knew. In a way, he was glad Marcus hadn't come by. He knew nothing, but he was sure the big guy would push hard until he was convinced that he knew nothing. But how long would Mike endure being pushed by Marcus? Mike opened the lower drawer of his desk. The Colt sub-nose .38 lay inside. He closed the drawer and went downstairs to the bar.

CHAPTER 46

Lewis picked up the phone on the second ring. "Where you calling from?"

"At the liquor store on Truman," Marcus said.

"Look around. Things normal, no unmarked PD lurking about?"

Marcus took the phone down from his ear, holding his hand over the one end. He looked out into the parking lot, into the street and traffic. He saw Latino mechanics in greasy overalls; Black women waiting for the bus; two homeless White guys shuffling down the sidewalk, their belongings swinging in plastic bags hanging from rusted grocery carts; nervous White women drivers stopped at the traffic light, their heads locked, eyes fixed on the road. "Man, I don't see anything suspicious. What now? I should be worrying about the pigs?"

"My connection downtown said the cops were looking for someone."

"What, me?" Marcus asked, his voice higher than usual. "What the fuck would I be doing in a queer joint?"

Lewis laughed. "You got something to tell me, big boy? You dressin' up real pretty at night?"

Marcus could feel his anger, but he didn't want to be disrespectful. "You're pimpin' me, man," he said in a calm voice.

Lewis continued to chuckle in a mocking way. Then he said, clearing his throat, "Yeah, man, I'm pimpin' you. Chill. I know your ways. They ain't looking for no big Black man, not in that place. But my spy says they're lookin'."

"What for?"

"She ain't sure, but she said two detectives from the drug unit are sniffin' around, and they arranged the raid."

"They on to us at the club?"

"Don't know. I don't think so, but I'm going to keep pressing my bitch for info. My guess is they're trying to see if they can get anyone to talk about anything in the neighborhood, or they're trying to get some snitch in place to get some information."

"Maybe they already got someone in place."

"I thought of that, so we're going to have to level some pressure, and see if everyone at the Repartee is a team player."

Marcus smiled. "What do you want me to do?"

"Nothing tonight. Stay away from the club. Don't know if they're watching that block. Let me think about it but I know it's time to bring in Mike and Russell my way. I'm tired of the lag. I've got to be satisfied. This shit needs to go down the way it should."

"How far on the muscle?"

"Not all the way," Lewis said. "But it's got to hurt, and they got to know their white-ass balls are in a vice. I ain't convinced about any one of those fuckers. You're going to have to put some fear in those honkies. Anyway, I'll get back to you. Call me after your run tomorrow — make it early and break your routine on the pickups and traveling about."

"You think I'm being followed?"

"My spy doesn't know if there's a tail on you. But check things out good when you go out."

"Okay." Marcus hung up the phone. He again looked over the cars in the parking lot and out on the street. He walked into the store. He needed cat food.

CHAPTER 47

Pinky was surprised that the walk back home was a little rambling. At one point, the curb seemed a little too high when he crossed Wyoming Street. The take-home burger went flying into the darkness as he hit the ground. Ah, *some dog will find it,* he said to himself as he got up. Fixing his eyes down the block, he did a mental count of his drinks at Lou's. *Let's see … five or six beers and three shots of Crown, or was it four? Damn, I'm getting to be a lightweight.*

Pinky looked down and saw his shadow. A bright light had fallen on him. He turned around, putting his hand in front of his face to block the light. Behind his hand, he could see the outline of a patrol car. He heard the car doors slam shut.

"Hey, buddy, how you doin'?" said a cop. "Bobin' and weavin' there."

"I'm okay. Just going home, that's all."

"Where have you been?" asked the other cop.

Pinky straightened up. "Been drinking, and I ain't driving."

"A little too much, don't ya think?" said the same cop.

"Yeah," said Pinky, his voice getting loud. "Why the fuck do you think I'm walking home?"

The two cops looked at each other. "Let's see an ID," said the first cop.

Pinky reached for his wallet, dropping it on the ground. He picked it up, teetering forward, and pulled out his driver's license. It was expired. One cop took the ID back to the patrol car. The other cop put his hand on Pinky's shoulder and said, "You need to sit down. Take a seat on the curb." Pinky slapped the cop's hand off and flopped down.

After five minutes, one cop got out of the car and pulled the other cop to one side. Pinky couldn't hear what they were saying. Then, one cop walked up to Pinky and said, "Did you know your license was expired, Mr. Grayson?"

"Well, yeah, maybe that's the reason I DONT OWN A CAR." Pinky felt a little sick. He wondered that if he threw up, the cops would go away.

"My partner here remembers you from that disturbance at Bain's Liquors some days ago. You were probably drunk then, I bet. You know, Mr. Grayson, public drunkenness is against the law. Maybe you need to dry out downtown." The cop then stood in front of Pinky, his hand on the nightstick hanging on his belt. "Okay, stand up, or we'll cuff you on the ground."

Pinky looked up at the cop. "Yeah, it was me," he said without moving. "And if you remember, OFF-FIS-SIR, two detectives came and took me out of your patrol car and sent you on your way. Call them, Jensen and Frederick, and see if they want me downtown."

The cop in front of Pinky stepped back and looked at his partner. There was silence. Pinky could hear his own heavy breathing. The cop by the patrol car shook his head. "Maybe next time, fuck wad," said the cop standing over Pinky. He threw Pinky's license at him and walked away.

"Have a nice day," Pinky said, picking up his license. The patrol car moved down the street. Pinky stood up and then flipped them off. "Assholes," he said aloud. It was three blocks to Corey's house, and he remembered the bottle of gin in the living room and figured there was beer in the refrigerator. He felt a little sober now.

Sitting in the living room, Pinky nursed the gin along with a beer. *This shit isn't going to get any better,* he told himself. *Jensen and Frederick are due to be in my face, and I really don't have anything. Giving up on me, they'll probably lean on Corey next, and that will just juice him up to find out more about the Repartee regardless. Won't take much to get him in a bind, and then some.*

Pinky decided he needed to get Corey out of the Repartee. He thought about telling him everything, how the detectives had leaned on him, how he'd fed them bullshit about the Slip, about how soon everything would come crashing down because the cops would eventually figure dope was going in and out of the place. *I could tell him Carolyn wants him back, and all he has to do is quit the Repartee. Will he do it? Does he love her that much? Shit, when was the last time I loved anybody?*

Pinky took a drink of his beer. He didn't know. *Corey's just now beginning to figure out he's been thinking with his dick for the last ten years. I can't be cupid here; got to be something else. Maybe just burn the place down.* Pinky laughed at the thought. He took a drink of gin. He remembered the flyers the Army would drop on villages from helicopters. A threatening note might work. Not that Corey was a chickenshit, but it would cause him to think, and give him a reason to quit without having to tell people the reason.

Pinky went around the house gathering up old magazines and newspapers. He made a pile on the coffee table. With letters from headlines and articles, he could string together a note and put it on the windshield of Corey's van. Yeah, it shouldn't be Mickey Mouse, or Corey might blow it off. It had to be short and serious. Pinky wrote out the note he was going to paste together. It read:

YOU BETTER WATCH YOURSELF, OR YOUR GOING TO GET HURT.

He cut and then pasted the letters onto a sheet of typing paper and folded it in half. He threw away the newspapers and magazines he used in the outside trashcan as he left the house to walk to the Repartee. Determination overrode the booze in his system.

Pinky stepped out into the street and came up on the driver's side of Corey's van so as not to be seen by the people leaving the club. Pinky slipped the note under the windshield wiper and turned and walked back up 39th Street. He felt good, and he felt tired. One more beer, then he'd crash. He wanted to be in his bed when Corey came home.

Corey had a pile of empty and half-full glasses dropped in a bus tub near the top of the stairs leading into the club. Fans of Rotten to the Core had done their best to sneak out booze as they left. He was sure a few people had gotten by, but he didn't care. It wasn't a fun night. The music was loud and bad, and there were ten guys for every girl. In Corey's mind, everyone seemed ugly and dumb. When it appeared the last customer had left, Becky came up and eyed the pile of glasses. "Gee, you caught a lot of people trying to take their beers out."

"Yeah, it was one of those nights ... like a bunch of newly graduated high schoolers straining their neck muscles as they kept time to loud, three-chord distortions."

"I don't know, some of them tipped real good," said Becky.

"That's because you were the only woman in the place worth looking at."

Becky frowned. "You really know how to build a girl up, Corey."

Corey watched her walk away. He picked up the tub of glasses and followed her to the bar. Mike was ready to do the nightly count, waiting for Becky and Corey's money. Becky separated out her bank and counted her tips. Corey handed the door money to Mike. "Good night, Mike?" Corey asked.

"I don't know. Maybe. Check the johns and walk the place. I want to get out of here quick."

Mike had the lights out in ten minutes and followed Corey and Becky down to the front door without saying anything. Out on the sidewalk, Corey asked if Becky's car was nearby. "In front of Nichelson's," she said. "I'm okay. Night."

Corey watched her walk away. *Now, why couldn't Carolyn have seen this instead of what she saw the other night?* He walked to his van and paused after seeing the note under the windshield wiper. He pulled it out, got in the driver's seat, and turned on the interior light. "What the fuck?" he said aloud. Corey looked around and then checked his side mirrors. There was no one around. He read the note again, and again, then laid it down on the seat next to him. He sat there a moment and then looked back to make sure the driver's door was locked. Corey went through the night's happenings. He hadn't gotten into it with anyone; he hadn't thrown anyone out. All and all, except for the constant hassle of stopping people from taking drinks out the door, nothing much had happened. No one had seemed mad at him; for metal heads, some had even been overly polite. *Maybe the note was meant for someone else.* No, Corey decided, it wasn't. *Maybe it was from that asshole Lawton. No, it wasn't his style; he'd just get in your face.*

Corey looked over at the note lying on the passenger seat. He started the van, did a U-turn, and drove up the street, checking his rearview mirrors. No one seemed to be following him. In his driveway, he looked around again before getting out. He picked up the note and went inside, locking the door behind him. As he sat on the couch fingering the note, he thought about seeing if Pinky was still awake. Then he decided not to. He was starting to believe it came from someone at the Repartee, maybe Mike. *Maybe his way of scaring me out of there. But why? Just fire me. Or maybe Mike knew nothing about it.*

Corey walked into his bedroom and threw the note on the dresser. He would go in early tomorrow and show Mike the note. Whatever Mike's reaction, Corey knew it was probably time to stop working at the Repartee.

Marcus finished his pickups before noon, checking at every stop whether he was being followed. Some of the corners were empty. Marcus made a mental note about who was missing, figuring he'd catch up with them later in the afternoon. He decided not to do a count at Millkin's. Instead, he pulled behind the barbershop and put the money he'd collected in the truck of the Cadillac. He then walked around the building to go into the barbershop.

Rupert Milkin was surprised to see Marcus and stopped cutting a customer's hair. Marcus looked around; three other men were waiting for a haircut and watching a baseball game on the TV. Marcus recognized them as from the neighborhood.

"Anyone been lookin' for me, Rup?"

"No one, Mr. Rudd. Need a haircut today?"

"Yeah, later. I'll be back." Marcus then went back to his car and drove to the liquor store on Truman. He called Lewis.

"Go over to that peckerhead Russell's apartment and get him," said Lewis. "He's probably still there suckin' on someone's dick. Have him call Mike and tell Mike I want to meet him at the club at two-thirty, then take Russell over to the massage house and lock him downstairs. He'll be shakin' — make him more scared."

"What about the bitches at the house?"

"I'll call over there and tell time to take the day off. Freelance out of their apartments if they want. The house should be empty when you get there with Russell."

"Then what?"

"Wait in the alley for Mike. You got your chrome, right?"

"Always."

"He shouldn't be holding. If he's got a piece, it's in his office. Anyway ... catch him before he goes in and take him to where Russell is at. Let them vegetate. I'll be by around three after I take my kids to McDonald's. And bro, what was the count today?"

"Haven't got there yet."

"Sounds like you had some absentees."

Marcus clenched the phone tighter. "You said to go out early. I did, and some of my people were still in their cribs."

"After this, Mike and Russell shit, go out again and get me a count tonight. Ah-right?"

Marcus didn't answer. Lewis let a few seconds go, then asked, "You hear me, nigger?"

"Yeah." Marcus hung up the phone. He got into his car and drove back to Millkin's. He got the money out of the trunk and put it in the back office safe and headed for Russell's apartment.

Russell was sipping tea and looking out the window when he saw Marcus' car pull up in front. He froze and thought for a moment about going down the back stairs. Russell knew Marcus was here because of the Slip. He unlocked the front door and sat down. He had nothing to hide. He decided he had to show that to Marcus.

Marcus turned the knob, found it unlocked, and stepped in. "Hello, Marcus," Russell said.

Marcus looked around the apartment. "You knew I was comin', motherfucker?"

"Saw you pull up," said Russell.

"You the only one here?" Marcus asked.

Russell nodded.

"Get your shit, you're leaving."

"Where are we going? To see Mr. Richardson?"

"None of your fucking business," Marcus said as he stepped toward Russell and then lifted him up off the chair. Russell squirmed away. "Let me get my jacket, okay?"

"Get it, but first, you need to call Mike and tell him to meet you at the club at two-thirty."

"Should I tell him you're with me?"

"Yes, motherfucker. Now do it, or I'm going to ram your fuckin' teeth down your fuckin' throat."

Russell walked into his kitchen to the wall phone. Marcus watched. It rang six times before Mike picked up.

"Mike, it's Russell."

"Yeah."

"How are you?"

Mike didn't respond.

"I'm here, err ... I'm here with Marcus. You know Marcus, don't you? And he asked me to call you to tell you..."

Just then, Marcus stepped closer and grabbed the phone from Russell. "Listen motherfucker. Be at your club by two-thirty. Mr. Richardson wants to talk to you and this fudge eater." Mike didn't say anything.

"You hear me, or do I have to come by your place and convince your ass?"

"I'll be there," Mike said. "Two-thirty."

Marcus hung up the phone. "Let's go," he said to Russell, grabbing him by the back of the neck.

"Huh, Marcus. We've got plenty of time. Maybe you would like some tea or something."

Marcus looked at Russell with surprise and disgust. "Are all you White people as stupid as you? You'll be lucky to be alive at two-thirty motherfucker. Now get your ass going."

Marcus pushed Russell out the door and kept pushing him at every turn as they walked out of the apartment building. With each shove from Marcus, Russell thought about running. He figured he could outrun Marcus. But by the time they got to Marcus' car, Marcus had his arm, squeezing his bicep. Russell knew this was about the Slip, but he knew nothing, and knew he had to stay calm and consistent to convince Mr. Richardson of that. Inside the Seville, Marcus pulled his Beretta from his waistband and put it on the seat between him and Russell. He looked over with a slight smile. Russell saw the gun from the corner of his eye but kept his head straight. "Go for it, mother-fucker. See how quick you are," said Marcus. Russell didn't move but felt pee dampen his underwear. Marcus let out a booming laugh and then said, "Put on your seatbelt. Don't want you to get hurt before we get there."

When Marcus pulled down the alley ten minutes later, and passed the Repartee to the massage house, Russell blurted out, "Why are we stopping here?"

"Shut up," Marcus said, getting out of the car after grabbing his gun. "Get out."

Russell couldn't move. Marcus grabbed him and pulled him from the car. He held his neck in a tight grip as he pushed open the back door to the house. He led him down a hallway, past several bedrooms with massage tables, to the basement door and pulled Russell down the stairs. An old sofa sat against one wall. Marcus pushed Russell onto the couch. Russell's face was pale, his hands shaking. In the strongest voice he could put together, he asked, "You going to kill me?"

Marcus stood in front of him. He brought his hands together, pushing down on the top of one hand, hearing the knuckles crack, then the other hand. "How come you a fag?" he said.

"What? What did you ask?"

Drawing the words out slowly, Marcus said again, "How come you a dick-sucking fag?"

Russell fell back against the couch. In a calm, almost confident voice, Russell said, "Because that's who I am."

Marcus didn't move for a moment. He couldn't think of anything to say back to Russell. He then turned to walk back up the stairs. "Wait," Russell said again. "You going to kill me?"

Marcus turned around. "Not unless Lewis wants me to," he said.

And he walked up the stairs. Russell heard the door shut and a key turn the lock.

Marcus drove his car down to the end of the alley and parked by the laundromat a block up from the Repartee. He walked back down the alley, staying close to the buildings, then stood against the back wall of the house. He was able to see part of the parking lot behind the Repartee and Nichelson's. He would see Mike when he parked and walk to the back door of the club. Marcus felt his .380 in his waistband and looked at his watch. It was ten after two.

Twenty minutes later, Mike pulled his car into the parking spot closest to the Repartee. He got out and walked to the club's back door. As he put in the key, he looked up the alley and saw Marcus walking his way. Marcus pulled up his shirt to show Mike his gun. Mike put his keys back in his pocket.

"I take it we aren't meeting here."

"No. Walk up the alley to the house. Be cool."

When they got to the back door, Marcus told Mike to open the door and walk down the hallway. At the basement door, Marcus told him to stop. He pulled his gun from his waistband and held a key out to Mike. "Open the door and then give me back the key." Mike did what Marcus asked and walked down the basement stairs. "Sit with your fag friend," Marcus said, pointing the gun at Russell. "Lewis will be here soon." Marcus walked back up the stairs and locked the door.

Mike looked around the basement. They sat on the only piece of furniture. Paint cans were stacked under the basement steps. In the center of the room was a drain. A stained, restaurant-duty sink on legs with a facet and attached hose was on the far wall. The basement ceiling was padded with thick insulation, and large pillows were duct-taped against the two basement windows. A single light bulb hung in the center of the room. Mike thought if he could imagine a torture room, this was it.

"They're going to kill us, aren't they, Mike?" Russell said. His voice was calm.

"No, they're not. They might hurt us, threaten us, but I don't think they'll kill us. They need me at least."

Russell looked at Mike in dread. "So, they'll kill me and not you. Jesus fuckin' Christ."

"Shut up, Russell. Who would miss you anyway?"

"My mother," Russell shrieked. "What about your mother, Mike? Would she even know?"

Mike turned to look at Russell. He thought about punching him, busting his mouth open. "Shut the fuck up. Nobody's getting killed, so shut up."

They sat there for a half-hour until they heard the lock turn and the basement door open. Lewis walked down the stairs with a smile, followed by Marcus. His gun was in his waistband. "Well, well, look at my business partners, my brother. Don't they look white with fear?" Both men then laughed as they slapped their hands together. "Lookie here, you boys got some explaining to do — don't they, Marcus? I mean, every time a Black man tries to trust a White man, it just doesn't fly. Always some shit tied to it, the White man always tryin' to get over."

"For real," Marcus said.

Lewis turned to Russell. "Russell, my man. What do you know about the Slip? Were you there when the cops came? You do go to that queer joint, don't you? Come on, Russell, tell me some stories about the Slip. Tell me the cops weren't looking for you there."

Mike turned and looked at Russell.

"I don't know what you mean, Mr. Richardson." Russell's hands trembled; his face was pallid. "Sure, I go there every once and a while. But I wasn't there then, and why would the cops be looking for me?" Russell turned to Mike. "Tell him, Mike. Tell him I'm trustworthy." Mike stayed quiet.

"Well, this is what I hear, Russell. The cops were looking for a guy maybe like you — nice threads, slicked-back hair, goatee, a real cool dude. But that wasn't you, huh, Russell?"

Russell put his head down. "No, Mr. Richardson, please, it wasn't me. I don't talk to cops."

"I hear ya, Russell. But I don't think Marcus is convinced." Lewis looked over at Marcus. He went and stood Russell up and took him across the room, a few feet from the drain. Russell stood there. His shoulders were slumped forward when Marcus hit him in the stomach. It was a strong hit, and Russell crumpled to the ground, coughing and vomiting. Marcus reached down and stood him up again. He steadied him by holding him by the neck, and then Marcus gave him a punch on the lower back, aiming for the kidney. Russell moaned. Next, Marcus tuned the ribs with quick punches, each side.

Mike started to stand up from the couch, then sat back down. "Don't you think that's enough, Lewis? He's got nothing to gain by hiding anything. You should know that."

"Maybe," said Lewis. "Break his arm, Marcus, and that will be it." Marcus stood Russell up, then took his right arm, pulled it behind his back, then jerked the arm up and out. Bones cracked. Russell screamed in pain, and Marcus dropped him to the floor.

Lewis and Marcus exchanged deadpan looks. Lewis turned to Mike. "Listen here, I hope you watched closely and learned something. 'Cause with you, Marcus just might cap your ass to expedite things. I know something is fucked up. The pigs are snooping around, and someone in the club or coming to the club is a snitch. Now if it ain't Russell, it ain't that skinny ass waitress you got, it ain't some regular who shows up for every gig, then maybe it that doorman of yours ... or it's you."

"It isn't me," said Mike.

"Okay. Then pull that joker in tonight before you open the doors, give him a test to see if he's a narc, then kick his ass out with a warning. If I hear a word on the street about our deal, he's dead. Marcus will be with you to make sure it all comes down clean. Am I making myself clear, White man?"

"You are," Mike said. "But are you going to kill him if he's a narc?"

Lewis laughed. "No, Mike. You offer him a line. If he does it, he's not a narc. But he's still gone. What did you say? He's a writer, motherfucker? Well, he ain't writing shit, especially if Marcus takes the ballpeen to his hands. That threat should make him get the message. If he doesn't do a line or makes some lame-ass excuses, he'll know he's been made, and then you somehow let him slip out. My guess is he's gone as soon as you both turn your backs. That means you get the coke out of there right then, and it means we fade out for a good while and not do anything. Word will get around quickly that writer-boy is a narc. With any luck, someone later on will cap his ass. 'All in all, it means you owe me a bundle, Mike, until the operation gets back on track."

Lewis looked over at Russell. He had passed out. Lewis then looked back at Mike. "Get his fag ass to the hospital. It's only a few blocks down the road. Say it was a bar fight. He'll likely need a few days there. Marcus will be back by four. Keep the back door to the club open."

Mike nodded and watched the two walking up the basement steps. He got Russell to a sitting position on the couch, then slapped his face to get him conscious. "Mike, I hurt bad," he said when he awoke.

"I know, man. Keep quiet about this. I'm taking you to the hospital."

Mike got Russell up on his feet and told him he had to walk. They both got up the stairs and down the alley to Mike's car. He drove to the nearby hospital to the emergency room. As he put him in a chair in the lobby, he told hospital personnel that he'd found Russell in an alley off 39th Street. He ignored the calls from nurses for more information as he went through the automatic doors.

When Mike got back to the Repartee, he went to the bar, made himself a tall vodka over the rocks and went upstairs to his office. He sat down and checked his wristwatch. It was three-thirty. He pulled open the bottom drawer of the desk and looked down at the .38. He could kill Marcus when he came through the door. Steady his aim on the top of the desk and pump two or three shells into his chest before he knew it. He'd have his gun with him, so it would look like self-defense ... say he was looking for last night's receipts. *With a good lawyer, I could get off any charge, and the publicity might even help the club. But what would Lewis do? That's the question. He wouldn't let it slide, and I owe him too much money for him to ignore everything. I could tell the cops about the whole arrangement, but there's no proof of Lewis' involvement and Russell and Becky would be too scared to say anything. It would be my word against him, and he could make me out as a racist, killing a Black man, and accusing another of being a drug dealer. It won't work. This whole thing is going down the tubes.* Mike took a drink.

CHAPTER 49

"Where have you been?" Corey asked when Pinky walked into the kitchen. Corey was stacking some lunchmeat onto a slice of bread.

"Did you leave enough for another one?" Pinky asked.

Corey slapped the bread together and left the meat on the counter. "Be nice if you bought some food every once and a while."

Pinky stepped around Corey and began to make himself a sandwich. "Touchy, touchy. I'll pick some food up tonight when I work at the store. As an employee, I got a tab and a discount."

"Work the store? I thought you burned that bridge."

"Nope. Gary's taken a shine to me of sorts. He's not such a bad guy. Plus, for some reason, Donni, the waitress down at Nichelson's, put a word in for me. At least that's what Gary said just now when I was up there getting cigarettes and him showing me how to close."

"Wow, man. You're getting to be a real community member," Corey said through bites on the sandwich. His tone bordered between complimentary and sarcastic.

Pinky smiled at Corey. "Weird, ain't it? But I'm going down to Nichelson's after I close the store. I think she's a vet or was a vet when she wasn't a she ... You know what I mean."

"Yeah, I've noticed that faded USMC tattoo on her forearm. Think she did a tour?"

"Maybe. Maybe she — or he — did the 'nam. I don't know." Pinky stared at the meat on his bread. Corey stopped eating his sandwich and stood behind Pinky. They shared the stillness. Then Corey said, "Might be good to get to know her, you know, shared experiences and all that."

Pinky didn't answer and reached into the refrigerator and got two beers. He handed one to Corey. "You're leaving kinda early to go down to the club," Pinky said.

Corey looked at Pinky. He knew it was time to leave Vietnam alone. "Yeah. Need to talk with Mike about something."

"Something happen?" Pinky asked.

"Yeah, something did, but I'm not going to talk about it right now. But I'm pretty sure I'm quitting the place."

"That's good," said Pinky. He was smiling. "You might tell Carolyn that when you do."

Corey froze. He knew she had asked about him. "Yeah, I might," said Corey. "You seem pretty happy about me quitting. You'd think you and I were dating."

Pinky laughed as they toasted each other. Then Pinky walked into the living room, taking the remainder of his sandwich and beer. "Going to sack out for a while. See you later," he said, going up the stairs.

"Okay, man," Corey yelled out loud enough so Pinky could hear him. He finished his sandwich and took another drink of his beer. He checked the kitchen clock above the refrigerator. It was a little after four-thirty. Carolyn went in at five to Lou's. Corey thought about catching her getting out of her VW to tell her he was quitting the Repartee. *How would she react? Would she throw her arms around him and kiss him hard, my penis rising in his pants like an anxious swimmer reaching for the surface after a deep dive?* Corey chuckled at his metaphor. *Or she could stare at him in disgust, giving him that look of tight-lipped contempt that only a woman made hard by hurt could give.* "Got to write this down," Corey said aloud, pleased with himself.

He downed the rest of his beer and went into his bedroom, but before he could find a pen and paper, Corey again saw the note Pinky had left on his windshield. He opened it again and read it. YOU BETTER WATCH YOURSELF, OR YOUR GOING TO GET HURT.

Somebody needs a lesson in grammar, Corey told himself, and he walked out to his van, taking the note with him.

This early, Corey knew the front door would be locked at the Repartee. He walked around back and was surprised to find the back door unlocked. He'd figured he would have to call Mike from the payphone in front of Nichelson's to get in. At the bottom of the stairs leading to Mike's office, Corey stopped and hollered, "Hey, Mike, it's Corey. Can I come up?"

A minute later, Mike opened the door and waved Corey up. When Corey stepped in, he saw Marcus sitting on the couch. "You busy?" Corey asked.

"No. Sit down, Corey." Corey didn't move, standing in front of Mike's desk behind the chair Mike had pointed at. He figured Marcus was the guy Becky had mentioned.

"Don't want to take up your time, Mike, but I need to show you something." Corey unfolded the note in his hand and placed it in front of Mike. He read it and then looked over at Marcus.

"What is this?" Mike said.

"I don't know, Mike. I found it under my windshield last night when I got off." Corey then gave Marcus a quick look and said, "You tryin' to tell me something, Mike? If you want to can me, just say so." His voice had gotten more forceful.

Mike fingered the note and kept glancing over at Marcus. "It didn't come from me, okay, Corey? I don't operate that way. Maybe it's someone trying to be funny, or maybe you pissed someone off while working the door. I wouldn't worry about it. Okay?"

"Yeah, that's what I thought," said Corey. "But why?" He then looked at Marcus.

"Who knows why people do the things they do," said Mike. "I think someone is just pimpin' on you. Look, it's early for you to be here. Calm down and come back in an hour, and we'll talk more. I've got some business with this gentleman here. He might be redoing the johns."

Redoing the johns, my ass, Corey thought. *The guy looks like he could bend iron with his teeth.* "Okay, Mike. I want to talk more. I'll come back around six."

"Good, Corey," Mike said, and he reached out to shake Corey's hand. Corey was taken aback. Mike had never shaken his hand. Mike then put his arm around Corey and led him to the office door. He stood there as Corey went down the stairs and waited to hear the back door shut. He then turned to Marcus. He pointed to the note on his desk. "This your idea or what?"

Marcus got off the couch slowly and went over and picked up the note. He read it, then tossed it back on the desk.

"Somebody is tryin' to play us, man," Marcus said.

"How?"

"I don't know. Let me call Lewis and see what he says."

Marcus called Lewis' home number, something he wasn't supposed to do unless it was really needed. Lewis was irritated and thanked "Mr. Rudd" for calling and said he didn't have time to talk because he had to get some medicine for his kid at the grocery store. Ten minutes later, Marcus called the number of one of the payphones outside the grocery store. Lewis listened to Marcus talk about Corey coming in with the note, and he then had him put his voice on speakerphone in Mike's office.

"Nothing's changed, motherfuckers. You're still going to test out that Corey dude. He might be the key. Now maybe the note signals that we're on to him, and it's his cue to leave, using the note as an excuse to cover his ass. Maybe the real person who wants to know our business left the note to get his ass out of the way. Maybe that fucker Russell wrote it. I don't know."

"He didn't," Mike interrupted. "The guy's hurting bad. Come on, Lewis. He's got no reason to."

"Right on, big mouth White boy. Ain't none of your fuckin' business. You were spared, but that might not always be so."

Marcus looked at Mike. His eyes brightened.

Lewis went on. "But get that Corey fuck out and get rid of the stash there. Capeesh, motherfuckers? Call me tomorrow, Marcus, and get me a count, nigger." Marcus frowned at Lewis' request. Mike noticed but didn't ask what Lewis had meant.

Mike clicked the speakerphone off and hung up the phone. "I'm getting a drink. You want one?"

"Don't drink," Marcus said.

"You want a Coke, some water, anything?"

Marcus shook his head. He leaned back on the chair and spread his legs out in front of him. Mike noticed how tight his slacks were around his thighs and that his stomach was flat under the silk shirt he wore. Marcus put his hands on his knees, tilted his head back, and closed his eyes. "Suit yourself," Mike said. "I'll be downstairs at the bar having a drink or two."

CHAPTER 50

Corey walked to Nichelson's. He ordered coffee and chocolate cream pie. He had almost an hour to kill. *Why did Mike want me to come back? Maybe because of that big Black dude in the room — secret business.* Corey looked around as he waited for his pie. He found the day's newspaper and began to scan the headlines. Three refills later and having picked through the newspaper, Corey checked the time. The urge to quit had faded from him. Maybe Mike was right; the note was nothing. He paid for the pie and coffee and walked back over to the Repartee.

Mike's office door was open when Corey looked up from the foot of the stairs. At the top, Mike told him to shut the door and sit down in the overstuffed chair in front of his desk. Marcus was still there, seated on the couch.

"I don't think there's anything to the note, Corey. Just someone having fun with you, that's all."

"Really, Mike? Do you know something I don't know?"

Mike ignored the comment. "Corey, let me introduce a business associate," he said, pointing over to Marcus. "Marcus here is joining our operation."

Corey looked over at Marcus. "Howdy." Marcus didn't respond but instead stood up and moved behind Corey. He wondered, *what kind of hick shit is "howdy"?*

"The big man likes to stretch his legs," said Mike. Corey was feeling uncomfortable. "Relax, Corey. Let me offer you something to set the mood. We're talking business here." Mike reached into the top drawer of the desk and brought out a flat tray with four lines of cocaine on it. "Little early for me, Mike. Thanks."

"Come on, give you a good buzz and set you right for working the door."

"About working the door, we need to talk about that, Mike." Just as Corey spoke, Marcus grabbed him, stood him up, and ran his hands around Corey's waist and down his back. He then turned Corey around and put his hand on Corey's chest, moving his hands out, touching both sides of Corey's body and under his arms. He did it so quickly that Corey didn't react right away.

"What the fuck!" Corey said, breaking away from Marcus. What's the deal feeling me up like that?" Neither Mike nor Marcus spoke. Corey looked at one and then the other. "Oh, now I get it. You think I'm a cop or undercover. You think I'm a fucking narc wearing some sort of recorder" Mike shrugged. "Okay, I'll show you," Corey said, and he went over to Mike's desk, held the shortened straw to his nose, and took in two lines. His head went back as a rush of pleasure hit his brain. Mike looked at Marcus with an expression of satisfaction. They waited for Corey to re-focus. "Nothing wrong with that shit, is there, Mike?" Corey said when he felt himself moving away from the coke high.

"Nope. Just good shit, as you've found out."

Corey sat back down in the chair. The buzz was still on.

Marcus moved close to Corey again. Mike held up his hand and said, "Corey, we're done. You're not the doorman anymore. In fact, you aren't welcome here at the Repartee, not even as a patron. Understand? You dig?"

Corey fixed his eyes on Mike. He felt Marcus standing behind him.

"You show up; you could find yourself in a ditch. And understand this, Corey, you say nothing about leaving here as the doorman other than you quit. No writing articles, no journal notes, no shooting the bull about the Repartee. You clam up and be safe. Otherwise, Marcus here will light you up real bad. If you wonder how bad, go visit Russell at the hospital down the street to get the picture."

Corey couldn't breathe. He wondered how badly Russell was hurt. He started to raise himself out of the chair, but then felt Marcus grabbed his arm and pull him over the back of the chair. At the office door, he pushed Corey. Corey stumbled but maintained his balance going down the stairs. Marcus followed him. At the club's back door, Marcus pushed him out and said, "You better be down with this honkey, or you'll be tattered so hard your mama won't recognize you." His voice was low and calm.

Corey stepped back from the doorway and just nodded. He could feel the sweat rolling down the middle of his back. The coke high had disappeared. He walked out into Nichelson's parking lot toward his van, looking back at the Repartee once or twice before getting in. He opened the glove box and got a cigarette. His hands were shaking. He got it lit, took a deep drag, and then dropped his head onto the back of the seat. It was done. He was out of there. He had no doubt Marcus was a bad man. As for Mike, it wasn't about the music; it was about the money. Now, they were pushing the dope. Corey didn't want to know. Eventually, the word would get around anyway and drift back to the cops. He just hoped he would have some distance from the club by then — let the suspicions of betrayal fall on someone else. Yet, more people got popped for weed and psychedelics than coke in this town, he reminded himself. *Fucking lawyers do it — why not the cops?*

Corey went back to his house. Pinky had gone to work at Bain's. He thought about going up to Lou's to see Carolyn. *Hey, babe,* he would say walking in, *I nearly got wasted by a huge Black dude, but I quit the Repartee. Love me now?*

Corey didn't chuckle at the thought. He looked in the refrigerator. He counted the beers — seven, plus the bottle of peppermint schnapps. He then went into the living room, reached under the couch, and pulled out a tray with a bag of pot and some rolling papers.

He took it into the kitchen, got a beer, sat down, and began to roll a joint. In all, there was enough to get him fucked up good.

Pinky came to the house around ten-thirty after closing Bain's. He found Corey nearly passed out on the couch. Five or six empty beer cans and a bottle of schnapps were on the coffee table. Pinky was glad he'd picked up some beer. "And I got some lunchmeat, too," he said to the sprawled-out Corey. The sarcasm had no effect.

"And the note, that was from me," Pinky said, standing over Corey. Corey didn't move, not quite conscious. *There, I told him,* Pinky said to himself. He then put the beer in the box and got a new pack of cigarettes from a carton in the freezer. He was sure Donni was working at Nichelson's, and he wanted to say thanks. Pinky felt good. *My shit is on a roll,* he said to himself.

Corey woke up around 2 a.m. and crawled into his bed. He stayed there through most of the day. Pinky went down to Bain's that afternoon just to talk with Gary and hang out. Pinky wanted to know if Gary knew Donni. He'd known her for a long time, even when she was known as Donald. At one point Carolyn came into the store to buy cigarettes and to see if Pinky was there.

"He did?" she said when Pinky told her Corey had quit the Repartee.

"Yeah, I think it was a hard thing to do," said Pinky, "'cause he pretty much got wasted bad last night at home."

Carolyn asked Pinky if she should drop by his house. "Be cool, lady," Pinky advised. "Let him get the Repartee out of his system, and he'll come around. When are you working next?"

"Tuesday, day. Lou is going to his doctor's."

"I'll mention it to Corey."

Pinky did later that day. Corey just nodded as he stared at the television. When Tuesday came, Carolyn waited but Corey didn't show. He knew if he saw her, she would ask about how Mike reacted when he told him he was quitting. Corey didn't want to lie. He knew Carolyn would see through it, and he didn't want to tell her he'd been threatened, that if he showed up at the club, he'd likely get his ass pounded. Corey figured if he gave it time before he saw Carolyn, the less she would ask about how he had quit the job. But it was hard. He wanted to see her.

One afternoon the following week, when Corey was at his house in between delivery runs, Jensen and Frederick knocked on the front door. They asked for Pinky.

"He's working at Bain's," Corey said. "Who are you guys?"

Jensen and Frederick looked at each other. Jensen pulled out his badge. "You his roommate, the guy who works at the club on 39th?" he asked.

"Not anymore. Quit there last week."

"Problems up there?" Frederick asked.

"No problems. I just quit." After dealing with Marcus, Corey didn't feel intimidated by the cops. "Now, if you want to see Pinky, he's up at Bain's. Me, I got to get in my van and get back to work." Jensen and Frederick turned and walked back to their car. They were still sitting in front of the house when Corey pulled out in his van. They didn't follow him.

"Looks like we're at a dead end," Frederick said.

"Yeah, maybe so. If he's still working at Bain's, it means any leverage we had to get him to cooperate is gone, and if his roommate isn't working at the Repartee, we're basically back to square one."

"How are you going to tell the sergeant, Jensen?"

"He wasn't too keen on focusing on the Repartee anyway. He liked hitting the Slip 'cause the arrest count went up with all the fags holding dope. Looks like we're back to leaning on the street lowlifes to get some traction."

"So, Marcus skated out?" said Frederick.

"Man, that thug has been skating for years." Jensen started the car, and the two detectives began debating where to get something to eat.

CHAPTER 51

That night, Corey told Pinky about Jensen and Frederick. Pinky wasn't concerned. "Ancient history," Pinky said. Corey didn't ask further. "I'm going up to Lou's to see Carolyn," he said.

"About time," said Pinky. He was smiling.

When Corey walked into Lou's, Carolyn was at the end of the bar. She turned and sauntered up to where Corey stood at the bar. "Hello, stranger," she said.

Corey reached behind her neck, making sure his hand was under her hair, and pulled her to him. He kissed her hard. She touched his face as they kissed. It was a long kiss. A few people clapped, and someone yelled, "Get a room." When they separated, Carolyn said, "Maybe I should quit my job and run away with you, stranger."

"Naw," Corey said. "One of us needs a decent job."

Corey stayed through her shift. Carolyn urged people to drink up as the closing time got closer. People didn't object. They knew the reason why.

That night, Corey and Carolyn found every inch of the other's body. Everything was touched by hand, by foot, by their lips. He didn't have to talk to her. She knew what he was saying, and at times, when he touched her, she would tear up a little. When he finally got inside her, she had an orgasm almost immediately, lifting her pelvis up, coming back down, eyes closed, smiling, his head next to hers, her legs around his, the back of her ankles rubbing up and down his calves. They made love a second time and then again in the morning. They hardly exchanged a word but never stopped touching one another.

The next day, she bought her stuff back to Corey's. Pinky complained that he couldn't walk around in his underwear anymore, but with his hours increasing at Bain's, he knew it was time to start considering a move of his own. When she didn't work, Carolyn had dinner for Corey when he ended his delivery day. He brought her home little gifts — flowers, body lotion, imported hand cream, and chocolate. But he found himself unable to drive by the Repartee. He wasn't sure if it was anger or fear. Either way, Corey didn't like it. He had never been a tough guy. His gamesmanship had always been about smooth talk and scintillating praise. Those tactics left him in control. Banishment from the Repartee gave him no control. What was it his mother always used to say to him in quoting Rabbi Heschel? "Self-respect is the root of discipline." And Corey needed discipline to keep Carolyn and to be a writer.

On a Saturday three weeks after the threat from Mike and Marcus, Carolyn asked if Corey was going to come by later at Lou's. He told her he had something to do. She wasn't worried about what he was doing; she knew he loved her.

"Be there by one to help close," she asked.

"Yes, baby, I will," he said.

Around ten, before Pinky got home after closing Bain's, Corey drove his van past the Repartee, turned, and parked in Nichelson's lot, closer to the street than the alley. He walked around the building, up the street, and into the Repartee. At the top of the stairs, Russell was working the door. He had a full cast on his right arm. Island Sound was playing, and the place was near capacity.

When he saw Corey, Russell's eyes widened, and he said, "Man, you can't come in here."

"What's the cover, Russell?"

"You can't come in, Corey. If Mike or Marcus sees you, you'll be in the dumpster out back."

"Here's five bucks. That ought to cover it." Corey walked in as Russell got off his stool and tried to grab Corey's arm. Corey pushed Russell away and then moved down the aisle to settle against the wall halfway between the door and the bar. With the crowd before him swaying and dancing in place to the reggae sounds, there was no clear sight to the bar. Straining a bit, Corey saw Mike working the bar and, looking to his left, he saw Marcus in the shadows near the bar. Neither saw him. Relaxing a little, he watched the crowd and saw Russell looking around, trying to find where Corey stood. The beat was infectious, and Corey found himself taking in the music some. A minute or so later, Corey turned his head, and Mike stood in front of him, his face into Corey's.

"What the fuck are you doing here? Didn't you understand?"

"What are you going to do, Mike? Call the police?" His voice held contempt.

Mike pushed him up against the wall and held him there, his hand hard against Corey's chest. Mike felt a hand on his shoulder. "Mike, don't," came a voice. "People are watching you." It was Becky. Mike lifted his hand from Corey. "It's your funeral, fuck head," and he walked back to the bar.

"What are you doing, Corey?" asked Becky. "You trying to ruin everything?"

Corey straightened up. "No, I'm not," he said. "But it's a public place, isn't it?" The anger didn't leave Becky's face. "This isn't all about you," she said and walked away. The band continued to play. A few people nearby saw what had happened. None thought much of it. The band kept playing, the beat near hypnotic.

Corey didn't hear the music. Panic was starting to well up. He moved toward the bar. Now, he wanted to apologize to Mike; he wanted to be able to be part of the scene again. As he moved into the most crowded part of the club close to the bar, Michelle, Lewis' girlfriend, stepped in front of him. "Hi, cutie. You're someone I'd like to get to know," she said while cupping his genitals in her hand.

Corey stepped away. Over Michelle's shoulder, he saw Marcus making his way through the crowd. Corey looked at her, a look of disgust on her face. The realization that he was trying to step back to what he once was came over him. "What makes you think I want to fuck you?" Corey said it as loud as he could. People nearby stopped dancing and talking and looked at Michelle. Corey turned around and moved to the door. Russell stood at the entrance but moved aside when Corey was on him. Down the stairs and into the street, Corey hurried to Nichelson's. By The Pink Slip, he looked back, but Marcus had yet to step onto the sidewalk. He was breathing hard when he sat down at the counter. Donni, with a perplexed look, came over with a cup of coffee.

"Just rob a bank, sweetie?" she asked.

Corey smiled as he caught his breath. "That might have been the easy thing to do."

"Hopefully, you ain't running from that sweet girl who works at Lou's. Corey shook his head and then looked over his shoulder. "You going to eat, honey?" Donni asked as she set a glass of water in front of him. She then looked up, and Corey turned. Marcus walked over to the counter and sat two stools away from Corey. He glared at Corey and didn't look at Donni when she brought him a glass of water and a menu.

"Can I help you, sir?" Donni asked.

Without looking at Donni, Marcus said, "No."

"Sir," Donni said, "you have to order something, or I have to ask you to leave."

Marcus turned to look at Donni. His growl softened, and a small smile formed on his face. "What the fuck are you? One of those transvestite bitches with a dick?"

Donni smiled, then turned and picked up a carafe of water sitting on the burner behind her. It was the hot water used when a customer ordered tea. She turned and calmly poured the water on Marcus' hand, which was laid outstretched on the counter. He jumped back, shaking his burning hand. He started to reach for his gun at his waistband when he saw two policemen stop eating and raise their heads in a booth in the dining area. Donni saw them, too. She smiled and waved, then formed her hand in the "okay" sign. She turned back to Marcus, leaning in close to him.

"Sorry about that, Mr. Rudd. Your name is Marcus Rudd, isn't it? You know that's a nasty burn; it might be second-degree and blister up. Maybe you should call Lewis, Mr. Richardson, whom I'm sure cares a great deal for you. He could send a car if you can't drive. If not, maybe Mike, Mike Smith, the enterprising owner of the Repartee, might have some salve in his office. I'm real sorry, Mr. Rudd."

Corey stared at Donni. She smiled back at him and then looked again at Marcus. He squinted at Donni, trying to see if he knew her or know how she knew his name. He then glared at Corey and said, "Watch your back, motherfucker." And as he stood up, still shaking his hand, Donni said, "You too, Mr. Rudd."

Marcus said nothing. He pulled his coat close. Donni and Marcus stood staring at one another. A few others in the restaurant stopped eating, watching the two. Then Marcus walked away. Donni put the carafe back on the burner and asked Corey, "You ready to order, honey?"

Corey had a puzzled look on his face. "How do you know all that? I didn't know that — his last name and the name of the other guy, Lewis, whatever."

"Oops, got a customer down the other end." Donni walked down the counter. Corey's eyes followed her, his mouth agape. When she returned, she said, "What was it you asked?"

Corey moaned, and his body went slack. "Come on, Donni."

Donni stepped closer to Corey. He looked up at her, and she glanced around the restaurant. "Your roommate is Pinky, right?" Corey nodded. "Well, Pinky, as you know, works for Gary of Bain's Liquors." Donni's voice was now girly-like. "And Gary has a close friend who got caught up in that Pink Slip raid, remember?" Corey nodded furiously. Donni put one hand on her hip and turned a foot to one side. "Well, Gary bailed his friend out of jail. That friend had just broken up with Russell. You know Russell Manger, don't you?"

"Yeah, yeah," Corey said.

"Well, Russell told that friend about Marcus and Lewis and Mike and what was going on at the Repartee. That friend told Gary, Gary told Pinky, and since Pinky and I are forever vets together, he told me. Information is gold, sweetie, and so are friends. Now, you going to eat?"

Corey stared at Donni.

Donni waited a moment and then picked up the menu. "Guess not. Coffee's on me, Corey. I would advise you to stay away for a while. The Repartee won't last long anyway. Now go see that pretty young thing at Lou's. By the way, how is Lou doing health-wise?"

"I'll find out and tell Pinky," Corey said, getting off his stool. He stood, still staring at Donni.

"Close your mouth, honey," said Donni.

Corey smacked his mouth close but kept his eyes on her.

Donni smiled and pushed up her hair at the back of her neck. "Got a date at the beauty parlor tomorrow," she said. The bell rang at the food pickup window. Donni turned, waved her hand at Corey, and walked down the counter to get a customer's order.

CHAPTER 52

Marcus thought he could wait out Corey and get him when he came out of the diner. Wailing on that, she-freak behind the counter could wait. But his hand burned, pushing away any immediate plan he had. Driving back to his apartment, Marcus forgot for now about getting revenge. Instead, the burn had him remembering the time he put his hand on a still-hot burner on Aunt Eve's electric stove while trying to snatch a cooling chicken leg. *What did she put on my hand? Petroleum jelly.* Marcus smiled. He had a jar of it in the drawer of his nightstand, kept for easing into a woman who liked a backdoor entry.

The throbbing hadn't lessened when he found the jelly and rubbed the top of his hand, covering it with gauze and white medical tape to hold it there. Thoughts of Aunt Eve hadn't left. The lights brought a couple cats to his patio door. It was a returning-home greeting he was beginning to like. He filled a bowl of dry food and stepped out into the night. "Damn, you guys keep hangin' here, and I'm going to have to give out names." Marcus scrutinized the kitties as they ate, thinking of names that might match them.

He decided it was too late to call Lewis. He didn't want to have to explain what happened. The hand would heal in a few days, and with things running fairly smooth at the club, it's unlikely Lewis and Marcus would meet in person. He also figured that Mike wouldn't call Lewis about him not being on hand when the club closed. Sure, Mike would ask him about Corey and what he did or didn't do. Marcus also figured Mike was angling to score some points by keeping his mouth shut so that he could cash in later. *Fat chance, honkey, 'cause I don't do favors for no White man.*

Marcus wouldn't mention Donni. She was his personal mark, something he would take care of on his time. But he needed to know what Lewis wanted to do about Corey. Having his little white ass running around was getting aggravating.

Marcus flopped down on the couch and reached for the TV remote. He looked over at the patio door. The cats had left, emptying the bowl. He thought about coaxing one of the cats inside. Maybe when it starts getting cold. Aunt Eve had her cats both in and out.

Sunday was no different from other days for Marcus. He still had to collect the proceeds from the street dealers and then head to the barbershop to count the money. Lewis would call him there in the afternoon.

"Everything good at the club last night?" Lewis asked.

"No problem. A lot of shakin' asses to the reggae band," said Marcus.

"White asses, right? And a white band playing Black music. Is there a brother in the band?"

"I didn't see one, but I got distracted. That White boy we scared off got some balls and showed up."

"How far you take it?"

"Didn't have the chance. He skated out before I got to him."

Lewis kept silent. Marcus knew he was thinking about what he had said. "You let him know you saw him, didn't you?"

"Yeah, that's why he ran."

"Okay. Let it go for now. Let him think we're around, and make the paranoia sink in. See how it plays out. I need to get the money train in motion with Russell out there, making the expansion happen. Right now, I don't need anybodies connected to the club turning up."

"I can dig it," said Marcus.

They continued talking about the money count from Saturday and if there were any problems out on the street. Marcus never mentioned his hand or Donni. It was one of the few times Marcus had kept anything from Lewis. It didn't make him feel any guilt, but keeping something to himself, separate from Lewis, did give him a sense of detachment from him. Before that, never telling Lewis about his fondness for cats had given him that feeling.

CHAPTER 53

Within a week, Marcus' hand had healed. He began watching Nichelson's, tracking the days and hours Donni worked. Marcus was in no hurry to even the score and even thought about letting it go. Taking out a transvestite, if that's what she was, wouldn't prove much, or likely get much attention from the cops, and it wouldn't do much for his street cred if somehow it became known he had taken her out. It wasn't until one of Lewis' street dealers asked about his hand that Marcus decided he had to rectify the situation.

"What did you hear?" Marcus asked the dealer.

Seeing his anger, the dealer stepped back and said, "Nothing, Mr. Rudd, nothing."

"Don't give me any shit, or I'll cap your ass right now."

"It's a rumor ... that some freaky-looking waitress at that all-night midtown diner poured boiling hot water on you, and you did nothing. I figure it's bullshit. I know you don't let anyone be that bold, Mr. Rudd. Please, I'm not trying to be disrespectful. I'll make sure that if I hear about it that people know it's shit."

"You do that, junkie, or I'll do your face in so that you won't be seeing or hearing nothing."

The rumor put Marcus in a dilemma. Kill her, she's found, and the rumor becomes true. Not kill her, and he would have to live with the contempt he received from her. He wasn't going to do that.

A few days later, Donni got off her 11 p.m. to 7 a.m. shift and walked a few blocks to a grocery store. It was on the way to her apartment. It was a bright, sunny morning. Traffic was light as usual, which meant the catcalls she sometimes got were absent. With two bags of groceries, Donni made her way from the store toward her home. With traffic now close to being rush hour, she decided to cut through some alleyways to help avoid any possible hassles from motorists.

Marcus left his car in the grocery store parking lot. He followed Donni, keeping a half-block behind and close to the buildings. Donni walked with a spirited gait, swinging both grocery bags back and forth as she watched the clouds roll by above her. Later that day, she was to get her hair done.

Marcus slowly moved toward her. Twenty-five yards from her, in a shadowy part of the alley, he burst into a full run and grabbed her from behind, throwing her up against a building. "Remember me?" he asked as he threw his fist with full power into her face, breaking her cheekbone. He continued striking her head and face, completely closing one eye and breaking her nose and jaw. Finally, holding her up against the wall by her neck, he gave her one hard blow to her solar plexus. She crumpled, finally releasing each grocery bag in her hands, the items spilling out. A can rolled across the asphalt and tapped against Marcus' foot as he stood looking at Donni. He looked down and saw it was cat food.

Just for a moment, Marcus felt remorse. "You got cats?" he asked.

Donni looked up. She could still see from one eye. She nodded. Marcus kept looking down. He had his hand on his Beretta. He again looked at the can of cat food.

"I ain't killed anybody yet, and I ain't going to start now." Marcus walked away, not looking back.

Donni died a few days later of a brain hemorrhage brought on by the beating, the doctor said. One of her coworkers took in her cat. Corey heard about Donni's death from Pinky after he and Gary had gone to her funeral. Corey hadn't told anyone, not even Carolyn, about that night in Nichelson's went Donni saved him from Marcus. He hadn't been in NIchelson's since then. The cops called her death a random hate crime. Corey tried very hard to believe that.

ACKNOWLEDGMENTS

I want to thank those who commented, good or bad, on my writing and encouraged me to keep at it, especially my son, Quinn. And I want to thank the characters I've known who gave me the inspiration to absorb some of their ethos, deliberately or not, and convey some aspect of them in my writing.

ABOUT THE AUTHOR

Many things aided Bruce Rodgers in developing as a writer: being an intercity substitute teacher, a correction officer, a military stint, a variety of blue-collar jobs and a run for public office. Call all such experiences teaching exercises. In addition to this novel, he has written for general interest and niche magazines, and was an editor for an 80,000-circulation newsweekly. He lives in Florida.